ARAB SOCIAL LIFE IN THE MIDDLE AGES

For Charles and the family

Shirley Guthrie

ARAB SOCIAL LIFE IN THE MIDDLE AGES

An Illustrated Study

Saqi Books

British Library Cataloguing-in-Publication Data
A catalogue record for this book is available from the
British Library

ISBN 0 86356 043 1 (hb)

This edition first published 1995
Saqi Books
26 Westbourne Grove
London W2 5RH

Contents

Illustrations

In-Text Illustrations

Colour Plates

Glossary

ḥadīth (pl. *aḥādīth*)	Traditions of the Prophet and his companions
ḥajj	the Pilgrimage to Mecca
jāmiʿ	congregational (Friday) mosque
khān	merchants' caravanserai
madrasa	religious school, college
miḥrāb	recess in mosque indicating the orientation of prayer towards Mecca
muqarnas	a honeycomb-type of vaulting
qāḍī	judge
sharīʿa	Islamic canon law
sūra	chapter of the Qur'an
ṭaylasān	head-shawl worn by judges

A Note on Transliteration and Pronunciation

The Arabic letters *d*, *s*, *t* and *z*, with a dot underneath, are known as 'emphatic', or 'velarized', consonants. Their pronunciation is similar to the equivalent letters without the dots, except that the back of the tongue is raised slightly (towards the velum) and they are articulated more strongly. The *h* with a dot underneath is a very strongly aspirated sound originating in the back of the throat.

The combination *dh* represents the sound *th* in the English word *then*; *kh* is similar to the *ch* in the German *ach* or the Scottish *loch*, but is somewhat more guttural; *gh* represents a sound similar to the Parisian *r*, more or less the sound made when gargling.

Bars over the vowels (ā, ī, ū) indicate that they are to be pronounced long.

The definite article is always shown as *al-*, regardless of whether or not it is assimilated to the following letter.

Foreword

by
Robert Hillenbrand

This is a book to be welcomed. Shirley Guthrie's study of the *Maqāmāt* book illustrations produced in Syria and Iraq during the thirteenth century departs from the usual practice, which is to study them with a view to establishing their date, provenance and stylistic variations. Instead, she focusses squarely on what they reveal about life in the eastern Arab lands in the high Middle Ages. Others before her have drawn on this wonderfully rich source to illumine this or that aspect of contemporary society; but she is the first to quarry this material systematically. Hers is a full-scale excavation rather than a mere *sondage*. The various headings under which she groups her findings tell their own story; religious life, the judiciary and ruling class, the role of women, urban life, the rural scene and the traditions of Arab hospitality.

Wherever possible, Dr Guthrie fleshes out the evidence of the paintings themselves with complementary information drawn from either the *Maqāmāt* text or from other relevant medieval literary sources—geographical, historical, biographical or *belles lettres*. She notes the visual echoes of verbal puns. She shows how the artists ring the changes on hackneyed subject matter. And thus the full achievement of these painters gradually emerges. They observe the world around them with an engaging blend of humour and sagacity. Ironic detachment allied to superlative technical skill allows the best of them, al-Wāsiṭī, to present an unrivalled cross-section of high and low life in all the teeming vitality which characterised Baghdad in its Indian summer. Under the caliphs al-Nāṣir and al-Mustanṣir it briefly recaptured—after centuries of eclipse—the self-confidence due to the premier city of Islam. Al-Wāsiṭī caught that buoyant mood a mere two decades before the city was sacked by the Mongols, a catastrophe from which it never recovered. And this book, which publishes the fullest selection of these works yet to appear in colour, gives us a ringside seat for the panorama which he and his fellow-artists unfold. There is something here for everyone interested in the mediaeval Islamic world. Dr Guthrie deserves warm congratulations for making this material available to a wider audience than the traditional group of specialists.

Robert Hillenbrand
University of Edinburgh

Preface

Al-Ḥarīrī's *Maqāmāt [The Assemblies]* are rightly viewed as a classical Arabic *tour de force*. Having engaged the attention of more Arab scholars than any Arabic text other than the Qur'ān, they are viewed as an almost unique homage to Arabic language and culture. Al-Ḥarīrī frequently used these tales as a subtle and indirect way of satirizing the prevailing social order and drawing a moral, and it is likely that they in some way gave a sophisticated voice to the urban bourgeoisie; in this may lie one reason for their considerable appeal throughout the Arab world.

My initial approach was sociological. I wished to examine the illustrations not merely as documents of style or iconography, as is so often the method followed by Western art historians, but rather as visual evidence amplifying and complementing literary and historical accounts of the medieval Near East.

Since miniatures need to be analysed in relation to the text, I have translated the Arabic narrative immediately surrounding the illustrations and established their precise place in the stories through recourse to Steingass' Arabic text. However, the final English translations given as quotations at the introduction to each miniature are those of Preston, Chenery or Steingass; I have chosen them for their particular suitability, or out of personal preference, with due regard to accuracy based on literary criticism. All Arabic terms, from whatever source, have been verified with medieval dictionaries such as *Lisān al-'Arab*, *al-Ṣiḥāḥ*, *al-Misbāḥ* and *al-Qāmūs*, drawing on Edward Lane's *Arabic-English Lexicon*. The transliteration is basically that of the *Encyclopaedia of Islam*, updated with minor modifications. (*Maqāmāt* is plural, while the singular form *Maqāma* is used synonymously with 'tale'.)

This study is a revised version of my 1991 doctoral thesis at the University of Edinburgh, which set out to provide the most comprehensive work of reference. In order to make the *Maqāmāt* available to a wider audience, it has been necessary to abridge the footnotes. Scholars may wish to consult the original for the complete bibliography and further technical data. Each illustration can be linked to Grabar's microfiches.

While every effort has been made to reproduce high-quality illustrations, it is hoped that the reader will be sympathetic to the ravages of time and climate, iconoclasts, and the wide dispersal of the manuscripts over seven centuries.

My thanks are due to Professor Robert Hillenbrand (University of Edinburgh), in particular, for his encouragement, guidance and constructive criticism and to Professor Oleg Grabar (Institute for Advanced Study, University of Princeton) and Dr Yasin Safadi (British Library, London) for reading the manuscript. I should also like to express my gratitude to Mme Monique Cohen (Bibliothèque Nationale, Paris), the British Library and the Suleymaniye Mosque Library, Istanbul for access to their treasures, among many other sources too numerous to mention.

Introduction

As a literary genre, the *Maqāmā* was not new in the late eleventh and early twelfth centuries, al-Ḥarīrī's time, and it is generally accepted that al-Hamadhānī's 400 tenth-century *Maqāmāt* represented a fully developed and independent literary form which provided the paradigm for al-Ḥarīrī's 50 *Maqāmāt*. Al-Sharīshī was of the opinion that al-Ḥarīrī's work was more elaborate and comprehensive and therefore superior to al-Hamadhānī's *Maqāmāt*.

However, al-Ḥarīrī correctly anticipated hostile criticism of his masterpiece on the grounds of caprice and his choice of a protagonist in an unheroic mould. He made no attempt to conceal his admiration for his unprincipled and thoroughly disreputable rogue, Abū Zayd al-Sarūjī. Nonetheless, he was insistent that his work had an underlying moral purpose, and he asked in mitigation, 'What blame can attach to one who has composed anecdotes with the motive of conveying instruction, not deceptive display, and sought therein the improvement of others, not mere fiction?'[1]

The genre reflects a fascination with those on the fringes of contemporary urban society, and continues a literary preoccupation with the lower orders since the ninth century, the age of al-Jāḥiẓ. It follows on from Abū Dulaf's poem in praise of the Banū Sāsān, the *Qaṣīda sāsāniyya*, which dealt with Abū Zayd's supposed roguish ancestors. Although trickery always loomed large in fables, goodness and justice ultimately prevailed. The thoughtful and discerning reader will surely overlook Abū Zayd's obvious subterfuge and appreciate his uplifting sermons and discourses, as well as his frequent vindication.

The credibility at this period of an anti-hero in the mould of Abū Zayd exemplifies a change of spirit, which found its parallel in the decorative arts. The illustration of secular manuscripts was already in vogue by the early thirteenth century and represented a new taste for adding narrative representations to works of art in other media. It may be that the inclusion of miniatures reflected merely a change of taste. Earlier scientific illustration played an important didactic role in identifying the properties of plants and animals, the location of the source of medical dysfunction and trauma, the utility of mechanical devices or military exercises and so on; thus it might have been the text which dictated the illustrations. Moreoever, it is certain that their explanatory nature imposed a degree of realism on the illustrations, where a correct identification and diagnosis were prerequisites.

On the question of readership, didactic works would have had a relatively limited appeal; these were the 'tools of the trade' of specialists. The relative cheapness of paper was a factor in the growing availability of books and the widening of the market. It should be borne in mind that the average bourgeois reader's interest in the text more than a century later was possibly quite different to that of scholars. Perhaps such a reader now sought to be entertained by images. All these points suggest a new, popular audience. Given the abstruseness of the *Maqāmāt* text, it could never be popular in the generally accepted sense of the word; its appeal would still presumably be confined to a literate and sophisticated metropolitan readership, namely someone in similar circumstances to the author, a prosperous Basran merchant. An ambitious and affluent bourgeoisie had developed in the third, fourth and fifth centuries of Islam (the ninth to the eleventh century AD), but it is not known whether its members were bound by ties of business, residence in a particular area of the city or affiliation to individual brotherhoods or religious sects. Although it was not an organized group which attained political power, it was capable of exerting a powerful socio-economic influence, which peaked at the turn of the tenth and eleventh centuries. This group could represent a significant source of patronage for scribes and illustrators. Whether this audience needed illustrations to elucidate the text in the early thirteenth century is an open question; textual exegesis does appear on occasion, particularly in the most sophisticated illustrated work of all, the BN 5847 manuscript of al-Wāsiṭī.

Despite the fact that similar threads run through the illustrated thirteenth-century *Maqāmāt*, as we shall see, a total of six manuscripts is far from adequate to determine a clear relationship between them. The relatively few manuscripts so far discovered and their wide dispersal pose challenges for their study. What is evident is that each manuscript represents an individual response by the artist to the challenge of its illustration, and that some are more successful than others. With the exception of al-Wāsiṭī—who was both scribe and painter—we do not know who executed these manuscripts, or who dictated the number of miniatures or their placing in the text. Nor is there any indication as to whether the artists were working speculatively and alone, under patronage, or in an official workshop.

The chart in Figure 1 attempts to analyse the placing of the illustrations in each manuscript story-by-story. It deals with the number of folios and the total

Figure 1: Comparison of manuscript sizes.

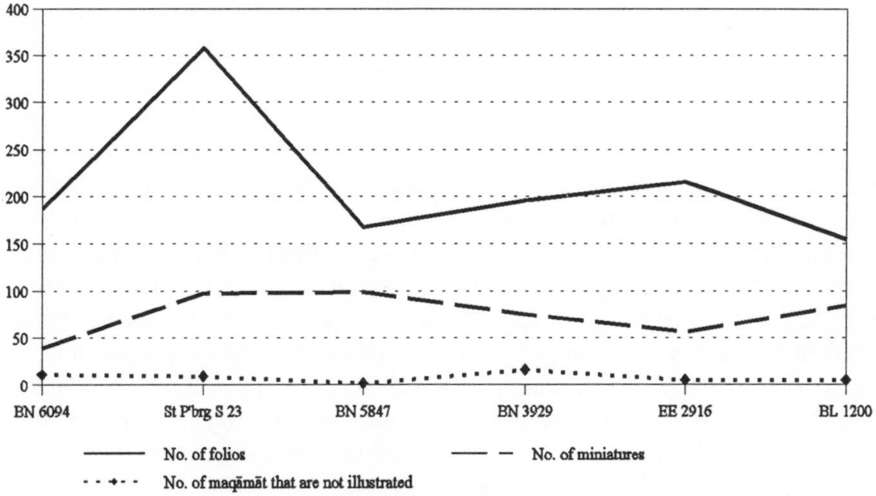

number of miniatures, to see if there was any attempt to tailor the text by the insertion of illustrations and allows a comparison of manuscript sizes. The aim is to discover how the manuscripts were constructed and, if possible, to establish stemmata between them.

An attempt to analyse the correspondence, if any, of the number of illustrations to the degree of difficulty of the text and/or the length of individual tales as defined by the commentators proved impossible to quantify in chart form. My conclusion is that there was none, and this agrees with Grabar's view that there is no correlation whatever between narrative complexity and the number of images.[2]

While it is possible to view the paintings simply as decorative adjuncts to the text, a knowledge of the text is, at the very least, advantageous. Even the unsophisticated BL 1200 manuscript threw up a surprising image, a woman lying on the ground in *Maqāma* 47. This illustration does not appear to have been noticed or commented upon elsewhere. It is a reference to the mother of the proverbial 'cupper of Sābāṭ' of the text, and presupposes a knowledge of the whole proverb on the reader's part. This brief phrase must have caught the eye of someone, although not necessarily the painter.

The conclusion must be that the time was ripe for the adding of images for their own sake and for their individual aesthetic appeal. The varied *Maqāmāt* settings in diverse lands, with their markets, caravanserais, lawcourts, and so on, provide ample scope for illustration and excited the interest of an appreciative audience. Al-Ḥarīrī's hope was that:

> whoever examines with an eye of intelligence, and makes good his insight into fundamental principles, must place my *Maqāmāt* on the list of profitable

> productions, and class them along with those [fabulous] compositions whose subjects are taken from animate and inanimate nature.[3]

Some of the illustrators have indeed succeeded in 'profitable productions'.

My aim has been to demonstrate that the illustrations of the thirteenth-century *Maqāmāt* are a reflection of everyday events in the Near East of the period, to clarify aspects of medieval Islamic culture and to provide a comprehensive reference work for further investigation of this complex text. This has been done by establishing broad categories of subject-matter and treating together the various illustrations that fall within them. Thus the illustrations themselves become the means of analysing aspects of medieval Islamic society, with reference to a wide variety of literary and historical sources. Grabar introduces some 450 miniatures from the thirteenth-century manuscripts on microfiche in his excellent study, in which he seeks to evaluate shared and diverse ways of dealing with the same topics and the relationship, if any, between different pictorial cycles, and to establish whether there was a distinct *Maqāmāt* idiom. An in-depth analysis of individual miniatures was outside the scope of such a brief.

I considered that an art-historical approach to specific miniatures could be enhanced and consolidated by analysing them within the literary context of the *Maqāmāt*. Grabar's study, while by no means ignoring this approach, has a somewhat different focus, so much close analysis of the interplay between text and image remained (and remains) to be done. Accordingly, I consulted specialist commentaries on the *Maqāmāt*;[4] they were extremely valuable in gaining additional insights. There was also a whole set of related issues to discuss. These included the possibility of investigating and evaluating the artists' approach to the challenge of a previously unillustrated and difficult text; the amount of freedom they had in deciding where to place the images; the means of visual expression available to them; the opportunity to create archetypes; the function of illustrations as *aides-mémoire* to a difficult work; and the means employed for the artistic embellishment of a given folio.

It should be borne in mind that al-Ḥarīrī's text was produced more than 100 years before illustrated versions appeared. This might have posed problems in the artists' visual interpretation of earlier events set in distant countries, although it is axiomatic that, as the *Maqāmāt* is basically a 'people-centred' work, human virtues, failings and moral issues are relatively constant factors that can be understood in all eras.

Once my framework had been determined, I chose illustrations to fit within it. This choice was necessarily subjective, but my aim was to reproduce as wide a selection of illustrations as possible. Many of the paintings in the *Maqāmāt* cycles are merely confrontation scenes between the hero and the narrator at the end of the tales. They are almost interchangeable and have largely been ignored. Unfortunately, both the St Petersburg S 23 and the Istanbul, Suleymaniye, EE 2916 manuscripts have suffered at the hands of iconoclasts. Inevitably, the genius of al-Wāsiṭī, the painter of BN 5847, carries the day, and this work is arguably disproportionately represented.

A preliminary examination of the miniatures revealed a wide variety of everyday situations and locations in the depiction of the 'low-life' adventures of the anti-hero Abū Zayd, who was possibly a prototype for the popular picaresque heroes of later European literature. The visual counterparts of his marvellous tales afford a glimpse of court life, litigation before *qāḍīs* (judges), religious and military pomp and ceremony and the true purpose of religious ritual, the bustle of the *sūq* (market), the routine of village life, bedouin hospitality and so on.

Al-Ḥarīrī's narrator, al-Ḥārith, is a peripatetic merchant who recounts his experiences on his travels. He invariably chances upon an altercation involving Abū Zayd, the well-known trickster type existing on the margins of society. Abū Zayd, who is usually in disguise, lives by his wits through exhibiting his many talents and dazzling his admiring audiences with displays of erudite poetry and rhetoric. Happily, there are a few notable exceptions when Abū Zayd's motives and conduct are beyond reproach. Generally regarded as a 'knight-errant' sort in literature, he represents a type who has assimilated characteristics from many of the most cultivated medieval minds.

'Abū Zayd' is one of the most commonplace of Arab names and in examples of Arabic grammar 'Zayd' denotes 'any man whatever'. Abū Zayd is versatile, a 'man for all seasons', and could be anyone; he represents the 'human interest' element in a tale. 'Al-Ḥārith' is as indeterminate a name as 'Abū Zayd' and is borrowed from an expression attributed to the Prophet, 'Each of you is a Ḥārith, and every one of you a Hammām.'[5] It has the extended meaning of someone who is a prey to care and anxiety. Abū Zayd represents the ordinary person, with all too human failings, who invokes in the reader the notion that 'There but for the grace of God go I.' Consequently, al-Ḥārith can be seen as the still small voice of conscience. Such an interpretation should have negated any disapproval of the stories on the part of the readers and would surely have struck a responsive chord in a sophisticated, much-travelled audience.

Many commentators consider that al-Ḥarīrī based the narrator, al-Ḥārith, on himself; this is entirely plausible, for al-Ḥārith also enjoyed a comfortable lifestyle and was a highly educated Basran with a great regard for feats of eloquence. It may not be a coincidence that departures from the architectural norm such as booths in the *sūq*, the caravanserai and a covered street outside al-Wāsiṭī's Rayy mosque all involve aspects of town life relevant to an urban mercantile class. This would be a prosperous and leisured group, and potential patrons of the arts. As such, they would be confident and self-assured, and unlikely to wish to change the status quo. To this extent, Abū Zayd perhaps offered his audience a sophisticated 'voice' whereas the scabrous shadow theatre suited the lower orders of society. Some degree of interdependence with the ruling classes is suggested. Merchants procured luxury goods, they were a source of income through taxation and customs dues, and they would also have been in a position to act as couriers with news of foreign places and events.

As we shall see, the manuscripts now in St Petersburg and Istanbul share certain attributes (although differing in many respects) and form a key set as a basis for comparison, since all the other *Maqāmāt* can be explained in relation to them. Here, the events of the narrative are sometimes relegated to a secondary role due to the overriding concern for setting, although the paintings almost always appear at the 'correct' place in the text. Architecture is prominent and the pictorial space highly developed, particularly in the case of the landscape in the Istanbul work. BN 5847 should be linked with both of these in its concern for backdrop setting and genre quality, and in that the majority of its unusual interpretations might suggest the modification of an earlier form of *Maqāmāt* illustration. The St Petersburg manuscript is generally regarded as the earliest. Both the iconography and certain postures or typical compositional devices such as figures organized on an elliptical base-line betray the influence of Christian painting. The people depicted are apparently Arab and are shown in repeated but lively poses. The architecture is decorative, a contrived 'set piece', and does not provide any real clue as to provenance. These three manuscripts are related stylistically and iconographically to the Dioscorides *De Materia Medica* work (dated 1224) from Baghdad.

BN 6094 is set apart from all other *Maqāmāt* manuscripts in that it is a reworking of Hellenistic art by a Byzantine school. The date 1222 appears in two places and the provenance of Syria seems certain. We have a *terminus ad quem* of 1242–58 for the Istanbul EE 2916 manuscript, which has not been attributed to a particular area. The mosques here appear to be the brick-built Iraqi types with squat minarets, and the presence of roll-up blinds, reed matting and wind-towers (which were also depicted in BN 5847) suggest at least a hot, dry climate like that of southern Iraq. The people and costumes appear to be Arab and an Iraqi provenance is possible.

BN 5847 is unique in that its colophon reveals that the same person, al-Wāsiṭī, copied and illustrated it in 1237. This is a luxurious work. Al-Wāsiṭī had great psychological insight derived from his knowledge of the text; he established a rare empathy with the characters and provided the greatest variety of imagery. He employed many double-page illustrations, and one wonders whether this was because he was somewhat less successful than the painters of the St Petersburg and Istanbul manuscripts in developing the pictorial space on a single folio. Nevertheless, his work is the undisputed 'jewel in the crown' of thirteenth-century Arab painting.

BN 3929 shares many of the features of the so-called 'Mosul' school of painting, such as flat compositions in strong colours, patterns similar to those on metalwork and uniformity of style. Mosul was an important Saljūq centre and Saljūq royal iconography has been drawn upon. A dating in the 1240s has been generally agreed, but assuming that Ward's revised date of 1206 for an Istanbul copy of the al-Jazarī manuscript, the *Treatise on Automata [al-Jāmi' bayn al-'ilm wa al-'amal fī ṣinā'at al-ḥiyyal]*, is correct,[6] the similarities in style and iconography may indeed point to an earlier date for this work in Paris.

There is more than a hint of the shadow theatre in the BN 3929 and St Petersburg manuscripts; both have lively, jerky figures and there is a definite sense of theatricality in the elaborate and formulaic architectural settings, and in the sea-going vessel in *Maqāma* 39 of the latter. These complement the clear impression of Abū Zayd 'play-acting' before a *qāḍī*, for example, or in the many other situations in which he finds himself. Ibn Dāniyāl's three Arabic shadow plays, written around 1267, are the oldest extant examples, although they were apparently based on older traditions and may be posited as a revival of this art.

The colophon of the BL 1200 manuscript mentions 1256 and the copyist's name, 'Umar ibn 'Alī ibn al-Mubārak al-Mawṣilī. It is in poor condition and the faces have been repainted in a schematic fashion. This manuscript is clearly derivative; it adheres to the Mosul tradition and shares landscape and other features with BN 3929. It is surprising to find a double-page illustration of the Samarqand mosque in *Maqāma* 28. However it is unlike al-Wāsiṭī's two-page spread of the Rayy mosque in *Maqāma* 21, being extremely simple, and the preacher and other officials are clearly based on Eastern Christian priests. No place of execution has been suggested.

Certain identifiable pictorial cycles are evident throughout the *Maqāmāt*. The princely repertoire is not a direct borrowing except in al-Wāsiṭī's frontispieces. It has influenced al-Wāsiṭī's satirical portrait of the governor of Raḥba in *Maqāma* 10, his tavern scene in *Maqāma* 12 and his drinking bout beside a water-wheel in *Maqāma* 24. One also finds it in the Istanbul portrait of Abū Zayd as a governor in the 26th tale. The rulers in BN 6094 and 3929 are Saljūqs. This cycle was extended to encompass other figures of authority such as *qāḍīs*, as well as beardless youths; portrayals of youths in general are influenced by these types. Costume obviously varies according to the function of the incumbent; for example, *qāḍīs* are universally depicted wearing the head-shawl. Governors are fairly uniform in dress, whether Arab or Saljūq, and the thrones of both are consistent, depending on the tradition. Adaptation of 'author portraits' has been noted in BN 5847 in *Maqāma* 2, in the depiction of the *qāḍī* in the St Petersburg manuscript for the 43rd tale and in the Istanbul sick-bed portrait of Abū Zayd in *Maqāma* 19.

There appears to have been a set formula for illustrating the texts, although at whose behest is unknown. My analyses show that illustrations throughout the corpus appear on many occasions at the same place in the text. Confrontation scenes occur at specific instances as dénouements and may have been created especially for the *Maqāmāt*. Even in crowd scenes there is a limited range of male types, and the conclusion must be that there was a relatively narrow band of visual experiences upon which artists might draw.

At a minimum, the text usually requires that settings be defined as outdoors or indoors. Where, for example, a cave, the Euphrates or a hill is mentioned, the artists complied, and to that extent created a specific *Maqāmāt* cycle of illustrations. The St Petersburg and Istanbul manuscripts generally establish the primacy and development of the setting, whether architecture or landscape. The St Petersburg painter repeats his architectural formula and depiction of people to the extent that they become types, and he successfully employs the elliptical base-line to create perspective. The Istanbul artist, on the other hand, frequently adds an abundance of architectural features and displays innovations in landscape in the exploitation of pictorial space which was to become evident in Persian painting. He also reduces his total number of illustrations by eliminating confrontation scenes, and includes elements which are absent in other manuscripts and are not required by the text, such as a suckling camel in *Maqāma* 31, the bastinado scene in the schoolroom in Homs and two fighting dogs in the market-place in *Maqāma* 47. Al-Wāsiṭī is sometimes faithful to the narrative but at other times he places illustrations in apparently arbitrary positions; on occasion his interpretation goes far beyond the text, probably owing to the insights garnered in his dual role as artist and scribe.

With the exception of the 25th tale, the painter of BN 6094 consistently provides one miniature per *Maqāma* within a schematic and repetitive type of 'architecture'. BN 3929 offers a strict, literal adherence to the narrative; the artist takes little account of natural or constructed settings and re-enacts the human drama. His large captions are superfluous and a reiteration of the text, which he may well have read. Illustrations in the derivative BL 1200 also usually appear at particularly apposite points in the tale. However, one cannot assume that the artists were necessarily conversant with the text.

The *Maqāmāt* may have been read aloud to an assembly or literary gathering (*maqāma*), in which case the narrative would make the setting clear. Although places in Iraq, Syria, Egypt and Persia are all mentioned in the text, there is no visual evidence that any regard was paid either to the setting in an area other than where the artist worked, or to an earlier period, when al-Ḥarīrī wrote the text. Artists seem to have produced their personal renderings of a setting in their own time and place. These could encompass anything from a rudimentary pair of spandrels to a full cross-section of a typical Iraqi brick-built mosque with a frieze inscription, from elaborate hillsides with multiple ground-planes to a single plant. Such devices formed a framework, developed space, anchored compositions to a base-line, and so on.

Ideally, one would wish to compare the *Maqāmāt* constructions with extant examples; this is extremely difficult, as so few have survived, but it is not impossible. Illustrations sometimes depict natural building materials, such as stone, brick, marble, stucco and reed matting. These are perhaps relevant pointers to the place where the manuscript was produced. Some artists clearly painted from observable surroundings: for example, al-Wāsiṭī's drinking bout in *Maqāma* 24 in a garden irrigated by an Archimedes-screw type of water-wheel, the Istanbul mosques, and the two distinct types of boats in *Maqāmāt* 22 and 39. It is impossible to say which of several different illustrations of the same setting is the 'true' rendering; what seems important is that the scene was in some way recognizable to the viewer.

In order to portray events outside their own experience, for example an appearance at a governor's court or before a *qāḍī*, artists would have had either to use or adapt an existing model, or create a new formula. It should be noted that no specific design for palaces or legal tribunals has emerged; recognizable cultural items such as costume, personal attendants or furnishings define the setting more precisely.

Textiles are also problematic. Costly fabrics were shipped from far afield and are well documented. Costume would be subject to the dictates of fashion and regional variation; contemporary dictionaries are a fount of information here. Enormous prices for textiles have been cited. It is likely that these were the preserve of the very rich and that some of the splendid, brightly coloured garments seen in the *Maqāmāt* in crowds and in agricultural settings in fact fulfil other functions. Colours are used for their aesthetic qualities and as elements of composition that define pictorial space. Colour symbolism does not appear to play a prominent part. One notable exception is provided by the mourners in al-Wāsiṭī's cemetery in *Maqāma* 11 who are not wearing the dark blue associated with bereavement. Instead the men are portrayed, unusually, in startling white garments which link them with the white-shrouded corpse and may indicate that they are kin.

The taverns depicted in the BN 5847 and St Petersburg manuscripts in *Maqāma* 12 are remarkably similar and detail all the processes of wine-making and consumption. Archetypes lurk behind these. First, al-Wāsiṭī's Abū Zayd is parodying a royal figure; drinking was so closely associated visually with royal imagery that this is the only appropriate depiction here. BN 3929 also shows the bibulous Abū Zayd on a type of throne, while BL 1200 further confirms an association of drinking with the princely cycle in its inclusion of the standard paraphernalia of flowers, cup-bearers and musicians. Second, the elaborate taverns in the BN 5847 and St Petersburg manuscripts may themselves be no ordinary drinking dens but wine-halls of some distinction, possibly with royal connections.

In preparing this work, I have made every attempt to use literary texts that are as contemporary in time and space as possible; this is extremely difficult for a Western art historian and there is undoubtedly a wealth of material yet to be unearthed. (Grabar is correct in asserting that no truly usable method of attempting to relate literature and art has yet been formulated.)[7] Nor can it be assumed that accounts of what held good for Egypt or Syria, for example, necessarily applied to Iraq; here quotations from such sources as the Hebrew manuscript in the Cairo *Geniza*, or storehouse for documents, or Ibn Munqidh's *Memoirs [Kitāb al-i'tibār]* come to mind. Customs might vary according to region, external influences and the interplay of various cultural strains. All these factors are counterbalanced by the great extent to which the tenets of Islam govern the minutiae of daily living. There is also a danger that earlier (or later) material may not be strictly relevant. A case in point is the ninth-century work by al-Jāḥiẓ, *The Epistle of Singing-Girls [Risālat al-qiyān]*, which I have cited on occasion. It should be borne in mind that al-Jāḥiẓ was a theologian, man of letters and satirist; as such, he is unlikely to have been an entirely impartial observer of society. In mitigation, the function of singing-girls, their tenuous position in society and their machinations to maintain the status quo may be assumed. I have also quoted extensively from al-Tanūkhī, a tenth-century *qāḍī*. In view of the proven link between anecdotage and the *Maqāmāt* literary genre, al-Tanūkhī's informal observations on the frailties of human nature, which are universal in all periods, frequently seem pertinent.

1

The Religious Life

Even today, no traveller to the Middle East can fail to be impressed by the very public nature of Islam and the extent to which it impinges upon daily life. Pious exclamations are on the lips of all, whether 'Praise be to God!', 'If God wills!' or 'In the safe-keeping of God'. The life of the Prophet and the early Muslims is at the heart of the community's collective memory as a paradigm for all in society. Social gatherings are preceded by 'In the Name of God, the All-Merciful, the All-Compassionate' (the *basmallāh*) and also frequently by a recitation from the Qur'ān. Five daily calls to prayer in the Sunni tradition punctuate the day, and on Fridays the pavements outside the congregational mosque are thronged with crowds of men and boys. The great festivals of Ramaḍān and the *ḥajj* (the pilgrimage to Mecca) are joyous communal and public celebrations of a culmination of rigorous deprivation and religious obligation. Coffee shops and restaurants are closed and the fasting population look tired and anxious. The pinched appearance of returned pilgrims is suffused with the quiet pride of the achievement of a lifetime's goal. All of these are highly visible symbols of the literal meaning of Islam—'submission to the will of God'—and foster the sense of belonging to a community.

The articulation of Islam into a body of religious sciences and practice took place largely in Iraq during the 'Abbāsid period. It is therefore not surprising that the illustrations in a work containing several hundred Qur'ānic allusions and numerous pious sentiments should feature rulers as upholders and defenders of the faith, mosques and preachers with great oratorical powers, lawyers expert in the Sharī'a and tableaux of Ramaḍān and the *ḥajj*.

Ramaḍān

The ʿĪd al-Fiṭr Sermon (Khuṭba)

Maqāma 7 is set in Barqaʿīd, which was a town of considerable size north of Mosul and south of Naṣībīn. The tale unfolds on the great feast of ʿĪd al-Fiṭr, which signals the breaking of the fast at the end of the month of Ramaḍān. It is possible that the author chose this location because it rhymes with the words *barq ʿīd* at the end of the next clause. These translate literally as the 'lightning of the festival' and are a metaphor for its approach. Al-Ḥārith is unwilling to resume his journey on this day of colourful ceremony without observing the obligatory and supererogatory rites. Mindful of a Tradition of the Prophet, he dons new clothes and sets out for the Great Mosque, where he joins the procession of people similarly attired in fine garments. As the congregation gather and arrange themselves in rows, an aged blind beggar appears, guided by an emaciated old woman who hands out petitions for alms.

The painter al-Wāsiṭī has produced a striking illustration in BN 5847 for the interior of the congregational mosque (*jāmiʿ*), where the preacher (*khaṭīb*) delivers the ʿĪd al-Fiṭr address. Textual commentaries are written at the sides in red ink in a decorative zigzag pattern. The three lines of text above the miniature are part of Abū Zayd's speech. They read:

> I am in God's hands and commit my case to Him;
> There is no power or strength but in Him;
> To Him alone I look;
> For in mankind a source of bounty now no more I find.

He continues in similar vein, then in the two lines of Arabic below, he instructs his companion:

> But nevertheless be cheerful and hope for the best,
> And now collect the papers together and count them.

She replies:

> I have already collected and counted them.
> And found that the hand of loss had destroyed one of them.

Whereupon he exclaims, 'Ruin to thee! Slovenly wretch!'[1]

Later on, the text indicates that the action takes place when the congregation is gathered and arranged in rows, presumably before the sermon (*khuṭba*), although none is mentioned.

Abū Zayd does not conform to the text's 'old man in two cloaks' (*shamlataini*) with his eyes closed as he feigns blindness, although his left hand

1. The preacher delivers the 'Īd al-Fiṭr address.

rests on his wife's shoulders. A cloak precluded the need for other clothing; it was therefore eminently suitable for the poorer classes and would have been the ideal garment for Abū Zayd, in this instance, to convey his poverty. This type of robe was also worn by the Jewish poor and it is cognate with the Hebrew term. Instead, Abū Zayd wears a plebeian white robe, albeit with *ṭirāz* bands on his sleeves. The *ṭirāz* was a richly embroidered band of material for the embellishment of garments; one would certainly not expect to find it on a poor man's robe or, as here, on the olive green turban (*'imāma*). Under his right arm he carries a coarse sort of wallet from which he produces his poems of supplication for alms. Despite his supposedly penurious circumstances, his hair and beard are well groomed, and his robe snowy-white, so he has evidently made an effort over his appearance. As he says, 'Far better poverty with patient pride than bitter scorn and insult to abide.'

Abū Zayd's companion looks neither emaciated nor old; she is well built and is the type of ample, middle-aged female who appears elsewhere in this manuscript, as we shall see. These women are invariably capable-looking and assertive, and here her vivid hand gestures leave no doubt that she is literally empty-handed. She wears an outer wrap (*ghilāla*) of everyday smokey-grey colour, but it is gold-trimmed and again inappropriate for the effect the couple of the text would wish to display, unless it represents her as a refined woman temporarily down on her luck. Perhaps al-Wāsiṭī sought to inject a vein of humour and to indicate to the reader—although it was hardly necessary by the 7th *Maqāma*—that these are no ordinary beggars. Alternatively, the garments may be used as compositional markers, to draw attention to the principal characters.

Alms-giving on ʻĪd al-Fiṭr is public, and the exploitative side to Abū Zayd's nature is well to the fore: fully aware of the obligation upon the faithful to be generous on this occasion, he is prepared to capitalize on this baser, but none-theless human, spur to giving. Ideally, the deprivations of the fast should afford the congregation some insight into the needs of the poor through their own experience of extreme hunger and thirst, and one would expect them to be moved by compassion to generous giving. That they do not do so serves to highlight the naivety of al-Ḥārith, who is the only member of the congregation to give the woman alms, namely 'a *dirham* [a small silver coin] and a mite'. This suggests that the congregation knows something that al-Ḥārith does not—in other words, that the pair are perpetrating a confidence trick.

From the ninth century onwards there had been an interest in the 'low life', in the form of itinerant tricksters. We know from *Maqāmāt* 2 and 49 that Abū Zayd considered himself to be a member of the self-styled 'Sons of Sāsān' (Banū Sāsān). Sāsān was the son of a petty ruler of a district in western Persia. He was disinherited, took refuge with the Kurds, and in folklore founded the begging fraternities and became their king; his clan apparently embraced all groups beyond the pale of law-abiding society. Abū Zayd and his wife are clearly not of the criminal class as such, but they are at least on the margins of society and make up the general collectivity of the Banū Sāsān. Abū Zayd's wife, therefore, is identifiable with a popular underworld female character, one of a begging duo who frequented mosques, who regaled the audience with tales of hardship due to her husband's blindness.

The viewer is linked to the pair by the pointing finger of the preacher, while the row of turbans emphasizes the outstretched postures of the begging couple. Al-Ḥārith stands at the left-hand side in the mosque, hand to mouth; he is anxious to make the acquaintance of the person who has woven 'the rich tissue of these verses' that outline hardship, but is unable to move forward because of the pressing crowd. His hand gesture is taken from Byzantine painting and here conveys a sense of unease and a feeling that all may not be what it seems. Al-Ḥārith is shown in three-quarter profile with the feature of the 'protruding eye', a curious feature of western Indian painting from the eleventh and twelfth centuries which also occurs in Coptic illustration. It is not until later in the tale that he suspects 'that Abū Zayd was indicated by all this' and his 'sorrow was excited for what had befallen his eyes'.

The congregation comprises a tight group of six men in the foreground. Four of them watch the couple, while the other two turn their heads towards the preacher; this has the effect of hinting at depth in the composition, and these people comprise part of the crowd who 'had become such as to be well-nigh suffocating'. Their self-coloured robes are in shades of red, pale blue, smokey-grey, pale saffron, pink/violet and dark green. Folds and patterns are gently delineated to suggest that the materials are fine.

The turbans are in a variety of these colours; two of them are white and belong to the two men who are turned towards the preacher. All the turbans have extremely long waist-length ends, with *ṭirāz* bands. White turbans occur elsewhere here, in the first tale and in the cemetery. White is uncommon for turbans in the *Maqāmāt* and it seems to have been employed to draw attention to a specific feature or as a compositional marker. Here, it may also indicate studied indifference to Abū Zayd or rapt attention to the preacher.

The tail (*'adhaba*) of the turban usually measured four fingers in length, anything longer being regarded as ostentatious,[2] but one should bear in mind that these people are both seeing and being seen in all their finery on a great public occasion. There is an obvious parallel with the artist's well-dressed women in the Rayy mosque discussed in the analysis of 'Women in the Mosque' (see Chapter 6) (Plate 5).

Al-Ṣābi' describes a typical Ramaḍān scene of worship in the *Rules and Regulations of the Court [Rusūm dār al-khilāfa]*: shortly after sunrise on 'Īd al-Fiṭr the people, clothed in their best garments, gathered in the mosque and performed the two prostrations in prayer (*rak'āt*) led by the caliph or his appointee, and the alms of the fast (*ṣadaqāt al-fiṭr*) were distributed. This was followed by much house-visiting of relatives and friends, the mutual expression of good wishes and the exchange of gifts of clothing and cash. Ramaḍān was, and still is, a time of the greatest hospitality and the wearing of new garments. Another source reveals how a vizier, Ibn 'Abbād, entertained several thousand people at this time and gave away more in that one month than he did throughout the remainder of the year.[3]

Several features indicate that this is an official occasion. The pair of black official 'Abbāsid standards which flank the preacher are twisted like silken skeins. It is likely that the fabric bears epigraphy, for they are identical to the furled standard borne by a horseman on the opposite page, which is clearly inscribed in white (Illust. 2). The finials of the flag-poles are also identical in both illustrations. In Chapter 5 of the *Rules and Regulations of the Court*, mention is made of the types of banners which were given to princes on their appointment; these bore pious inscriptions on both sides and read, 'The upholder of Allāh's command. The Commander of the Faithful'.

Al-Wāsiṭī's preacher is clad in the black robes which stamp him as an 'Abbāsid appointee; the sleeves are wide and bear deep golden *ṭirāz* bands on the upper arms. According to Ibn al-Athīr, when an official sought to be inconspicuous he removed his black clothing. The black turban with gold ornamentation here is quite different from those of the congregation, and it is perhaps fastened with a form of gold clasp. Ibn Iyās reports that the black turban was also known as the Baghdadi turban.

In his right hand the preacher clasps a black encased sword of office. Ibn Jubayr describes the preacher in the Cairo mosque in Ṣalāḥ al-Dīn's time as dressed 'after the fashion of the 'Abbāsids', namely, wearing black and girt with a sword.[4] One wonders if the appearance of the sword in the *minbar* (pulpit) is associated symbolically with the staff (*qadīb*) upon which the Prophet leaned; this practice was adopted by his immediate successors and emulated for some time elsewhere. A staff and turban were evidently indispensable for a preacher.

Even if the *amīr* (prince) was in the capital at the time, his name was not invoked, as he was subservient to the caliph. Adherence to this practice was strictly enforced, for in the mid-tenth century al-Rāḍi bi-Allāh dismissed three senior Baghdadi clerics who mentioned the name of *Amīr* Muḥammad ibn Yāqūt immediately after the invocation of the caliph himself.[5] The presence of standards and black official garments on a festival day all suggest that this *khaṭīb* is preaching as the official representative of the *amīr*. Al-Wāsiṭī's preacher (later on in the Samarqand mosque) wears a girdle (*minṭaq*) encrusted with jewellery and with two clasps of gold or silver, and this is perhaps an additional item of rank. However, there are no banners on the Samarqand *minbar* on that ordinary Friday. This seems to confirm that the banners in our illustration indicate 'Abbāsid officialdom and a special occasion.

The *minbar* is shown two-dimensionally, and the preacher has entered it through the small crenellated arched doorway at the foot of the stairs. This pointed archway has been considerably reduced in scale, as it would otherwise intrude to an unacceptable degree at the centre of the miniature.The reduction in scale of the *minbar* also allows for the inclusion of the *miḥrāb* (architectural focus of orientation of prayer towards Mecca); it focuses attention on the famous preacher and the black standards which emphasize the festival and provides a decorative backdrop for the drama. The whole structure has been swung round 90°, perhaps to counteract the somewhat flat effect of the six men with their backs to the viewer, but it also allows us to see two of them glancing towards the preacher. There is no canopy at the head of the stairs. It should be noted that, like the *miḥrāb*, the *minbar* curiously lacks inscriptions.

The small portal is further distorted, for it has been swung round 90° to echo the *miḥrāb*. It serves to separate the preacher from his flock and underscores both the official setting and the impudence of Abū Zayd and his wife by placing them, in a sense, on a par with the preacher. A *minbar* is constructed in two distinct sections; the first is the tall, box-like structure on a square base, which is composed of three horizontal divisions per side.[6] The upper division (*taqfīsa*) forms the balustrade and the lower portion carries the platform. The tall rectangular side panel flanking the platform is elaborately decorated with polygonal wooden insets which are carved in a variety of geometric patterns. The upper part of this panel has been repainted, but the decoration has not been restored. The tall side panel may also have been repainted.

The second section is the large triangular side which carries the staircase; very detailed examination shows that it has been elaborately worked in a floral arabesque similar to that on the *miḥrāb* and contrasts sharply with the geometric designs of the insets. It is not possible to see how many stairs there are. Ibn 'Abd Rabbih's *The Unique Necklace [al-'Iqd al-farīd]* mentions a plank fastened to the top of the *minbar* of the Prophet at Medina, to prevent anyone else sitting there. Abū Bakr sat one step down from the Prophet's stool and 'Umar chose one step below that. 'Uthmān, however, later in his caliphate, chose to preach from the top. Mu'āwiyya raised the Prophet's *minbar* six additional steps. It seems that the practice of sitting lower than the Prophet's place was never officially prescribed and it was ignored on at least one occasion before the twelfth century.[7] In the illustration, the preacher stands below the topmost step.

There are eleven balusters, some of which appear to be carved; the banister and other parallel sides are known in Iraq as *kīfsij* and they, too, are devoid of pious inscriptions. The various sections of the structure are joined by iron brackets with iron nails; examples of these are clearly found on the 'Amādiyya *minbar*. Nails on a door from the 'Amādiyya mosque were in the form of an eight-petalled rosette, a popular contemporary motif, and other decorative nails had been popular in Sāmarrā.[8] Al-Wāsiṭī has omitted these features. The position of his *miḥrāb* to the left of the *minbar* is correct. This may account for the placing of what, strictly speaking, in both textual and chronological sequence, should have been the first illustration, namely the mounted cavalcade, after the sermon in the mosque, facing to the right. Al-Wāsiṭī has thus produced a mosque interior in a fairly simple form. Although devoid of an architectural framework, the requisite features of *miḥrāb* and *minbar* set the scene. This format was to be expanded as the artist worked through the range of 50 tales.

The main focal point, the *miḥrāb*, takes the form of a semicircular niche known as *mujawwaf*. This architectural feature first made its appearance during the reconstruction of the Mosque of the Prophet in Medina by the caliph al-Walīd and the governor 'Umar ibn 'Abd al-'Azīz in the early eighth century. It is still unclear whether a *miḥrāb* had existed in any mosque before that time, and this niche form owes much to late antique decoration. The *miḥrāb mujawwaf* therefore represented a genuine formal innovation in the mosque.[9] Since its inception, the *miḥrāb* has been the focus for the *imām* (prayer-leader) and its primary function is liturgical. Its symbolic focus is perhaps comparable in meaning to the symbolism of the address from the *minbar*.

Al-Wāsiṭī's *miḥrāb* is an elaborate structure composed of several different panels deeply carved in various styles, with a double row of crenellations: all these features accord well with the associated symbolic values of the *miḥrāb* and its commanding position in the mosque. Similar crenellations appear on buildings throughout this manuscript. Crenellations are unusual in the context; the only other example of a similar *miḥrāb* I have been able to find in the *Maqāmāt* is in the illustration of this 7th tale in the badly damaged fourteenth-century BL 9718 manuscript. There, too, the archway is rounded, although it almost verges on the horseshoe shape, and not the more usual slightly pointed four-centred arch found elsewhere at the period.

In al-Wāsiṭī's fairly simple mosque, it is plausible to view the crenellations as suggesting a cross-section of the whole building, in the absence of fuller architectural elements. The Iraqi *miḥrāb* at this time was generally executed in brick, stucco or marble but al-Wāsiṭī's prayer niche is in the red wood of the *minbar*. There is a wooden *miḥrāb*, 1.98 metres high and dating from 1103, in the Masjid-i Maydān, Abyaneh, which is reasonably close in scale to that of the illustration.[10]

The usual pious inscriptions are absent here. The inset ochre-coloured panels may be terracotta; apparently, these were frequently designed and fabricated to defined dimensions and proportions for a particular building. They were placed on panels with a fixative that was applied only on the back of the terracotta piece. Contemporary terracotta decoration was also applied in the form of tiles known as *shashsha*. Examples are found in Baghdad on the mausoleum popularly known as Sitt Zubayda, built by al-Nāṣir and dated 1179–1225, as well as on the Madrasa al-Mustanṣiriyya. All of these elements feature fairly simple, pleasing floral scroll patterns.[11] (I have found no parallels for a mixture of wood and terracotta.)

Only one of the two pillars for the *miḥrāb* arch is visible; its bell-shaped capital appears to be constructed in the grey/blue soft marble which was plentiful in the Mosul region and lent itself to elaborate carving. This technique in marble may represent an artistic link between the earlier stucco-work of Sāmarrā and the Saljūq brickwork of Baghdad. Ornamentation within al-Wāsiṭī's niche consists of a heart-shaped pattern which is also reminiscent of contemporary stucco-work. Al-Wāsiṭī depicts grey/blue pillars in the Samarqand mosque and the Basra mosque in *Maqāma* 50, where these columns have bell-shaped capitals and bases. Similar capitals are found in the St Petersburg manuscript. The theme was also taken up in in Egypt,[12] and appears in the niche of the main *miḥrāb* in the Great Mosque in Mosul. That structure is strikingly similar to al-Wāsiṭī's *miḥrāb* with two exceptions: the lack of crenellations and a slightly pointed, four-centred arch. Bell-shaped capitals are a feature of contemporary *miḥrābs*, particularly in the Mosul area. They occur on a flat *miḥrāb* in the Shaykh Fatḥī tomb, on a *miḥrāb* in the Nūrī mosque, and on another *miḥrāb* in the tomb of Imām 'Abd al-Raḥmān.[13]

Most of the *Maqāmāt* illustrators found it difficult to portray the correct physical relationship of *minbar* to *miḥrāb*; this may have been due to lack of expertise in exploring pictorial space within the confines of the text. Alternatively, because the *minbar* in real life is so monumental a feature, it might tend to overshadow the setting, and the issue is therefore evaded by painters.

Al-Wāsiṭī has produced a striking and elaborate image which leaves no doubt that this is a great mosque of the period. However, without the miniature on the opposite folio (Illust. 2), a reading of the text and evidence concerning banners on the *minbar*, there is nothing to suggest that it took place on 'Īd al-Fiṭr, for the worshippers elsewhere in the manuscript are equally well dressed.

1. The pilgrim caravan arrives at Juhfa.

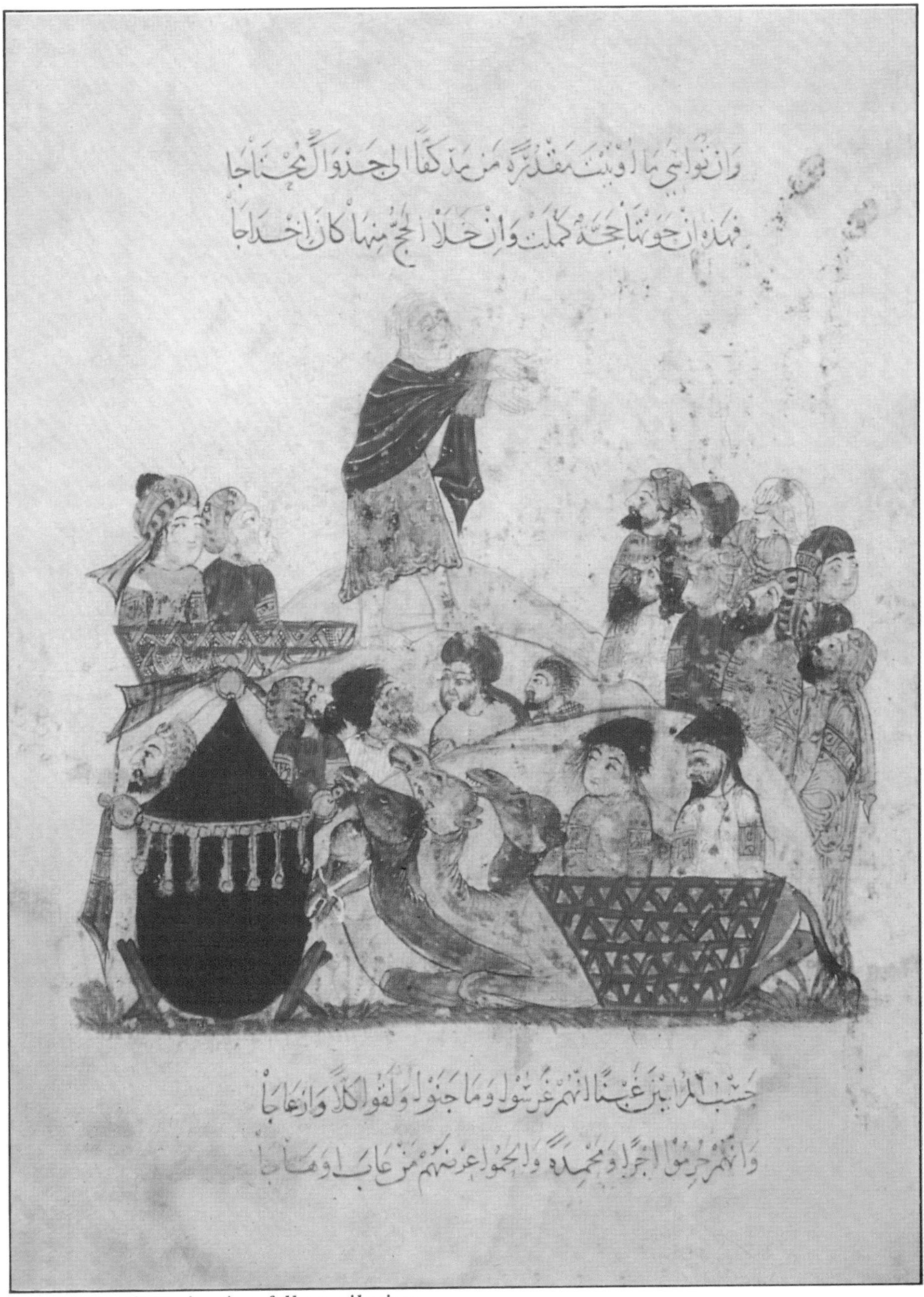

2. *Abū Zayd castigating fellow pilgrims.*

3. Abū Zayd in sycophantic mood before a governor.

4. Abū Zayd living like a lord.

5. Abū Zayd in the guise of a great preacher.

2. *The imperial military Band.*

The Imperial Military Band (Ṭabl Khāna)

In *Maqāma* 7 only al-Wāsiṭī illustrates the ruler's mounted military band (Illust. 2). This immediately follows his scene in the mosque (Illust. 1) and the three lines of text above it continue Abū Zayd's castigation of his wife and also record al-Ḥārith's ensuing conversation with the woman when, in reply to his insistent questioning, he learns that her companion is 'of the people of Sarūj', namely Abū Zayd.

The red commentary at the left-hand side refers to the horses (*khayl*). It draws attention to the Qur'ānic allusion to *sūra* 17 in the opening words of the tale, when al-Ḥārith tells of his determination to witness the festival ritual to mark the breaking of the fast on a day which 'brought up its horses and footmen', that is, its pomp and ceremony. This evocative image seems to have fired al-Wāsiṭī's imagination.

The miniature is not placed in the exact centre of the page, for there are three lines of text above and two below. The dialogue correctly runs on from the text of the mosque scene; the artist has ignored the intervening text of alliterative poetry in an appeal to the congregation for alms as a possible location for the image, as well as a prose section and another short piece of poetry. The caption runs:

Shall we lose the net as well as the prey,
And the wick as well as the brand to light it with? . . .
So she began to retrace her steps and seek the scroll . . .
I said, 'If thou desirest the burnished and engraved,
Thou must reveal a matter which is as yet a secret.'[14]

Assuming al-Wāsiṭī's inspiration did lie in the earlier Qur'ānic allusion, then it is clear that the miniature is misplaced in the text, for this mounted group has evidently assembled to announce that the breaking of the fast is to be officially sanctioned, and presumably a fanfare is about to be played. Strictly speaking, it should therefore have appeared before the scene in the mosque. Because al-Wāsiṭī, as calligrapher, could have inserted the illustration in the correct context, at the beginning of the *Maqāma*, it was not necessarily created for this volume and might have been copied from another manuscript. However, there seems to be a plausible alternative explanation. Al-Wāsiṭī laid out his pages with care. His title headings were in the large script known as Thulūth and lines of poetry were usually centred, although this is not the case in the Barqa'īd mosque miniature. Chapters did not necessarily start on a fresh page and equal, larger spacing than usual was generally left between headings and narratives, both above and below the title: an example is his illustration at the end of the 4th tale, where the title of the 5th *Maqāma* appears in handsome gold Thulūth between two lines of text in Naskhī script. Al-Wāsiṭī may therefore have concluded that he was unable to make the visual impact he sought, due perhaps to a necessarily 'top-heavy' introduction, for the reference to the pomp and ceremony of the occasion is very close to the beginning of the tale.

Four mounted horsemen, three of whom hold standards, are in the company of three musicians. All the riders wear Arab turbans, and four of them have Semitic features. Three of the men at the left-hand side have almond-shaped eyes. Two of these riders bear black pennants and the furled black standard of the 'Abbāsids is also borne aloft; perhaps their non-Arab appearance is significant, in that they are representatives of the court, where foreigners were employed, and they may have been modelled on Turkish figures in royal iconography.

Despite the exhortation to rejoicing and celebration, the standard-bearers have rather glum faces and they display little of the sense of joyful anticipation which is normally evident on this occasion. This is understandable in light of the effects of a rigorous month of self-denial. The Prophet said, 'Fasting is one half of endurance' and 'Endurance is one half of the faith,' and their faces reflect this aspect of Ramaḍān. Further, like the Muslim pilgrim, the observer of Ramaḍān should remain in suspense between fear and hope, since he does not know if his fast will be accepted.[15]

The elaborate preparations of caliphs, viziers and other high-ranking officials to celebrate the start of the 'Īd are set out in the *Rules and Regulations of the Court*. The people assembled at dawn in colourful procession, splendidly attired, and set out from the residence of the vizier or the military commander, making their way through the city to the place of prayer (*muṣallā*). This scene could represent such a group and, in the absence of architecture, they may have gathered either at a setting outside the official's residence or outside the city walls. *Muṣallā* could also mean a large patch of bare ground, usually outside the city bounds. Apparently it had a wall which oriented the prayer towards Mecca (*qibla*) and an open-air *minbar*. In other words, it had the function of a mosque reduced to the barest essentials. *Muṣallā* might be interpreted as any place where one might pray, but where it was not recommended to say the Friday prayers.[16] It would be a suitable site for an official retinue to gather to announce to the populace that the long month of fasting was over; indeed, the dry, uncultivated earth with minimal vegetation which forms the groundline in the illustration suggests such a setting. The two images would be identified by the Muslim reader in the context of a great religious festival.

All the men wear turbans, shown in hues of gold, russet, green, grey and white. They appear to have a fairly short piece of winding cloth, for the endpieces do not hang down over the shoulders like those of the congregation in the mosque. This suggests that the men are officials, for the preacher wears similar headgear in his capacity as an appointee of the state. The standard-bearer at the extreme left and the trumpeter in the centre of the illustration may be wearing a *midra'a*, which the medieval dictionaries *al-Qāmūs* and *al-Layth* describe as 'a certain garment [a tunic] like that called *durrā'a*, never of anything but wool'. Al-Wāsiṭī's rendering may be a sartorial compromise, for the standard-bearer's orange robe is clearly split across his saddle, yet it has no obvious chest fasteners, and the buttons and loops of the Egyptian version noted by al-Maqrīzī are not illustrated. Instead, the garment is secured by a gold-coloured belt whose roundel design hints at Persian influence. This belt may identify the wearer as the most senior member of the group.

The trumpeter in the centre wears a similar tunic, while the other members of the procession are wearing a simple type of shirt (*qamīs*) which came in varying lengths and had a round neck-hole and no opening at the front. According to the Sharī'a, the shirt should have been long, but Ibn al-Ḥajj reports that in the fourteenth century it frequently reached only to the knees.[17] One sees clearly that the player of the kettle-drum (*naqqāra*), whose white trousers (*sarāwīl*) are tucked into his boots, is wearing a waist-length shirt. This outfit would make it easier for him to strike the pair of kettle-drums than the tight-fitting coat described above, and would also be more expedient on account of the larger saddle and saddle-board of his mule. Sleeves had become wider in the ninth century, during the reign of al-Musta'īn, and al-Mas'ūdī later describes sleeves as measuring three hand spans. Curiously, the fashion reached its apogee as the caliphate's power plummeted; al-Rāghib wryly observed that when the tall hat (*qalansuwa*) became very long, turbans extremely elaborate and sleeves too wide, the people would perish.[18] Al-Wāsiṭī's illustration shows shifts with both narrow and wide sleeves, so an element of personal preference or practicality may be evident here. He has employed a bright palette for his costumes. Robes of orange, brown, dark green, gold and shades of grey are distinguishable, which aptly recall the text's 'arrayed, agreeably to traditional practice, in new apparel'. In the medieval period, textile production in the Near East rivalled that of steel and other metals today and fine garments commanded enormous prices. For example, the *Rules and Regulations of the Court* reports that the highest category of robe of honour (*khil'a*) presented to a regional governor in earlier days might have cost 300 *dīnārs*; in the 'Abbāsid period such robes were much more costly, due to the fashion for jewelled embellishment.[19]

Fine clothing is mentioned in works of *belles-lettres*, and the implication must be that it was the apparel of the leisured class. Al-Washshā' had earlier produced several chapters on the types of clothes worn by his contemporaries, including a section on 'The dress of the elegant: the costume affected by men of position', while the *Book of Curious and Entertaining Information [Laṭā'if al-ma'ārif]* of al-Tha'ālibī of Nīshāpūr includes a list of elegant clothes in the context of the Buwayhid court. Even among the poorer classes, clothing was not cheap: a pledge document from the Cairo repository of Jewish manuscripts (*Geniza*) dated *c.* 1213 itemizes several garments which were pawned for the not inconsiderable sum of 4 *dīnārs*.[20]

The orange tunic falls into the category of cloth of one colour (*musmaṭ*). The lack of highlights, other than the shading for folds on the lower left arm and right thigh, perhaps indicates that it is woollen. Other tunics seem to be made from figured materials (*wāshī*) and may be brocade (*dībāj*), a cloth with both warp and weft of silk. However, *mulḥam*, with its silk warp and cotton weft, would also have a sheen. All these upper, outer garments bear decorative *ṭirāz* bands.

The striking backdrop is composed of five large banners with legible epigraphy which are a triumphant confirmation of the doctrine of the Oneness of Allāh (*tawḥīd*), a theme that was to be reiterated in the sermon. They are likely also to contain some of the 99 names of God. Like the black banners in the mosque, the standards have metal hexagonal finials, but there is no sign of their bearers.

The banners are rigid and must be made from a fairly robust material. The two at the right-hand side bear the first half of the profession of the Muslim faith (*shahāda*), 'There is no god but Allāh.' The central grey banner also shows the word 'Allāh', among less legible words, and it is likely that the blue and orange banners to the left may also bear religious inscriptions. The highly decorative, ornamental type of Kūfic script employed here evolved from the twelfth century onwards into even more intricate patterns. A careful study of the word 'Allāh' in the top line of the orange banner reveals it to be identically written to the inscription that al-Wāsiṭī has placed in a frieze on his village mosque in *Maqāma* 43 (Illust. 13). However, there the Kūfic inscription is less floriated, for brick or stone would be less amenable to elaboration than cloth.

There are three possible interpretations of the fabrics used for this backdrop. If the banners are of cotton, they have been painted with a brush or stylus, using stencils or blocks, and outlined in lighter hues or white. Linen, which originated in Egypt, is an alternative explanation; it was not until what Kuhnel terms 'dynastic times' that pigments which did not dye the fabric, but merely coated the surface, were employed. The third fabric may be wool, with a woven inscription.[21]

A very long standard with pseudo-epigrapy at the left-hand side acts as a frame and counterbalances the furled 'Abbāsid standards on the opposite page; both of these devices close the extremities of an extremely large double-page spread. Al-Wāsiṭī has carried this long banner well up the page, out into the margin and past two lines of text, which represents an early instance of invasion of the margin. Such experimentation is possible in the absence of a ruled frame.

The black furled banner is the standard (*'alāma* or *rāya*) of the 'Abbāsid caliphs. The *Qāmūs* and *Tāj al-'arūs* dictionaries also describe *'alam* as the ornamental or figured borders of a garment or piece of cloth. It is significant that the root of this word means 'to know', which confirms the notion of the standard, like the *ṭirāz*, making a political and religious statement. The *Book of the Virtues of Baghdad [Faḍā'il Baghdād al-'Irāq]*, written by al-Fārisī for the caliph al-Mu'taḍid in the eleventh century, sets out the various expenses in the caliphal palaces. Provision was made for the bearers who carried the standard at the Two Feasts, namely the lesser feast here, 'Īd al-Ṣaghīr, and the great feast, or 'Īd al-Kabīr, at the end of the pilgrimage.[22]

Al-Wāsiṭī's standard-bearers are perhaps paid officials of the state. The furled banner appears to be silken and the epigraphy is white. Given that this is a caliphal emblem, the inscriptions may have been applied by silk tapestry weaving; they seem to read 'Allāh'. The finial of the pole is hexagonal in shape and is apparently made from pale grey metal; it would presumably be inscribed, although no inscription is evident.

The black pennants, which are fringed (*ḥāshiyya*), are possibly silken and sport *ṭirāz* embroidery at their ends. The pseudo-epigraphy on the pennants generally resembles that on the very long black banner. The *ṭirāz* band on that long banner, to an extent not possible on garment folds, fulfils exactly al-Muṭarrizī's twelfth-century definition of the Arabized Persian word which meant 'even measurement'. A plausible reading of the epigraphy which runs the length of the field in a repeating motif is 'Allāh', if one sees the final letter of God's name as a very decorative evolution of the Arabic. This long banner might have been woven in the manner of a woollen carpet with a heavy fringe of coloured cottons and a gold field.

Embroidered bands feature not only on all the men's garments and the banners but even on the mule's grey felt saddle-cloth. This cloth in turn covers another thinner cloth which absorbed the animal's sweat. Both these items are placed below the saddle. The *ṭirāz* of the grey saddle-cloth provides a foil for the striped dark grey pattern. As the most prominent animal in the parade, such a decorative covering for the mule is appropriate, although it may also serve the more plebeian task of covering the wooden boards which bear the weight of the drums. It is unlikely that the embroidery featured on such a profane item would carry any religious invocation, so its appearance here may be a purely decorative element. A similar, smaller saddle-cloth, also in light grey, with an abstract pattern, is clearly seen below the horse's saddle, but it is unadorned.

Al-Wāsiṭī shows the remainder of the paraphernalia of riding in some detail. The bridle, for example, can be clearly seen. In the *Book of the Saddle and Bridle [Ṣifāt al-sarj wa al-lijām]*, Ibn Durayd uses 'bridle' for all the various forms of horse trappings.

The mule's grey girth is plaited. Here it has to be strong enough to support the not inconsiderable weight of the boards. Undated remnants of medieval girths have been excavated at Fusṭāṭ; these were double-woven from wool and consisted of two separate weaves of coloured wools which formed interchanging geometric patterns. They were produced with shafts and heddles, that is a series of vertical cords or wires. Girths were in wide use throughout the Near East; examples from Homs were exported and sold in fourteenth-century Cairo.[23] The word for girth, *ḥizām*, is also used for a belt. The horse in the foreground has no girth; this is surprising, but girthless horses were depicted even in fourteenth-century cavalry manuals, perhaps in order to develop greater powers of control. A two-stranded breast strap is attached to the pommel at the front of the saddle. Stirrups appear to be brass and are probably made in one piece; the riders, unlike those in the cavalry manuals, wear no spurs.

The kettle-drums (*naqqārāt*) have a footed base and are supported on a wooden board (*daffa*) at either side of the beast. The kettle-drum is beaten with two drumsticks which, through use, become bent at the ends; it is still used in Morocco.[24] The board is dark blue and elaborately carved; its upswept shape matches the pricked-up ears of the mule, as well as providing another link with the illustration on the opposite page.

Drums played an important part in religious festivities: as well as forming part of the spectacle of a band and being used to keep the populace awake during the long hours of the fast, they were an extremely effective means of communication and an affirmation of the ruler's might. Significantly, the verb *ṭabala* (to drum) has connotations of propaganda and the inference must be that these men are people of some official standing. The drumsticks are probably wooden, with a small round knop: the same type of drum and drumsticks persisted in Turkish military bands until at least the early eighteenth century.

The musicians' group includes two trumpeters. The trumpet (*nafīr*) is a long, harsh-sounding, single-reed instrument. Here, it appears to be of brass; a knop is clearly seen on one trumpet, and both have decoration on the stem and at the fluted opening. The interior of the instruments is reddish in colour, but there is no way of knowing if this is artistic licence.

Similar musical instruments are found on the water-clock in al-Jazarī's roughly contemporary *Book of Writing, Knowledge and Practice in the Profession of Mechanics [Kitāb fī ma'rifat al-ḥiyal al-handasiyya]*. The trumpet was used with double-reed instruments and kettle-drums in the military context and is found in Turkish, Persian and Mughal manuscripts. Trumpets had been in widespread use throughout the Mediterranean world since metalworking was introduced.[25]

Both trumpeters have their instruments upraised and at the ready for the announcement of the beginning of the 'Īd. Mounted trumpeters have also survived from Egyptian shadow-play figures; one was riding a horse while the other was mounted on a mule.[26] It may be that the kettle-drummer's mule is of a more even temperament than a thoroughbred horse and less liable to be upset by the vibrations and noise from the drums, the raucous trumpet blasts and the excitement of a large crowd. Mules are also stronger than horses, and the combined weight of the drums and wooden side supports might be too much for the average horse.

The mule and horses in the miniature are realistically depicted, with an intelligent, almost anthropomorphic sensibility that appears to render them independent of their masters. Thus they have more character and appear to be from a less formulaic mould than, for example, those found in a slightly earlier illustration from Baghdad, in al-Aḥnaf's *Book of Farriery [Kitāb al-bayṭara]*, dated 1210. The horse and rider on a late twelfth-century lustre dish from Kashān still betray a rather stiff heraldic quality (as does the floral decoration).[27] Al-Wāsiṭī's animals are perhaps symptomatic of a new realism in painting. The tail of the grey horse is plaited at the end, although the others hang loose. In the case of cavalry horses, the tails were looped and tied back on themselves, and one wonders why in that instance they were not simply cut, for practical reasons.

Close examination of the miniature reveals that, although there are seven horses and a mule, only seven riders are depicted. Further, it seems that al-Wāsiṭī has had to make room in the composition for the trumpeter in the centre, for he cannot be sitting on any of the three mismatched horses at the right-hand side; he sits both behind and to the left of the kettle-drummer. This would allow the trumpet to be included within the limitation of the page width and would also reinforce the balance of the composition and provide a link with the mosque illustration. In order to make this less obvious, the artist seems to have chosen deliberately to 'blend' the trumpeter in with the grey banner at the centre by making his tunic a similar shade of grey.

The massed heads of the four horses at the left-hand side emphasize patience, as does the solid phalanx of banners in the background. Anticipation is hinted at by the upward sweep of the elaborate board carrying the drums; this in turn is echoed in the pricked-forward ears of the mule. The upraised trumpets and banners counterbalance the horizontal rows of horses and banners, and these elements allay any sense of monotony arising from the multitude of horses' legs in the foreground. This vivid illustration suggests that the musicians and the restive horses at the right-hand side have sensed that the long wait is almost over. The anticipation of the electrifying reaction to the announcement of the ending of Ramaḍān in an indescribable cacophony of sound, as all the tensions and austerities of the month dissipate in preparation for several days of rejoicing, therefore seems apt and entirely predictable here.

A similar massed phalanx of riders is found on a polychrome glazed tile from Kashān, now in the Museum of Fine Arts, Boston, but the treatment of the theme there is very different. Gone is al-Wāsiṭī's preoccupation with the human drama. The tile composition is necessarily circumscribed by its 'star' shape and the impersonal, static quality in the over-large oriental features of the personages is characteristic of both Kashān lustreware and Persian polychrome pottery. The major difference lies in the iconography: whereas the *Maqāmāt* miniature reflects an interest in everyday Arab life, the Kashān tile depicts a theme (the Persians leaving the fort at Furūd) from Firdawsī's *Book of Kings [Shāh-nāma]*.[28]

The choice of subject-matter in the *Maqāmāt* and the realistic artistic style of these two miniatures may help to explain the popularity of the tales, the nature of their audience, and also that of patronage; just as Persian artists were patronized by the court, namely the subjects of the illustrations, the artists of the *Maqāmāt* manuscripts may have been commissioned by the bourgeoisie.

As scribe and artist, al-Wāsiṭī was aware of the social context, so he is once more taking an original leap of the imagination to illustrate the 'attendant circumstances', that is the ceremonial rites of the festival, and to exert his prerogative to determine exactly the placing of his miniatures. He has executed two contemporary scenes which would, in conjunction, be readily identifiable to his medieval audience. The underlying sentiments of Ramaḍān are as valid today as they were at his time and his appeal, on this occasion at least, is therefore timeless.

The Ḥajj

In *Maqāma* 31, the narrator tells us that while he camped at Ramla, which was an important town between Jerusalem and Jaffa, 'I found there a caravan of camels preparing to depart [by night], with loads being girded on, in readiness to go to Mecca.' Despite his earlier predilection for wandering in the course of his business, 'well knowing that foreign travel replenishes the stores and generates a constant increase of prosperity', al-Ḥārith is sufficiently inspired by the pilgrims to disregard his business in order 'to gain a sight of the holy wall' at Mecca. As his party dismount at Juḥfa, a lone figure appears to them from the hillocks and fires their imagination by promising to tell them what conduct will save them on the Day of Judgment. The old man climbs up on a rock and delivers an edifying sermon, first in rhymed prose and then in verse, on the true nature of the *ḥajj*.

Al-Wāsiṭī has again provided two illustrations in this tale which combine in the manuscript in an impressive tableau. The one to the right shows a mounted procession, while the left-hand painting features an elderly man preaching from a rock to a more motley crowd of pilgrims.

The Maḥmil *Procession*

The first painting (Plate 1) shows a procession with mounted musicians, and it appears at the point where Abū Zayd reiterates his earlier theme of the true nature of the *ḥajj* and his castigation of the other pilgrims. The illustration is placed below two lines of narrative, which read:

> Then he raised his voice loud enough to make the deaf hear
> And almost to shake the mountain-tops, while he thus indited:
> 'The *ḥajj* is not to journey day and night
> With camel choice and litter richly dight . . .'[29]

The text continues with a reproach to the pilgrim band. An exegesis of al-Ḥarīrī's text down the right-hand side includes an alternative verb which seems to refer to the pilgrims' mode of travel; the commentary forms a decorative outer frame, when taken in conjunction with what may be a similar commentary on the accompanying illustration.

This image is unique in the *Maqāmāt* cycle. A group of men mounted on camels is accompanied by a horseman and two footmen. Two men carry aloft standards bearing black pennants with *ṭirāz* bands and pseudo-epigraphy; a third, vertical, standard is perhaps being borne by one of the trumpeters. At first glance these standards appear to be made from black fringed silk with applied bands of embroidery.

The section on the 'Turkish lands' in the *Book of Curious and Entertaining Information* mentions the use of hair from the shaggy coat and the tail of the yak at the end of flag-poles and spear shafts;[30] al-Wāsiṭī's banners may have been trimmed with this material. The length of the standard seems to have remained constant since the thirteenth century: according to Lane's description of nineteenth-century religious processions in his *Account of the Manners and Customs of the Modern Egyptians*, the standard was 'a pole about twenty feet in length, like a large flagstaff . . . with a large conical ornament of brass on the top'.[31] However, the standards here have a hexagonal-shaped grey metal finial like those in the Ramaḍān group and may be of steel. It is possible that these hexagons bore inscriptions. The *Rules and Regulations of the Court* also describe the flag-pole of an earlier 'Abbāsid period that mentions the name of the Commander of the Faithful, 'Abdallāh ibn Ja'far al-Imām al-Qā'im bi 'Amr Allāh, invokes God's aid and pledges the ruler to God's cause. Indeed, the outlining of the hexagons in off-white in the illustration suggests that there would be inscriptions.

Trumpets and kettle-drums comprise the band's instruments. The form of trumpet here appears to be a type of *karna*, a raucous, double-reed instrument used in the context of outdoor military music. The drums are different in shape to those played by the Ramaḍān group; they are long and cylindrical, not wide and tapering. Here the drumsticks are club-shaped. Three are fairly rigid, but one is more flexible, and they are possibly made of leather.

The musicians and standard-bearers wear similar Arab robes with gold *ṭirāz* bands bearing pseudo-epigraphy on the sleeves. No definite patterns can be made out, although folds are delineated and texture hinted at by gradations of tone and delicate outlining in a contrasting colour. The folds indicate that a fairly fine material was used. The artist's preference for solid blocks of colour, as opposed to pattern for its own sake, is once more evident. This suggests that al-Wāsiṭī's primary concern lay in the context of the tale and the human drama being enacted. A similar disregard for textile pattern occurs in the contemporary *Romance of Warqa and Gulshāh* manuscript, a love-story by 'Ayyūkī where human interest and realism are also in evidence, and where the same techniques for folds and texture are employed.[32] A comparison of textile and other patterns in, say, the Mamlūk Vienna *Maqāmāt* reveals how an emphasis on ornamentation there led to a static quality of human representation and a notion that many of the miniatures were interchangeable, regardless of the story.

Al-Wāsiṭī's palette includes blues, dark green and gold for the garment fabrics; the turbans are shown in shades of russet, violet and blue. Definitions of the turban as a 'badge of Islam' (*simāt al-islām*) and a 'divider between belief and unbelief' (*ḥājiza bayn al-kufr wa al-īmān*) are particularly apposite here, in the context of a religious festival. Al-Wāsiṭī may have chosen colours without regard to the conventions of the day, when Jews, Christians and other members of the protected non-Muslim (*dhimmī*) class wore distinctive, prescribed colours. It should not be forgotten that in manuscripts of the Mamlūk period Muslims are depicted as wearing yellow, red and blue turbans. Other *Maqāmāt* illustrators also used colours for clothing that were normally associated with the non-Muslim *dhimmī* class. It seems that the regulations concerning dress were periodically renewed and that legislation affecting these 'people of the book' (*ahl al-dhimma*) who lived under Muslim protection was not always consistently enforced and frequently remained so much 'ink on paper'. Under al-Nāṣir ibn Qalawūn in the fourteenth century, the Samaritans were directed to wear red, the Jews yellow and the Christians blue head-bands.[33]

One unusual feature of costume in BN 5847 that has not been noted before is the white sash falling from the right shoulder to the left-hand side of the waist of the kettle-drummer in the green robe. This garment may be a *wishāḥ*, which was worn by both men and women; according to the *Miṣbāḥ* dictionary, it should properly be worn over the left shoulder and under the right arm, presumably to allow freedom of movement for the right hand, which is ritually clean. Al-Wāsiṭī's *wishāḥ* may be artistic licence, to follow the thrust of the trumpets and pennants in their emphasis of forward movement.

The three men in the foreground, who are dressed quite differently from the musicians and flag-bearers, wear blue knee-length tunics with gold *ṭirāz* bands on the sleeve. At least two of the robes, those of the horseman and the footman at the right foreground, open from the neck to the waist and are similar to a type of garment already portrayed in the Ramaḍān painting (Illust. 2). In the absence of drapery, one presumes that a heavier material, perhaps wool, was used for these garments. Al-Wāsiṭī therefore appears to have reproduced contemporary costume. The footmen also wear a plain gold-coloured belt or girdle (*minṭaq*) and striped stockings or leggings with hoops of gold, cream, purple and violet. The leggings are known as *muzāj*, which Dozy defines as an Arabized Persian word.[34] They differ from *jurāb* or *jawrab*, which were socks worn beneath shoes or boots, and here they clearly resemble spats and cover the footwear. *Muzāj* were made of wool, silk or leather.

The leading member of the group walks before the horseman and carries a staff with a knop. His companion brings up the rear, his staff holding a dark green and gold-coloured cloth bag hanging over his shoulder; perhaps this contains provisions, or at least the wherewithal to purchase them *en route*. The bag might also open out into the portable tablecloth with rings or loops (*simāṭ*) which occurs uniquely in the BN 3929 manuscript illustration of the 30th tale.

Both footmen wear a type of conical hat that is unlike the musicians' heavy, round turban; this must be the *dānniyya*, so-called in the dialect of Iraq because it was similar in shape to the long, tapering wine-jar (*dānn*). Sartorial fashions obviously varied according to place and era. For example, al-Ṭabarī's *History of the Messengers and Kings [Tārīkh al-rusul wa al-mulūk]* reports that while the *qalansuwa* with turban formed the only mark of sovereignty during al-Mutawakkil's reign in the ninth century, his successor al-Musta'īn confined the wearing of the *dānniyya* to *qāḍīs* because it had become so popular with the common people.[35]

By the thirteenth century, we see Abū Zayd wearing the *qalansuwa* with his turban elsewhere in *Maqāmāt* manuscripts. The horseman in the *ḥajj* procession possibly wears a tall dark *qalansuwa* beneath his blue turban; this is not entirely clear, as the base of the camel-saddle is behind his head. He sports light knee-length riding boots.

The musicians and standard-bearers have Semitic features; the exception is the beardless youth, who has an East Asian countenance and resembles people in a slightly later thirteenth-century work from Mosul, the Vienna *Book of Antidotes [Kitāb al-ṭiryāq]*.[36] At least two of the men in the foreground seem to be Saljūq Turks, an impression confirmed by their distinctive headgear. On the face of the leading footman one sees again the protruding further eye, a device representing the gradual replacement of the three-quarter view by the profile. It also appears in the St Petersburg manuscript.

Perhaps the artist deliberately sought to accord prominence to the lone grey riderless camel bearing a covered litter by depicting the other four camels as ordinary, workaday sand-coloured riding beasts (*ru'āhl*). There are no other examples of the species here, such as the fleet-footed red and very valuable *mahrī* camel from Yemen which could outrun a horse—one can be seen in the herd of camels that, together with a singer, form Abū Zayd's reward in *Maqāma* 32. The chestnut horse bears all the necessary paraphernalia and trappings of horsemanship that have been discussed elsewhere and can also be observed in the *Book of Antidotes*. These items also appear in other art forms, as, for example, on a Mosul candlestick; on polychrome pottery; on a beaker in the Freer Gallery of Art, Washington; and on a Kashān polychrome glazed tile.[37] In those media, too, the horses and their trappings have been carefully observed and realistically portrayed.

A grassy knoll defines the outdoor setting on two distinct planes. The horizontal groundline consists of vegetation where the grass is merely suggested. It is punctuated by a variety of stylized plant forms, with flowers that serve as space fillers or compositional markers, for they appear precisely between the horse's legs and then between the horse and the two characters travelling on foot. The same device of the crossing-over of two plants may be observed in the BL 1200 and BN 3929 *Maqāmāt* manuscripts. However, it is not seen in BN 6094 where, on the five occasions where vegetation appears, it is in the form of a highly stylized tree and closely packed grass bands. The stylized grass band on the right-hand side of the illustration accords fairly well with Nassar's description of 'small, obliquely placed, fleshy leaves, packed close together', which she notes in Saljūq and Syriac manuscripts of the same period.[38] In none of these manuscripts does there seem to be an interest in landscape features as such; they are used as a compositional device or to indicate an outdoor setting.

Al-Wāsiṭī repeats the division of the composition into two registers by a grassy hill elsewhere, and the artists of the Istanbul and St Petersburg manuscripts do likewise in the 36th and 39th tales respectively. The convention of animals appearing from outcrops of landscape prefigures Persian miniature painting. Al-Wāsiṭī has set his two disparate pilgrim groups apart by several means: the two registers; the different styles of costume; the diverse modes of travel; and the physical characteristics of the men. These elements may represent a deliberate attempt to highlight each group, and one must try to understand his motives.

The horseman may simply be a high-ranking person of means who is travelling in style, or he is possibly enjoying high patronage, as was Ibn Baṭṭūṭa while on an excursion in Turkey in the fourteenth century. However, there is an alternative interpretation. The cortège of the caliph, which appeared on Fridays when he presided over the community prayers and on festive occasions, was extremely impressive. The imperial military band (*ṭabl khāna*) marched before him with banners unfurled, trumpets blaring and the beating of drums. Instruments included the trumpet, the drum, the tambour, fifes and the hautboy.

During the later Mamlūk period, apart from the sultan, the military officers and the governors of five Syrian provinces, there was a further category of *ṭabl khāna* princes (that is, those who had forty Mamlūk slave-soldiers serving under them) who were entitled to be accompanied by a band.[39] Military bands, then, have more than an air of officialdom about them and the most important personage here may be a government official appointed by the caliph himself.

As the spiritual head of the Faithful, the caliph had to meet the expenses of the pilgrimage (among other things) out of the privy purse. The official in charge of the pilgrim contingent was known variously as *amīr al-ḥajj* or *ra'īs*, terms indicating high rank. Among his duties, he oversaw the journey, supervised the conduct of the pilgrims and led his particular group in the pilgrimage ritual. This post was evidently both a privilege and a great responsibility, for the *amīr al-ḥajj* was appointed by the government at a ceremonial gathering of the caliph, the chief *qāḍī* and his deputies, and other dignitaries.[40] One would therefore expect him to travel with a retinue under the patronage and protection of the ruler. Ibn Baṭṭūṭa records his own experience thus in his *Travels in Asia and Africa [Tuḥfat al-nuẓẓār fī gharā'ib al-amṣār wa 'ajā'ib al-asfār]*:

> I left Baghdad with the caravan of Sultan Abū Sa'īd, on purpose to see the way in which the king's marches are conducted, and travelled with it for ten days, thereafter accompanying one of the princes to the town of Tabrīz.[41]

This interpretation is given credence if the grey camel bears what is commonly known as a *maḥmal*. Strictly speaking, the term should be *maḥmil*, as defined by medieval dictionaries, and this term will be used in the interest of accuracy. These dictionaries give its primary significance as 'a place of bearing or carrying'. *Al-Miṣbāḥ* says it is the kind of vehicle known as *hawdaj*, and consists of a pair of panniers bearing two more or less equal loads with a small tent. Perhaps significantly, the twelfth-century *Mughrib* dictionary describes the *maḥmil* as 'the large *hawdaj* termed *ḥajjājī*', which places it specifically in the context of the pilgrimage. The object borne by the grey camel has a conical, domed cover, an almost drum-shaped frame with pommels, and possibly gold ornamentation. It is draped in a soft golden-coloured silky fabric and is adorned with three black pennants identical to those carried on the three standards in this painting. These hint at 'Abbāsid officialdom and suggest that this is a state-sponsored group of pilgrims who are escorting the official *maḥmil*. The problem is what, or who, was carried in this vehicle?

Is it likely that al-Wāsiṭī's painting, or a model, was an official rendering of an important official occasion? Opinions differ as to the origin of this procession. Al-Suyūṭī's *Perfection [Ḥusn]* credits the Mamlūk sultan Baybars, who ruled from 1260 to 1277, with the organization of the Egyptian *maḥmil* on a systematic and permanent basis. Baybars was apparently the first ruler to dispatch a *maḥmil* as a political symbol.[42] This opinion is reinforced by the fact that Baybars was renowned for his zeal and religious orthodoxy, and our particular cavalcade would make both a religious and a political statement. Baybars ruled some 20 years after al-Wāsiṭī executed this manuscript. The Syrian prince Abū al-Fidā' recorded in his *Epitome of the History of Mankind [al-Mukhtaṣar fī akhbār al-bashar]* that Sultan al-Mālik al-Nāṣir was attended by 60 princes when he undertook the pilgrimage in 1320.[43]

In the thirteenth century the *maḥmil* became a symbol of sovereignty and independence and not only the Egyptian but the Syrian, Iraqi and Yemeni caravans brought tented carriers to Mecca and 'Arafāt.[44] Given the trappings of royalty, such a procession seems to be symbolic of power and dignity. The *maḥmil* which accompanied the Syrian pilgrim contingent was not only smaller than its Egyptian counterpart but it had a domed top. It can be assumed, then, that the object on the riderless camel in the illustration is the Syrian *maḥmil*, because the incident took place at the Juḥfa of the text, which was 'a station on the pilgrimage, between Medina and Mecca, where the pilgrims from Syria assemble'. If this is so, then al-Wāsiṭī's illustration may well be the only extant example of the official Syrian pilgrim caravan. There may be a correspondence between the medieval *maḥmil* and the pre-Islamic tribal small domed tent (*qubba*) of red leather housing a sacred stone, which had the function of a portable sanctuary or tabernacle. There may also be a connection with the Jewish Ark of the Covenant.

Although al-Wāsiṭī frequently took an original leap of the imagination in his interpretation of the text, the accounts by Ibn Baṭṭūṭa and Ibn Jubayr of pilgrim caravans in the medieval period have no apparent reference to an official unoccupied *maḥmil*, or at least to the politico-symbolic aspect. For example, Ibn Jubayr says in his *Travels [al-Riḥla]*:

> The most remarkable of these *hawdaj* that we noticed were that of the Sharīfa Jumana, daughter of Fulayta and aunt of the *Amīr* Mukthir, which drew a long train over the ground, and those of the harem [*sic*] of the ruler and the harem of his principal officers, as well as other *hawdaj* whose number we cannot record because of the impossibility of counting them. On the backs of the camels these *hawdaj* appeared as raised pavilions, and the beholder would conceive them to be an encampment with its pitched tents of every lively colour.[45]

A twelfth-century painting of the two camel-riders in the Cappella Palatina, Palermo, conveys the notion of riding in a procession, and the second figure is clearly a woman in a tent-topped litter. Again, these camels face to the left.[46] However, none of these litters in any way approximates to al-Wāsiṭī's carrier, and the personal nature of the litters is emphasized. Unfortunately, it is impossible to say what al-Wāsiṭī's source was, or whether the practice of sending an empty, but politically significant litter to Mecca was instituted before the time of Baybars.

The dynamism created by the forward thrust of trumpets and flags in the miniature reflects the sense of triumph on arriving in the Ḥijāz and the anticipation of the approach to Mecca, the Mother of Cities, which is evident in the text. Al-Ḥārith's description of his companions, 'whose rapidity in travelling was like the current of a flood, and alacrity for the good work like that of swift steeds', may also have fired al-Wāsiṭī's imagination in his attempt to capture the mood of the occasion. That there is a sound reason for this urgency, and for the exultation on the arrival at sacred territory, can be gleaned from Ibn Baṭṭūṭa's personal account of the hazards which would have faced earlier Syrian pilgrims. Here he describes the rigours of his own caravan from Damascus which set out on 1 September 1326:

> From Tabūk the caravan travels with great speed night and day, for fear of this desert. Halfway through is the valley of al-Ukhayḍir, which might well be the valley of Hell (may God preserve us from it). One year the pilgrims suffered terribly here from the *samūm* wind; the water supplies dried up and the price of a single drink rose to 1,000 *dīnārs*, but both seller and buyer perished.[47]

There is nothing in the text of the *Maqāmāt* to suggest that the narrator either saw or travelled with an official caravan. The artist's inspiration seems to have derived from the contrast between the great pomp of a caravan's annual departure for Mecca and the haranguing of the pilgrims by the half-naked Abū Zayd.

The Pilgrims

In al-Wāsiṭī's accompanying miniature (Plate 2), Abū Zayd's speech reads:

> Thy generous aid to all who need a friend.
> Such true religion must thy *ḥajj* contain,
> Or else abortive prove, and end in vain:
> For know that utter loss alone requites
> The pilgrimage of heartless hypocrites:
> They plant, but on the soil no fruit is found;
> Their toil by no reward or praise is crowned.

Though sore distress and exile they endure,
They vainly hope advantage to procure;
Their only gain is but to doom
Their name to justly merited reproach and shame.[48]

A very small, incomplete portion of the textual commentary appears in the margin at the top left-hand corner. The painting encapsulates a moment earlier in the text, when al-Ḥārith tells how 'no sooner had we made our camels kneel down and loosened the ropes wherewith their loads were bound' than an old man appeared from among the hillocks. This is Abū Zayd, standing on a rock to address the pilgrims. Although he is bare-headed and unshod and may therefore have started to undress and change his clothing, he does not conform to the description of 'a person stripped to the skin'. Abū Zayd's pale blue shift with long sleeves falls down to mid-calf. The *qamīṣ* is a sewn garment; as such, it cannot be worn by the person in a state of ritual consecration (*iḥrām*). Over this robe he wears a russet shawl with black and white stripes, which could be a type of striped blanket. According to al-Fayyūmī, this was very thick and made of wool or goats' hair. The shawl is draped decoratively over Abū Zayd's forearms in a stylized manner, serving to draw attention to him and to link this illustration with the cavalcade on the preceding page. It also lends a sense of balance to the two illustrations. There is no sign of any other of Abū Zayd's belongings; he must have travelled austerely, eschewing the comforts of al-Ḥārith's group. Abū Zayd thus exemplifies his paradigm:

He whom his daily morsel satisfies
Alone is blest in life and truly wise.

Al-Ḥārith is not readily identifiable among the surrounding group of pilgrims, who are largely attentive to Abū Zayd's harangue and who listen in the 'silence' of the text; even three of the four camels at rest have their heads upraised. This may be a compositional device to counterbalance the downward slope of the hillock, or it could be an amusing diversion, for camels are notoriously intractable beasts. None of the other people is in consecrated clothing.

In the St Petersburg manuscript, a similar pilgrim scene was depicted. The text tells us how Abū Zayd ascends a hillock and, having first cleared his voice, says:

> O concourse of pilgrims who hasten on the broad tracks, know you what is before you and to whom you are going? Are you aware into whose presence you are approaching? . . . And on what a great undertaking you are venturing?

He goes on to point out to the pilgrims the error of their ways in their approach to the pilgrimage.

That painting, which is damaged, was therefore correctly placed in the text (it occurs at an earlier stage than al-Wāsiṭī's illustrations). Unfortunately, the reproduction is too poor to use, but it does allow an examination of the pilgrims. Here, Abū Zayd has changed from his profane garments on his arrival at Juḥfa before confronting the other pilgrims. In his austere, consecrated robe, he fulfils the textual description of being 'stripped to the skin'. There is no indication in the text that the other travellers have changed their clothing beyond a mention of Juḥfa and 'pilgrims'. It is clearly stated, however, that the caravan arrived at Juḥfa, a gathering-point at the entrance to the 'sacred land' (*al-balad al-ḥarām*) and the place where pilgrims from Syria, Egypt and the West congregate and prepare to consecrate themselves. It is at Juḥfa that the transition from the profane to the consecrated state occurs before setting out for the general meeting-place of Muzdalifa, next to Mecca.

Silk and ornamented fabrics are proscribed. The prescribed garments are preferably white; they come under Ibn Manṣūr's class of unsewn Arab costume and are known by al-Jāḥiẓ's designation of *shi'ār*, namely clothes worn next to the bare body. The consecrated robes comprise a close-fitting wrap (*izār*) which falls from the waist and covers the legs, and the type of cloak which medieval dictionaries define as a single, uncut garment (*ridā'*). The *ridā'* is worn over the left shoulder, to cover the back and breast, and to leave the right hand (which is ritually pure) free. Unlike the drummer in al-Wāsiṭī's procession, whose garment falls from his right shoulder, the pilgrims here correctly wear the *ridā'* over the left shoulder, to cover the back and breast and to leave the right hand (which is ritually pure) free.[49]

Again, there is a division of the composition into spatial planes of rocks, and what can be made out of the encampment in the foreground conforms to this artist's merchants' caravan in *Maqāma* 4. The people in the St Petersburg manuscript are generally lively and, because they usually wear long, everyday clothing, their legs are not seen. In this particular context, the short robes and thrusting of bodies and limbs are reminiscent of poses in Byzantine art; one thinks in particular of representations of Moses on Sinai receiving the tablets from Yahweh. Such a connotation ties in with the use of the double ground-plane and the elliptical base-line, which were employed in Byzantine and Syriac manuscripts, and indicate that a significant number of the St Petersburg miniatures are indebted to Christian iconography.

However, because the audience of pilgrims is jostling around Abū Zayd, this composition is less successful than al-Wāsiṭī's on two counts. First, the turbulence of milling bodies and upward-stretched arms is a distraction from the content of Abū Zayd's sonorous and heartfelt speech. Second, and crucially, if one seeks to understand the text and the significance of Abū Zayd's sermon, Abū Zayd has now been reduced to the rank of any pilgrim which, on this occasion, he clearly was not.

Al-Wāsiṭī's youth at the right-hand side turns away and faces the miniature of the military band; this not only provides a visual link across the two folios, but perhaps affords al-Wāsiṭī the opportunity to experiment yet again with the 'protruding eye'. It could be that the turning away from the central event by this figure, and the man peeping out of the black litter, represent a rare feature and are a misunderstanding of the theme. The majority of the pilgrims are Arabs and they do not look travel-stained or weary. They wear Arab robes with embroidered bands. Their turbans have very long endpieces, indicating that much material was used and that the wearers are probably men of some means. Ibn Khallikān, in his contemporary *Biographical Dictionary [Wafayāt al-a'yān wa anbā' abnā' al-zamān]*, describes the eminent tenth-century grammarian al-Naḥḥās as 'a man of sordid habits, parsimonious and niggardly towards himself; on being given a turban-cloth, he would cut it into three out of avarice'.[50]

Once again, costumes and turbans are of the hues commonly found throughout this manuscript, namely gold, russet, white, pale blue and violet. Three of the characters wear what seem to be black fur caps. I have found no identical headgear elsewhere, but several varieties of fur cap can be seen in the Demotte *Book of Kings*.[51] As two of the youthful pilgrims, who include one wearing a fur cap, are of non-Semitic and East Asian appearance, these factors suggest a Far Eastern influence, possibly through Persian painting; perhaps they were modelled on youthful attendants at court. All the youths wear the usual Arab robes and two of them have turbans. Al-Wāsiṭī has portrayed the two litters of the text, which appear to be of a kind used by women. These clearly have a wooden frame covered all round with cloth. The camel-saddle and two girths which support the litter are not shown. One final point needs noting here: the panniers would obviously be balanced across the camel-hump by carrying two people, one on each side.

Visual confirmation of this form of transport for women is found in the lower frieze of the *Book of Antidotes* in Vienna and on a metal ewer in the British Museum dated 1232. Both works, which were executed in Mosul, show the camel-trappings. An open dome-shaped litter bearing a woman occurs on a Fatimid ivory which is now in Cairo; this camel, alone of the examples noted, faces to the right. Figures, who are possibly female, are depicted in a litter on a thirteenth-century Persian lustreware figurine of a camel.[52] The litter has a crenellated crosspiece; one might perhaps drape a hanging over this, in the manner of a ridge tent, for privacy. Al-Wāsiṭī's illustrations appear to indicate that both occupants are inside one compartment, but this could not be the case.

Ibn Baṭṭūṭa provides a further personal insight into his experience of a pilgrim caravan: he tells us how, on his arrival at Mosul *en route* to Baghdad, he joined one such party. Although he does not say whether the litter was covered, he makes it clear that it was for two people. At Baghdad he:

> found the pilgrims preparing for the journey, so I went to visit the governor and asked him for the things which the sultan had ordered for me. He assigned me the half of a camel-litter and provisions and water for four persons, writing out an order to that effect, then sent for the leader of the

> caravan and commended me to him. I had already made the acquaintance of the latter, but I remained under his protection and favoured by his bounty, for he gave me even more than had been ordered for me.[53]

The 'half' confirms that one person was borne on either side of the beast.

It may be significant that so many depictions of camels show them facing to the left: this might point to a common source. There is also a black litter in the left foreground of the miniature, which is similar in size and shape to the golden-draped specimen on the facing page. This is clearly meant to be occupied, and a man's head is visible as he strains to catch Abū Zayd's speech. It fulfils the textual description of a richly decorated litter, bearing two sets of dark green pennants with *ṭirāz* and gold-coloured trappings; these are fine and probably silk. The small wooden camel-saddle to which it is fixed is also shown. This saddle must necessarily differ from those in the Mosul works of art discussed above, for al-Wāsiṭī's camels are the one-humped Arabian dromedaries, while the latter are the two-humped Bactrian variety.

Al-Ḥarīrī's pilgrims, then, were by no means unique in their choice of an easier path to Mecca than that taken by Abū Zayd. 'Easier' is, of course, a relative term: no journey of several weeks' duration across desert wastes on camel is by any stretch of the imagination 'easy'. A type of covered litter was in current use, for Ibn Jubayr describes the mounting anticipation of pilgrims in Mecca in 1183 concerning preparations for the sighting of the new moon and on the following morning. Saying that this occasion was 'a sight that asks to be recorded for its strangeness and wonder', he continues:

> We saw the streets and by-ways of Mecca to be filled with *hawdaj* bound to the camels and covered with various silk drapings and other trappings of fine linen, according to the circumstances and affluence of their owners, all of whom gave to it all the care and attention that was in their power.[54]

Not for Ibn Jubayr and his ilk, then, what Abū Zayd considers the arduous path of the true pilgrim, and this is precisely the style and spirit of the *ḥajj* undertaking against which he inveighs. Al-Wāsiṭī has successfully drawn a sharp contrast between the pilgrims' worldly goods and mode of travel and the paucity of Abū Zayd's belongings and style. Abū Zayd seeks to remind the pilgrims that they are fulfilling a fundamental religious obligation and taking a significant step towards the attainment of eternal bliss through self-abnegation. Al-Wāsiṭī thus provides a fitting vindication of al-Ḥārith's oft-maligned friend. It should be noted that the artist invariably portrays Abū Zayd in a sympathetic light, capturing the true essence of the man through his deep knowledge of the text.

Al-Wāsiṭī has exploited the different spatial planes which are here identified by outcrops of pale rocks, as opposed to the more usual bands of grass and vegetation which he employs, for example, in the village scene in the 43rd tale (Illust. 13) and the camel-slaughter scene in the 44th (Plate 20). He has achieved this by the skilful grouping of figures between rocks and by massing a crowd at the right-hand side; their gold *ṭirāz* bands form a curve parallel to the rock face, while the straight lines of the litters counterbalance the curves and echo the groundline. Finally, the black conical top of the covered litter emphasizes the two highest rock surfaces and lends Abū Zayd greater prominence (once more, these pictures are reversed in the original manuscript).

In order to understand the theme of Abū Zayd's speech, it is important to consider the reality of the pilgrimage for a great many travellers at that time. The appearance of these pilgrims who have travelled in style might be contrasted with a roughly contemporary description of the hapless less fortunate. Again in 1183 Ibn Jubayr describes the dreadful hardship of Egyptian pilgrims, some of whom 'stray on foot through the wayless desert and, being lost, die of thirst . . . Those who survive and reach 'Aydhāb are like men quickened from the shroud.'[55] Their ghastly physical appearance was a salutary reminder and a 'portent, for those who observed carefully', of the fate of all mankind. Abū Zayd's eloquence seems to have been successful, for the man in the white turban at the right-hand side is weeping with contrition. A touching and uncanny refrain in many contemporary biographies is 'He died on the pilgrimage.'

Finally, we should not overlook in this same tale what is probably the most touching portrait of the vindication of Abū Zayd in the whole of the *Maqāmāt* corpus. In BN 3929, the illustration is correctly placed much later in the tale, at the point where al-Ḥārith 'recognizes the style of Abū Zayd' and says how a 'thrill of joy' runs through him. It represents a confrontation scene in a non-threatening sense, as al-Ḥārith recounts in the surrounding text (using Preston's translation):

> When I saw that Abū Zayd was the object of my curiosity,
> And the man who had composed verses like a string of pearls,
> . . . I embraced him as closely as *lām* cleaves to *alif*,
> Esteeming him as much as health is valued by the sick;
> And I invited him to join company with me; but he refused;
> Or to ride on my camel with me; but he declined the offer;
> Saying: 'I have made a vow that in this my pilgrimage
> I will neither ride on the same camel with anyone
> Nor ride or walk alternately with a companion.'

The caption in large gold Thulūth script with black outline that appears immediately above the illustration might have been dispensed with, for it runs,'A picture of al-Ḥārith and Abū Zayd fondly embracing'.

Despite the textual description earlier outlined, Abū Zayd has not yet changed his everyday clothing. He wears a calf-length crimson unpatterned robe over light trousers, a pair of leather sandals with thongs and a long black pointed hat of the type known as *qalansuwa ṭawīla* or *qalansuwa dānniyya*. These descriptions refer both to the length and to the pointed shape. A young

3. Al-Ḥārith and Abū Zayd fondly embracing.

attendant holds his sheepskin bag for dry provisions and his staff. Somewhat surprisingly, the artist has dispensed with the prerequisite *par excellence*, the animal water-skin, although it clearly appears in his illustration on the following page. Abū Zayd is thus attired according to al-Sharīshī's definition of a pilgrim in the 1st tale.

In the 40th tale, in another context, Steingass says that 'the sweat of the carrier of the water-bag' is a proverbial expression for hardship and misery, which reinforces the view that the pilgrim must undergo severe deprivation. The attendant is therefore superfluous and has perhaps been created as a prop for Abū Zayd's belongings in order to facilitate the embrace; an onlooker appears at the left-hand side, possibly to suggest the crowd. Although the youth is in Arab clothing, he is not an Arab and the artist may have adapted a court scene with a young attendant (*ghulām*).

When written together, the Arabic letters *lām* and *alif* form *lā*, a particle of prohibition. They are particularly apposite here during a month of severe proscriptions. In fact, the embrace itself can be interpreted as a visual metaphor for 'do not' and evokes the outline of monumental inscriptions. It is likely that the Muslim viewer would make the necessary connection when reading that the friends embraced 'as closely as *lām* cleaves to *alif*'.

One can well understand al-Ḥārith's anxiety as he later searches for his truly penitent friend 'in vain'. The full meaning of the embrace is clear from the lines:

> Nor did I suffer in all my travels an affliction like this,
> Nor was visited in my journey by such poignant grief

as Abū Zayd declines his proffered assistance.

The anguish of waiting relatives and friends is well conveyed by Lane's nineteenth-century *Account of the Manners and Customs of the Modern Egyptians*:

> It is very affecting to see at the approach of the caravan the numerous parties who go out with drums and pipes to welcome and escort to the city their friends arrived from the holy places, and how many, who went forth in hope, return with lamentation instead of music and rejoicing; for the arduous journey through the desert is fatal to a great number of those pilgrims who cannot afford themselves necessary conveniences.[56]

There is for the discerning reader and viewer an undercurrent of poignancy here. Abū Zayd's speeches serve as a salutary reminder that before God on 'the day of mutual outcry' all mankind is as one. Extravagant pomp and ceremony should be eschewed, 'since wealth may fail thy hope, or prove thy bane'.

This *Maqāma* reveals Abū Zayd as a paradigm for all pilgrims and provides an insight into the real nature of the pilgrimage and the plight of the less fortunate. The universality of this message to all creeds throughout every era explains the continuing appeal of al-Ḥarīrī's masterpiece. Al-Wāsiṭī and the BN 3929 have captured the true spirit of the pilgrimage and Abū Zayd's critics should be silenced.

2

Power and Authority

There is no sense in the *Maqāmāt* of a celebration of great national heroes, as in the Persian epics. Where figures of authority such as governors, *qāḍīs* and preachers appear, they are treated in a somewhat irreverent fashion. In his appointed role as 'any man', Abū Zayd seeks to point out the error of their ways through erudite and eloquent outbursts and shows them up as rather naive characters. In fact, there is a definite de-emphasizing of the royal role in the iconography itself, and where it has been employed, it has been adapted as a framework to set off a leisured lifestyle. There is no obeisance on the part of Abū Zayd; indeed, his right to a personal audience is taken for granted. Together with their robes of office and the physical settings (which merely suggest a palace, a government office, and so on), these figures obviously represent a significant niche and crucial element in Islamic society.

If overlords in particular are treated less than sympathetically, it may be because the Saljūq dynasty were aliens who sought to impose their rule within an established framework of Islamic values and attitudes. The Islamic state is a religious body established under divine law where God is the supreme ruler and the primary task of the ruler is the promulgation of Islam as the basis for the whole civilization. That some failed to uphold these precepts in their public lives is only human and inevitable. In many cases, these rulers and their deputies had a poor command of Arabic and some resentment in Arab society is manifesting itself here in literary and illustrative forms.

Abū Zayd is able to masquerade as an official preacher on two occasions in the tales, and in the Rayy mosque he challenges the ruler from the pulpit to mend his ways. Such are his powers of oratory that the ruler improbably agrees to do so. On five other occasions he preaches informally to spellbound congregations, who are only too happy to reward him.

The attitude of the public—and, indeed, of many jurists themselves—towards the judiciary was highly ambivalent. *Qāḍīs* were official appointees and regarded with some suspicion in that they were deemed to have forfeited their moral authority by complying with the state. Five *Maqāmāt* recount Abū Zayd's exploits before a *qāḍī*, with al-Ḥārith as witness. This is not mere whim on the part of the author. The complex organization of business in the 'Abbāsid era required the intervention of *qāḍīs*. Jurisprudence (*fiqh*) governed contracts and ethics and all aspects of commerce and manufacturing. In particular, al-Ḥārith would have sought clarification of local customs and up-to-date news of market conditions.

Abū Zayd's skirmishes with authority are entirely consistent with the views of many of his contemporaries—anecdotal Arabic literature abounds with 'moral stereotypes' such as the religious charlatan, the just monarch, and overbearing *qāḍīs* as servants of the state. What is surprising, as we shall see, is the extent to which an ordinary member of the public apparently had access to such people.

The Ruler

The Arab Governor

Maqāma 38 takes place in Merv, in Khurāsān: al-Ḥārith relates how when he was at the governor's court he came across his old friend Abū Zayd, who was praising the quality of liberality in glowing terms. The illustration in the St Petersburg manuscript (Plate 3) appears close to the beginning of the tale, and the text is Abū Zayd's opening speech. After gently reminding the governor of his obligations towards his subjects, Abū Zayd continues:

> Truly thou has become, praise be to Allāh, the support of thy city and the pillar of thy age, to whose sanctuary the saddle-beasts are driven and from whose generosity bounties are hoped, to whose courts requests are carried . . .

There is an element of irony here, for Khurāsān was a byword for stinginess. An anecdote about a merchant from Merv tells how he would not allow his son to eat cheese; instead, he merely permitted him to rub his bread on the glass which covered it. This psychological classification of towns also occurs in *Maqāma* 46, set in Homs, which was a synonym for stupidity, as we shall see later (Chapter 4). As the audience must have been well aware of such connotations, their appreciation of text and image would be enhanced. What ruler, however much maligned his province, could resist such an eloquent plea? Abū Zayd capitalizes on this and goes away 'with a full sleeve and a merry heart'.

Arabic literature deals extensively with rulers. As al-Ghazālī points out in his *Counsel for Kings [Naṣīḥat al-mulūk]*:

> Nothing is more damaging to the subjects and more prejudicial and sinister for the king than royal inaccessibility and seclusion . . . Nothing impresses the hearts of the subjects and officials more than ease of access to the king.

One presumes that in the absence of the supreme ruler, his representative performed the same function. In his late eleventh-century treatise on the proper conduct of rulers, *The Book of Government or Rules for Kings [Siyar al-mulūk]*, the illustrious vizier Niẓām al-Mulk describes how. . . 'time passed. Bahrām Gūr came out and sat on the throne and gave audience. The chamberlains took the man's hand and led him to the audience hall.' Later in the thirteenth century, the Mamlūk sultan Lājīn sat for two days a week in the Hall of Justice to deal with the petitions and complaints of his subjects.[1] Abū Zayd is therefore merely exerting his rights as a not-so-ordinary citizen, and the manuscript appears to illustrate a contemporary occurrence in an official context.

Given the status of Merv as a Saljūq capital and the seat of the governors of Khurāsān, one might expect to find an elaborate setting for the governor's court. Palaces of governors or notables were apparently usually sited directly on the banks of rivers or in a main *sūq*. It may be that this reception room in the miniature was purpose-built in a quite separate building, for a tale concerning Hārūn al-Rashīd in the *Book of Government or Rules for Kings* tells that 'he returned from the audience-hall to his private palace'.

Abū Zayd makes his petition with outstretched hands, his small, slight figure not in the least intimidated by the almost monumental size of the governor. His self-confidence is matched by his eloquence. Al-Ḥārith describes his friend as 'in the rags of one poverty-stricken', and Abū Zayd's pointed hood may indeed indicate that he is dressed as a mendicant. As required by the text, Abū Zayd stands pleading in close proximity to the governor (here described as *wālī*), at 'the seat of the circumciser', which is a metaphor for closeness. Yaḥya ibn Faḍl, a twelfth-century 'Abbāsid courtier, considered the mass of the people to be 'filthy refuse' and a 'torrent of scum', when compared to the rulers. The governor of Merv is shown here as a powerful and imposing figure. Although royal personages were portrayed 'larger than life', he seems to exemplify the ideal of the period for one of his station: he has a large head (unlike that of a clerk), a thick growth of hair on his forehead, a high nose and a broad-cornered mouth. In addition, a broad chest and shoulders, a long forearm and long fingers were all deemed desirable physical features in a figure of authority.[2] It is interesting to note that this is not a portrait of a particular governor of Merv, for an almost identical figure is found in the same manuscript for the governor of Ṭūs. The artist was clearly painting a type, without imputing any individual characteristics to the person concerned. It also suggests that he had a limited number of models; similarly, his architectural compositions are repetitive.

The governor of Merv's black turban must be the *'imāma musmata sawdā'* which the *Rules and Regulations of the Court* describe as showing allegiance to the 'Abbāsid cause, and it has gold ornamentation or a gold clasp. The billowing outer cloak is of a plain deep blue, with gold braid at the hemline and neck; this fits the description of the robe of a single colour (*sawād*), with lining and collar, which formed part of the robes of honour from the caliph. It is impossible to say whether the gold edging at the neck is on the fabric or if it represents a chain of office. The governor is wearing a white undergarment which might be the *qabī'a* of fine Dabīq linen, also outlined by the *Rules and Regulations of the Court*, and black sandals. These clothes were probably presented to him on his appointment, for the same source also informs us that military commanders were frequently presented with a *khil'a*—this can refer to a single robe of honour or an ensemble of garments. The set might also include a red-sheathed sword with silver mounts, red Sūsī cloth, armbands and a collar, among other items.[3]

These accounts suggest that at least some of these very costly garments were not ready-made. This is borne out by an account of a man's dream on the 8th of Ṣafar (the second Islamic month) in the eleventh century:

> I saw in my dream as though a man had come to me and said, 'You will rise and come with me; the robes of honour have already been prepared for you . . .' Then we entered a great palace . . . Fine cloths were brought, fine linens and other such things. Then he said, 'We will call the tailor for you; he will cut, and you will wear them—God willing!' Then I awoke.

Al-Dhahabī's *Book of the Dynasties of Islam [Kitāb duwal al-Islām]* mentions 'attributes of power' and 'presents of honour' which the caliph al-Qā'im bestowed on Arslān al-Basāsīrī in the mid-eleventh century.[4]

The governor's throne appears almost to be an amalgam of throne and pulpit, and the back is covered in a golden brocaded fabric with large vegetal motifs. A similar textile occurs on al-Wāsiṭī's throne for his foreign governor in the 39th tale (Illust. 16) as well as on the curtains in the lower register of the miniature. In the early tenth century the caliph al-Muqtadir had an ebony throne covered with a gold-embroidered fabric from Dabīq. Literary sources reveal that he also had curtains of gold brocade, embroidered with gold thread and decorated with lions, birds, elephants, horses and camels. These were manufactured in Armenia, Wāsiṭ and elsewhere, and came both in plain colours and in variegated hues.[5] In the Istanbul 2916 illustration for this tale, the textiles are particularly outstanding and include addorsed birds, which were rare at this early period of miniature painting. A similar type of throne with a heavily patterned backcloth in a stylized flower motif appears in the later *Chronology of Ancient Peoples [Kitāb al-āthār al-bāqiyya 'an al-qurūn al-khāliyya]* by al-Bīrūnī, in the University of Edinburgh. Chapter 4 of the *Rules and Regulations of the Court* reveals that the caliph traditionally sat on an elevated seat on a throne covered in Armenian silk or a woollen and silken fabric; and his representative in the above miniature is granting an audience in similarly luxurious style. No cushions are visible. The carved wooden feet of the throne are bell-shaped; that form can also be seen on the throne on page 22 of the BL 1200 manuscript and on an early twelfth-century Syrian carved wooden screen. This bell-shaped motif is repeated in the miniature under discussion on the capital to the right of the governor.

Column bases with the same motif occur on the *miḥrāb* of the late tenth-century al-Azhar mosque in Cairo, and bell-shaped capitals appear in the Baḥrī Mamlūk period from the mid-thirteenth century. Columns with bell-shaped capitals and bases occur in the late thirteenth-century Istanbul manuscript of a religio-political association, the *Epistles of the Sincere Brethren [Rasā'il ikhwān al-ṣafā]*. More decorative bell-shaped columns with curvilinear zigzag bands were executed on a wall painting in al-Jawsaq al-Khāqānī and on columns at Sāmarrā, and they also appear on the *miḥrāb* of al-Juwayshātī mosque in Mosul. The repetition of the same form on column bases was typical of ninth-century Sāmarrā.[6] This motif, therefore, appears to be a long-established common architectural feature and its inclusion here should occasion no surprise.

A large dark curtain with a deep *ṭirāz* band has been tied back to admit Abū Zayd to the reception area. In al-Tanūkhī's report of the visit of Abū al-Ḥusayn ibn 'Ayyāsh to his friend, the vizier Sulaymān ibn al-Ḥasan, Abū al-Ḥusayn mentions:

> various nobles, state secretaries, generals and courtiers, who, not being admitted, were seated in the corridor, whilst the chamberlain was standing at the door of the staircase which led to a private chamber wherein the vizier was. When the chamberlain saw me, he ordered the curtain to be raised.

Al-Tanūkhī also reports how his father and the same Abū al-Ḥusayn frequently saw the vizier 'Alī ibn 'Īsā in his latter days when his salon was crowded. The vizier was:

> by an open door, leaning upon a bolster between the doorposts. A curtain was let down to reach the ground and conceal the bolsters, to screen them from the audience's view. This was because the old man wished to preserve his dignity and did not wish to be seen having to lean on anything.[7]

This raising and lowering of a curtain at audiences in the 'Abbāsid period is further confirmed by the *Rules and Regulations of the Court*. Thus the miniature represents contemporary practice, whether at the caliph's court or at that of his personal appointee.

A well-dressed, beardless youth with a black turban and long black boots stands behind Abū Zayd. His robe is of the same brocaded material as the fabric on the throne, as well as the the draped curtain in the alcove, so one assumes that he is an important personage. He is lolling languidly around the framework; this is surely a device to introduce depth to the composition, for such behaviour at an official audience would have been insubordination and a dereliction of duty. If the report of the regulations concerning the appointment of a chamberlain (*ḥājib*) have been applied here, this youth could not have been the chamberlain for, ideally, he would have been shown as 'a middle-aged man [between 30 and 50], wise and experienced; or a sturdy elderly man who has been tested and moulded by time'. He may have been the 'crier' who summoned those who had plaints.

Another smooth-chinned attendant in turban and boots is obviously an 'Abbāsid dignitary, as he wears a black robe and is girt with a sword. Ibn Khaldūn reports that in the ninth century the caliph al-Mutawakkil introduced the 'Persian fashion', which was to wear the sword at the waist. The use of the shoulder-strap (*najd*) was the typical Arab way of wearing the sword;[8] it is seen to good effect in the BN 3929 illustration in *Maqāma* 32 in the section on the bedouin, where the great legist addresses two tribesmen (Illust. 14).

Al-Ḥārith sits on a small platform to the right of the miniature; three men are sitting on the ground nearby. They may be petitioners, although it is highly unlikely that they would be seated in the governor's presence when even his courtiers are standing; this must mean that they are waiting outside, in a separate chamber. One should therefore view the two alcoves at either side of the reception chamber as separate antechambers. In the composition these three figures serve to establish the groundline and to counteract the stepped throne.

Niẓām al-Mulk's *Book of Government or Rules for Kings* reveals that:

> There is always a large crowd of complainants frequenting the court, and even when they receive the answers to their petitions they do not go away. Any stranger or envoy, arriving at the capital and seeing this clamour and tumult, will think that at this court gross injustice is done to the people. These doors must be closed to such crowds.

The vizier was further of the opinion that 'five persons should then come to the court, state their case, explain the circumstances, hear the answer and receive the judgment'.[9] The three seated men, together with Abū Zayd and al-Ḥārith, make up the necessary five people, although it is impossible to say whether this is by design or coincidence.

The audience chamber is housed in a very elaborate building that seems eminently suitable for a figure of authority. A somewhat similar lawcourt appears here in the 37th tale. In both of these tripartite compositions the separate areas are used as frames for the composition, with the base-line being set by a yellow brick floor. The massive ornamental frieze of the central chamber features a trilobed foliate design; al-Wāsiṭī has produced an almost identical frieze in his Basra public library in *Maqāma* 2. Such intricate and obviously costly ornamentation seems to indicate that the setting under discussion is an official building.

Al-Gailānī has pointed out a variation of this design on the minaret of the thread market (*sūq al-ghazl*) in Baghdad. An analytical pen drawing of yet another variation, perhaps intended for tilework and possibly dating from the ninth century, has survived.[10] This frieze, then, is apparently no mere invention on the artist's part.

Here, the two small antechambers are topped with leaded, ribbed domes with clerestory windows and pointed finials; the central chamber should presumably have had a large, well-lit dome although there is no sign of this. Small carved stucco panels adorn the façade of the antechambers. They are heavily carved and may perhaps be openwork, for ventilation purposes. Their ornamentation seems to owe something to woodwork and moulded stucco-work dating back to the mid-ninth century.

The reader is viewing the vestibule (*dihlīz*) of the reception area, which is the antechamber or vestibule situated between the outer gate or door and the main building. This is confirmed by the Arabic text of the description of the beggars' mansion in *Maqāma* 30, which this artist has depicted as a very similar tripartite composition. He therefore repeats a fairly standard formula which is capable of elaboration by the addition of specific elements relating to occupations and so on—this is one more shared feature with the shadow theatre. This approach may well extend to his portrayal of human beings, where he relies on 'types'; his portraits lack the sympathetic appeal to character, in spite of what is known of Abū Zayd's motives, which is obvious in BN 3929 and 5847.

Despite Preston's assertion that the literary content of this *Maqāma* is 'of inferior interest', the St Petersburg manuscript painter has successfully conveyed something of the contemporary ostentatious surroundings and the authority of a provincial governor. This Arab governor could be compared with another in *Maqāma* 26 in Istanbul 2916 (Plate 4). There, the artist seems to have misunderstood the text in his portrayal of Abū Zayd as a governor, as al-Ḥārith finds Abū Zayd living well, under the patronage of a governor, 'prospering in guestship with him, and pasturing in the oasis of his bounty'. In fact, Abū Zayd seems almost to be masquerading as a governor there. Alternatively, the painter has appropriated features from a standardized princely repertoire as a metaphor for Abū Zayd's successful lifestyle. There are two further examples of a 'transformed' Abū Zayd: in the 12th tale, both BN 5847 and 3929 show him drinking and clearly modelled on a 'ruler at ease' (Illust. 18 and Plate 14 respectively). Such transformations demonstrate that a royal iconography—albeit with a relatively limited repertoire—preceded the *Maqāmāt* and other twelfth- and thirteenth-century illustrations.

The Saljūq Governor

In *Maqāmāt* 10, 23, 26 and 38, Abū Zayd has resorted to the higher judicial authority of the governor. It appears that all matters in which the authority of a *qāḍī* was considered too weak or where a more authoritative hand was required were decided in the court of appeal (*dīwān al-naẓar fī al-maẓālim*), which sought to rectify extortionate demands. The earlier Umayyad practice of dividing the empire into provinces under an *amīr* or *'amīl* seems largely to have been adhered to by the 'Abbāsids. In theory, the governor held his post at the pleasure of the vizier, who had recommended the appointment to the caliph, and he remained the incumbent so long as the vizier was in office. In practice, however, the governor's authority tended to become supreme and his office hereditary. Governorships were not merely bestowed, but might be purchased; for political reasons, they could also be refused.[11]

Maqāma 10 finds al-Ḥārith in Raḥba, a town on the Euphrates between 'Āna and Raqqa. He comes upon a crowd which has gathered round an old man, who is dragging along a handsome youth whom he accuses of killing his son. In al-Wāsiṭī's illustration Abū Zayd is making his plea before the governor of Raḥba. The text above reads:

> 'Demand of him the oath.' The old man said, 'Surely he struck him down remote from men and shed his blood when alone. And how can I have a witness [when on the spot] there was [no beholder]?'

Abū Zayd is barefoot and fairly simply clad, despite the ostentatious long end of his turban. He is conducting his own plea (as was the established practice, according to al-Tanūkhī, who was a *qāḍī* in a family of *qāḍīs*), since he appears to make no mention of legal advisers or advocates. Presumably a single spokesman was also employed if several parties were involved. In matters pertaining to the community, representatives were appointed, a practice confirmed by the source material. Legal precedents were obviously recognized; al-Tanūkhī recalls a case where a widow 'came forward eagerly as one with an answer prepared', referring to a case recorded by al-Jāḥiẓ. Abū Zayd's oratorical success here is founded on precedents stretching back to the Graeco-Roman world, where many of the greatest examples of oratory were delivered in the courts.[12]

The governor has just told Abū Zayd that if he is unable to produce the statutory two male Muslims to testify for him, then the boy's evidence will be heard on oath. In this, the procedure differs from the court of the *qāḍī*, where only the plaintiff adduced evidence and questioned witnesses. This was the theory; in practice, local custom and law seem to have prevailed. When the boy refuses to take an oath, Abū Zayd dictates one to him.

Eventually, the governor agrees to 'liberate' the boy for 100 *dīnārs*, to which Abū Zayd agrees. Presumably, some sort of warrant would be made out to a

4. Abū Zayd makes his plea before the governor.

cashier, for al-Tanūkhī again records how a paymaster withheld payment of 200 *dīnārs* to a female petitioner for alms because he was unwilling to pay out such a large sum to a woman of her social class.[13]

Preston's nineteenth-century sensibilities prevented him from publishing a translation of this tale, which he says was omitted 'for an obvious reason'. This is because Abū Zayd deliberately sets out in the terms of the oath to make his son as alluring as possible to the governor; the homosexual inference is clear from both text and painting. Despite the fact that homosexuality is proscribed in *sūra* 26, examples from Arabic literature reveal that its practice was not unknown, and al-Ḥarīrī doubtless has his reasons for his choice of theme. According to al-Balādhurī, an early Muslim ruler who was effeminate and bisexual was known as 'the lady' (*al-khudayna*).

The 'accused', a beardless youth (*shawdar*), is well-dressed. He has the drooping (*saqīm*) eyelids and straight nose described in the text and conforms to al-Ḥārith's description of being 'in the mould of comeliness and clothed by beauty in the garb of perfection'. There is a definite hint that all is not as it seems. Here the reader will recall the description of Joseph in *sūra* 12, his innocence and his betrayal by Potiphar's wife. The lad wears an extremely elaborate robe with unusually delicate folds. Although his hair is not particularly long, his appearance recalls a poem recited to al-Tanūkhī by al-Sarūrī that provides a paradigm for youthful male attractiveness:

. . . a fawn,
With a cheek that ever reddened at our gaze,
Like a maiden who when gazed at stretches out one hand
To shield her face, and the other to replace her sleeve
Upon her heart. His locks hung down over his cheeks,
Wherein the gazelles might seem to have sewn their eyelids
And their tongues.[14]

The red zigzag lines of text at the left-hand side of the illustration are a commentary on the Arabic text, explaining that the governor glanced at the youth in a certain way; there are homosexual connotations. The curious protruding further eye is thus used to good effect here, both on the lad's face and on the governor's. The commentary acts as a framing device and one wonders to what extent the artist was influenced by Far Eastern painting, where the text was written from top to bottom of the page.

Several features in the illustration suggest that the governor is a Saljūq Turk. The red beard (which might, of course, be dyed out of vanity), moustache and hair indicate that he may not be an Arab. This is borne out by his tunic, which appears to be slit down the middle in the form of a coat, although he does wear a turban. He also has long black boots. There is no mention of the governor's racial origins in the text.

According to the *Book of the Dynasties of Islam*, when the caliph al-Mustanṣir bi Allāh Abū Ja'far died in 1242 or 1243 he was 52 years old and had reigned for 17 years. He was 'fair-skinned, with red hair' and 'born of a Turkish mother.' Sultan Lājīn of Egypt, who ruled in the closing years of the thirteenth century, was marked out as a foreigner by his tall, imposing stature, blue eyes and ruddy complexion. The Arabs appear to have been somewhat prejudiced against light-eyed foreigners, since many of their northern enemies had blue eyes. In the ninth century, al-Jāḥiẓ describes in his *Compendium of the Turkish Language [Dīwān lughat al-Turk]* 'the excessively lanky, thin and reddish hair of the Franks, Greeks and Slavs, the redness of their locks and beards, the whiteness of their eyebrows and eyelashes', which he found loathsome and ugly.[15]

A further Turkish influence is suggested by the governor's 'pendant leg' pose, which, although technically correct, emphasizes his foppish, dainty appearance. The postures of Turkish princes and their retinues appear to be connected with conventional Indian postures of the lower limb (*āsanas*). These possibly originated in an earlier period, when the world was seen in relation to the cosmos, and they represent some aspect of a complicated ritual in the establishment of seniority in rank. This convention is found in Turkish iconography from the Buddhist period, as, for example, in a gilded bronze plaque from the Buddhist temple of Aq-bešim. It is also seen in an Uighur mural dating between the ninth and the twelfth century which depicts a warrior paying homage to a Buddha. It survived in religious iconography until at least the early sixteenth century.[16] The pose appears in BN 6094 and 3929 for this story, as well as in BN 6094 for the governor in the 23rd tale (Plate 7).

However, although it represents an iconographic borrowing, the 'at ease' pose may also be a deliberate attempt by this artist to sabotage the governor's authority and a satirical depiction of an unpopular foreign ruler. According to the eleventh-century *Epistles [Rasā'il]* by al-Kāshgarī:

> I have seen that God caused the sun of empire to rise in the mansions of the Turks, and turned the heavenly spheres around their dominion, and named them Turk, and gave them sovereignty, and made them kings of the age, and placed the reins of the people of this time in their hands, and ordained them over mankind, and sustained them in the right . . .[17]

The visual de-emphasizing of the regal aspect now mirrors the declining importance accorded to the ideology of royalty. In this, the *Maqāmāt* seem to represent a withdrawing of the Arabic-speaking world into its own ethnic fold in response to a growing non-Arab influence in the Muslim world.

There is no elaborate relationship between Abū Zayd, his son and the governor, but the spear links them; it also represents a visual pun on the textual verb *jaddala*, which medieval dictionaries define as 'to pierce with a spear or the like; to throw someone down'. The spear has replaced the carved wooden post of the throne, but its tip reflects the post's finial; the substitution is perhaps deliberate on the artist's part, to emphasize the play on words, and it may be intended as a coarse joke for an exclusively male audience. Somewhat similar thrones with spear-shaped finials and pointed backdrops appear in the *Book of Antidotes* of 1199 from northern Iraq, as well as on contemporary Persian polychrome wares and metalwork.[18]

Al-Wāsiṭī may have added the carved post to allow the page-boy from the princely iconography to peep through, adding a sense of depth to the composition. This 'peeping' convention is a forerunner to later Persian miniature painting and it also appears in the BL 1200 manuscript. It has also been noted in the BN 3929 illustration of the 6th tale, where another small boy is at the side of his master's throne (Illust. 5).

The governor is perched on a plump bolster on a very elaborate red carpet or drape, which has a dark green reverse side. This drape is decorated with a *ṭirāz* band of pseudo-epigraphy within a roundel border; the heart-shaped motif, which contains a leaf, is reminiscent of the Chinese *joo-e* head which appears on a thirteenth-century Anatolian carpet. The motif, and indeed the whole of the red area of the rug illustrated, may be woven in relief. If this is the case, then Yāqūt's term *maḥfūra* was the correct name for this rug; *maḥfūra* in turn had displaced *qaṭīfa*, meaning a textile with a pile, used as a carpet.[19]

The unusual feature of this throne is the brick dais, which serves two purposes: first, it establishes a necessary groundline to hold the composition together; and, second, the contours of highlighted, undressed bricks counteract any tendency to flatness in the composition, in the absence of architectural elements. Al-Wāsiṭī had already produced an almost identical throne for the *qāḍī* in *Maqāma* 9 (Illust. 17). It also sits on a brick base, and a small al-Ḥārith replaces the page at the right-hand side. The standard royal iconography was capable of being adapted to a variety of plots.

We might have expected a more lavish setting for the official court, for we know that from the eleventh century onwards there was a revival in the prestige and power of centres such as Merv and Damascus. However, the absence of architectural distractions serves to accentuate the anecdotal aspect of the human drama being played out.

The little page-boy, beside his master, would have been well advised to heed al-Ghazālī's advice to royal servants in his *Counsel for Kings*: 'If the service of kings you enter, put very strong garments of discretion on! When you go into [royal courts], go blind! When you come out, if come you do, come dumb!'[20] In his case, discretion would obviously be the better part of valour.

Al-Ḥārith recounts in *Maqāma* 21 how, when he was visiting the Persian city of Rayy, he was swept along in a crowd hurrying to hear a preacher whose fame surpassed even that of the great Ibn Sam'ūn. Athough the only textual indicator of the setting is *nādi*, or 'meeting-place', al-Wāsiṭī has set his stunning scene in the Friday mosque (Plate 5), where the provincial governor is attending public worship. After an uplifting sermon, a member of the congregation tries in vain to gain a fair hearing of his plaint by the prince. Abū Zayd, in the guise of famous preacher and perhaps mindful of his reputation as an orator, takes it upon himself to deliver a public rebuke to the ruler.

The miniatures illustrate the sermon proper, for the preacher is gesticulating to the congregation in general.

Part of al-Ghazālī's advice to a ruler in his tractate, *Fitting Conduct in Religion [al-Adab fī al dīn]* runs:

> The sultan should show kindness in dealing with his subjects and not treat them harshly. He should reflect carefully before giving a command. When with his own household, he should not act as though he were better than everyone else, yet at the same time he should forestall undue familiarity. He should show regard for common folk, yet inspire them with respect.[21]

Needless to say, his appointed representative would be expected to do likewise and, naturally, advice to the official in this vein is put much more eloquently by Abū Zayd.

This 'preacher' delivers his oration while seated on the steps of an elaborate pulpit; the absence of a handrail emphasizes his hand gesture. The stair treads have elaborate triangular insets of blue, white, brown and black. Carpets were strewn on mosque floors for the faithful, and the geometric forms and colours here are reminiscent of Saljūq rugs. However, the stair treads suggest regularity and rigidity and in reality these triangles may be insets of wood which have been coloured for decorative effect; they also resemble mosaic work. Geometric insets of contrasting woods (and ivory) were featured on the side panels of pulpits, and these have been already been commented upon in the context of the mosque in Barqa'īd in Chapter 1.

Blue and white recur on the panel behind the preacher; they tie together and complete the pulpit, close the extremity and frame the image. The painter of BN 6094 has also depicted an elaborate flat panel behind his preachers in *Maqāmāt* 21 and 28. There, the designs appear to be square tiles in geometric patterns in blue and white and may be based on lustreware, such as those on the *miḥrāb* of the Qayrawān congregational mosque.[22]

In al-Wāsiṭī's second illustration (Plate 6) the governor is sitting comfortably and listening attentively. He has not yet become 'sullen at what he heard', nor has his colour 'changed and changed'. He would, of course, have sat in the screened-off portion of the mosque (*maqṣūra*) which was reserved for his personal use. Al-Wāsiṭī suggests this exclusive space by placing the governor 'in seclusion' at the top of the composition, just as he has correctly 'secluded' the ladies upstairs; he has achieved this by extending the mosque masonry over the throng outside. (These women are discussed at length in 'Women in the Mosque' in Chapter 6.) He might otherwise have correctly seated the governor downstairs, but this would have been at the expense of the large crowd, whose attentive presence adds so much to the mood of the composition and emphasizes the brilliant oratory of the preacher.

The governor is solidly built, whereas men in this manuscript are usually shown as of slim build. He has a very full face and a thin moustache and his head is framed by a 'halo'; there is, of course, no religious significance in this. (The 'great preacher' is similarly highlighted, and this linking by halo indicates that the sermon is now directed at the governor, as the text requires.) It is not clear whether the governor has a beard or if he is wearing a balaclava-type head-covering under his cap. If this is the case, his hair is covered. He wears a bushy black fur hat with gold ornamentation to the front; because of his high status, it may be of sable, which was very fine and costly. The *Book of Curious and Entertaining Information* lists several kinds of furs, including 'the sable of Bulghār' in the context of the tenth-century Buwayhid court of 'Aḍūd al-Dawla. Alternatively, the fur could be marten. Ibn Jubayr's *Travels* record how, on a visit to Baghdad on the sixth day of Ṣafar:

> We saw this caliph, Abū al-'Abbās Aḥmad al-Naṣīr li Dīn Allāh . . . in the western part of his belvedere there . . . On his head was a gilded cap encircled with black fur of the costly and precious kind used for [royal] clothes, such as that of the marten, or even better.

This hat is both flatter and wider than the examples which occur in other manuscripts and on metalwork.[23] These variations may reflect variations in fashion, the availability of the pelts, or stylistic traditions according to the places of execution of the manuscripts. Al-Wāsiṭī shows yet another variety of fur hat on the first folio of his double frontispiece.

Our governor in the Rayy congregational mosque wears a dark blue robe of ankle length with *ṭirāz* bands and tight sleeves; it does not cross over his chest. He is probably a Saljūq Turk. He is in a frontal pose, but an element of informality in his depiction now appears, for his head is slightly inclined towards the left as he regards the famous 'preacher'. He sits on a long bolster with pointed ends, one of his ankles resting daintily on the other in the cross-legged position. The ruler should, of course, have removed his shoes; however, as his retainers wear boots, it is possible that his footwear is on view. This may be a satirical touch, to suggest ignorance on the ruler's part. Alternatively, if the throne scene has been directly appropriated from elsewhere as an artistic 'short cut', it may be an oversight by al-Wāsiṭī. One should also bear in mind that the ruler would normally be screened from public view, and some aspersions are possibly being cast on his religiosity here.

The throne has the usual pointed corners, apparently carved from wood and featuring a floriate pattern. A similar throne with bolster appears in the early thirteenth-century illustrations in the *Romance of Warqa and Gulshāh* in Istanbul. A handsome red and black carpet or fabric with a leaf design covers its back. Behind the throne one glimpses a circular drape or rug, and al-Wāsiṭī later shows a scalloped circular drape behind the throne in *Maqāma* 39 (Illust. 16). These may be an adaptation of the rather similar rug on which the prince sits in the frontispiece of the contemporary *Book of Antidotes* in Vienna. A circular edge reminiscent of the Sāsānian roundel motif is also obvious on a rug in a royal audience scene in the Istanbul *Romance of Warqa and Gulshāh*.[24]

Five beardless, long-haired youths (*ghilmān*) attend the governor in an amusing and disrespectful rag-tag manner. It is difficult to say how old these pages are. Although they are wearing Arab clothing, their long hair and full round faces suggest they are of non-Semitic origin; they also conform to an idealized notion of male adolescent beauty. They too wear fur hats with gold ornamentation which are of the flatter type found in the *Book of Antidotes* miniatures. Four of them carry swords, and they must be bodyguards, for there was always the risk of an attempt on a ruler's life. Al-Hādī is credited with the institution of the caliphal bodyguard (*ḥaras*), which in the late eighth century was drawn from Khurāsān or from among loyal Medinans. In ninth- and tenth-century Baghdad, the regiment of bodyguards (*mukhtārīn*) performed military service at audiences and acted as escorts of the caliph.[25] It is possible that caliphal appointees, although lesser dignitaries, also merited a guard. In the early thirteenth century Muḥammad al-Rāwandī wrote in his *Repose of Hearts and Signs of Joy [Rāḥat al-ṣudūr wa āyāt al-surūr]*, 'In the lands of the Arabs, the Persians, the Romans and the Russians, the sword is in the hands of the Turks and the fear of their swords is rooted in men's hearts.'[26]

In his *Travels in Asia and Africa*, Ibn Baṭṭūṭa's account of his visit to the

Emperor Takfūr in the fourteenth century emphasizes the security aspect of a court visit. A slave led him through four gateways, each guarded by armed foot soldiers, and:

> when we reached the fifth gateway, Sunbūl [the slave] left me, and going inside returned with four Greek youths, who searched me to see that I had no knife on my person. The officer said to me: 'This is a custom of theirs; every person who enters the king's presence, be he noble or private citizen, foreigner or native, must be searched.'

The swordsman in the black clothing is perhaps the most senior. We find in the *Rules and Regulations of the Court* that "'Abbāsid dignitaries wear black outer garments and shoes; and they adorn themselves according to rank with girdles and swords.' Black was proscribed for lower-ranking dignitaries, who could choose other colours.

The question of rank is confirmed by the official standing nearest to the governor. Close proximity to royalty and its bearing on seniority also applies to the unarmed page, whose function is not clear. His distinctive belt or girdle suggests that he holds a special rank; Niẓām al-Mulk's *Book of Government or Rules for Kings* reports that by the third year of training a page was presented with a girdle.[27]

The page has a red cloth (*mandīl*) with a gold band (*muṭarraz*) knotted or tucked into his belt. The *mandīl* was a rectangular piece of cloth which had various uses, such as a napkin or towel. When serving its basic function, it was detached from the body; when attached to the person, its function became secondary, as here. It had connotations of refinement. In time, the napkin became indispensable for a properly attired person, and it was a desirable and costly possession. This illustration seems to be a fairly early depiction of the napkin attached to the belt as an item of apparel. There was a gradual progression in the training of a page, with increases in rank expressed through the clothing and accoutrements and the entrusting with further duties. By the third year the page had a girdle, and by the fourth year a quiver and bow. In theory, an ambitious youth could become a troop-leader and progress to chamberlain. By early middle age, a really capable man might reasonably expect to be promoted to the rank of provincial ruler. For example, Badr al-Dīn Lu'lu' was virtual ruler of Mosul in 1210 and became sovereign in his own right in 1233.[28]

The institution of the category of personal attendants (*khāṣṣakiyya*) in the context of the Bahrī Mamlūks was perhaps more highly developed than that of the earlier class of household servants (*dāriyyat al-ghilmān*) and more orientated towards the military. There, too, the personal emblems adopted for individual posts were symbols of achievement, appearing in manuscript illustrations, on metalwork and on stone reliefs.[29] In both categories a small élite was raised at court in close contact with the ruler; mutual affection and trust sustained self-interest. The development of sexual bonds in such a tightly circumscribed, exclusively male social circle is hardly surprising.

Four of the pages in the Rayy mosque wear long boots, while the fifth wears shoes. This is unthinkable in a mosque, so they are, technically, improperly dressed. Their costume, rank and physical orientation in relation to the ruler may presuppose a knowledge of court procedure on the part of al-Wāsiṭī.

The densely packed congregation in the public (downstairs) part of the mosque interior and the overflow outside is all male; most faces are hirsute and Semitic, although occasionally one finds features from the farther corners of the empire. They are well-dressed, urban types, with the exception of a bedouin at the top right-hand side of the crowd who is distinguishable by his turban, which is fastened under the chin. Three horsemen reinforce the notion of a crowd hastening to hear a famous preacher who has run 'with the running of steeds' and invaded the mosque precincts 'with the spread of locusts'.

Abū Zayd is clearly not heeding al-Ghazālī's definition of 'proper conduct' in the presence of one's ruler:

> Subjects should stand in awe of their ruler, even when he is kindly, and must refrain from undue familiarity, even though he be lenient. When the sultan appears, all conversation should cease and those present should call out blessings upon him.[30]

There is a possible explanation for Abū Zayd's outburst: the illustration may represent once more a satirical, or at least humorous, portrait of a foreign ruler by author and painter. It was well known that many of these officials spoke and understood very little Arabic, and al-Wāsiṭī's governor of Raḥba (Illust. 4) in *Maqāma* 10 has already been shown in a most unflattering light. However, the governor of Rayy seems more enlightened. Although his colour has changed in anger or consternation, he is impressed by Abū Zayd's exhortation to repentance and mercy. Acknowledging the error of his ways, he 'was courteous to the preacher and gave him gifts and urged him to visit him'.

This is a highly successful montage which has captured a spellbound audience, a 'distinguished preacher' and the ruler and his retinue in the personal enclosure. One can sense the dusty clamour outside the mosque. A late tenth-century anecdote from al-Muqaddasī sums up the atmosphere well. The caliph 'Abd al-Malik reportedly said, 'It would be splendid to rule without the clatter of the post-horses and the hard wood of the pulpit.'[31]

In *Maqāma* 23, one of the longest tales, al-Ḥārith finds himself in an unidentified government office. An old man is accusing a youth of plagiarism of his poetry before the governor, here referred to as *wālī*. The BN 6094 manuscript has a single miniature (Plate 7), which is framed by one line of text above and one below. A literal interpretation to set the scene, it tells how an old man:

long of tongue but short of cloak held by the collar a lad fresh in youth but worn in tunic. So I spurred on the track of the spectators until we arrived at the gate of the Prefecture. And there was the Master of Protection sitting squarely on his cushion, awing by his deportment. Then said the old man to him, 'God magnify the governor and set his foot [on high].'

Abū Zayd is grasping the youth by the shoulder and his upraised arm and forward-leaning posture suggest vigorous movement. Over his violet robe, with *ṭirāz* bands on the upper sleeve, he has thrown a shorter brown robe casually over his right shoulder. According to the text, this is a head-shawl (*ṭaylasān*). Although al-Ḥarīrī was writing in the twelfth century, by the thirteenth century, on the visual evidence of the *Maqāmāt* manuscripts at least, the *ṭaylasān* had apparently come to be associated only with *qāḍīs*; it was shown in white or black and draped over the turban and shoulders. Elsewhere in this manuscript *qāḍīs* wear a white *ṭaylasān*, as do *qāḍīs* in the contemporary *Kalīla wa Dimna* manuscript in Paris.

A variation of a sun motif (*shamsa*) is printed on Abū Zayd's overgarment. It occurs at the hip and accentuates its line, and it will become clear later that a feature of the artist's depiction of costume is that he treats it as a flat surface capable of decoration, and that garments are 'figure-forming'. Abū Zayd's adolescent son wears a short green shift with gold braid and a gold-coloured or yellow turban. Both the youth and Abū Zayd are barefoot, and one of Abū Zayd's feet extends over the base-line.

The governor grants his audience in a reception chamber. He is seated beneath a central, dark blue dome with honeycomb vaulting (*muqarnas*), a smaller dome lying to each side of it. The spandrels of the archway are decorated in violet and black, with a floriate scroll pattern which may represent stucco-work. Similar schematic architecture and decorative motifs appear in two contemporary Syriac Gospels, British Museum add. 7170 and the Vatican *Siriaco* 559 manuscripts and also in the *Kalīla wa Dimna* fables. From an architectural viewpoint, the construction is rudimentary, serving merely as a frame for the governor; it suggests the perspective of a central chamber. A tripartite framework is more common in this manuscript. The building itself, according to the text, is situated in an open space around a city or a castle.

Despite the caption's clear description of the governor as 'sitting squarely' (*mutarabbi'ān*), namely with his legs crossed beneath him, his right leg is again in the curious pendant position. Chenery translates the last line of the caption as 'God magnify the governor and set his foot on high.' He elaborates by stating that the governor sets his ankle on high 'so that the lowest part of him may be higher than the highest part of his companions', although this would be difficult to illustrate literally within the confines of a folio. The invocation was a synonym for prestige and might, and thus confirms the previous discussion of the pendant-leg pose in the context of Turkish sedentary postures, which served to establish a hierarchy according to social class. Although this pose may arguably represent a visual pun on the text, this artist paid little attention to the text and merely used an existing model as a type for his governors.

Apart from the youthful attendants, one further confirmation of the adaptation from royal iconography derives from the inclusion of the bowl of fruit in the foreground. One might compare the Saljūq ruler 'at ease' on the frontispiece of the contemporary Vienna *Book of Antidotes*, and Barzuya's audience with King Nūshirwān in the contemporary *Kalīla wa Dimna* in Paris.

The governor sits on a long, flat, dark blue cushion with golden pointed ends. His ebony throne has short carved ogee feet and pointed corners. In the twelfth century, the geographer al-Idrīsī mentions ebony growing in 'unbroken forests' on the banks of the Nile in deepest Africa, and it is possible that African ebony was exported to Arab lands. However, ebony was certainly imported from India. Covering the back of the throne is a fine, black, heavily brocaded cloth, worked in a pattern of palm leaves and other vegetal motifs. Al-Muqtadir had earlier favoured an ebony throne, which was covered in a fine Dabīqī cloth with gold embroidery.[32] Kings in the *Kalīla wa Dimna* pose on similar thrones. There are three striking similarities in the miniature of the king and Ilādh: the single archway with a large central dome and two smaller domes; the fact that this construction serves as a frame for the king; and its occupying the left-hand side of the composition;[33] however, the throne has no solid back. Both artists perhaps drew on the same iconography.

The ruler has long dark hair, a full beard and a moustache, and he wears the characteristic Turkish tall dark fur cap. The fur seems to be sketchily drawn with circles. The best sable apparently came from China, followed by that from the Caspian region. He also wears a red, knee-length slit tunic, with gold braid round the neckline, down the front and around the hem; it has *ṭirāz* bands on the upper arm. The fabric may have come from Sūs, for the *Rules and Regulations of the Court* mentions that 'red Sūsī cloth, gilded or plain embroidery', was included in the investiture robes of governors. However, a very fine, luminous crimson material was also manufactured in Armenia and 'the more gold is woven into [these varieties], the better the quality and the higher the price'.[34] Despite the fact that identical hats are found on Saljūq metalwork, the coat shown here differs, for it is not crossed over and fastened. Around the governor's waist is a golden belt of roundel design. He wears flat black shoes, with striped stockings in various shades of violet. They resemble those in al-Wāsiṭī's pilgrim procession (Plate 1).

Two young pages stand behind the throne. They belong to the category of personal or private attendants (*khāṣṣa*) within the household servant class. The youth nearest Abū Zayd is very girlish-looking, with what resembles a female head-covering tied under the chin. His mustard-coloured robe has a deep grey quilted-looking edging and is split down the middle. Perhaps this is a female attendant after all—according to al-Jāḥiẓ's *The Epistle of Singing-Girls*:

A caliph, or someone else in a comparable position of power and influence,

> used never to be without a slave-girl standing behind him to wave fly-whisk and fan, and another to hand him things, in a public audience in the presence of other men.

He continues:

> An indication that looking at women in general is not prohibited is that a middle-aged spinster will appear before men without any bashfulness. Were this prohibited when she is young, it would not be permissible when she is middle-aged . . .[35]

The possibility therefore is that these were female servants, but one should bear in mind the long time lapse between that utterance and the appearance of the miniature.

The second page wears a turban and a long-sleeved, similarly coloured shift; the face is incompletely drawn. One hand is curled around the throne and this device, together with Abū Zayd's projecting bare foot, gives the composition a small measure of depth. Again we read in the *Rules and Regulations of the Court*, 'Slavic servants stand behind the throne and on its sides, chasing flies with gold and silver-capped fly-whisks.'[36]

A fly-whisk fitting this description is found in the portrait of Badr al-Dīn Lu'lu' in Abū al Faraj al-Iṣfahānī's *Book of Songs [Kitāb al-aghānī]*, which is now in Istanbul. The *Book of Curious and Entertaining Information* reports that shaggy fur or tails of the yak were used for fly-whisks mounted on poles. They came from the 'Turkish lands', by which al-Tha'ālibī means India, on account of the 'profusion of their specialities'.[37] It is interesting to note that, in the royal context, the type of fly-whisk in this BN 6094 work invariably appears in the thirteenth- and fourteenth-century *Maqāmāt*, when the governors wear the same type of fur hat and Saljūq costume. There is thus a recognizable Saljūq 'style' associated with royal iconography. The fly-whisk here is angled in counterpoint to Abū Zayd's hand gesture and, together with the curved arch, serves to soften the angularity of the reception chamber and the throne. It also adds force to the dialogue.

The text makes it clear that the governor was far from amused at being duped, so there is an element of humour in that a man who has taken such pains to flaunt his superior rank is taken in by Abū Zayd. However, in view of the fact that the artist has drawn heavily from other traditions, the humour is probably only understood by the reader, for this manuscript lacks the 'personal' touch that comes over so well in the other works.

The illustration of a governor in BN 3929 (Illust. 5) for the 6th tale shows the Saljūq official filling Abū Zayd's mouth with pearls as a reward for his eloquence. This represents a visual metaphor for a literary aphorism and may be an indication that the painter was conversant with the text to some degree. As in the miniature just discussed, the surface of the textiles here is treated as an area of composition which is amenable to decoration. However, the governor's headgear is quite different from that of Saljūq officials in the other *Maqāmāt* manuscripts.

These illustrations of governors in both the Arab and Saljūq manner show great diversity in iconography, costume, architecture and landscape, yet they manage to give what appears to be an accurate impression of local custom and practice in the context of the audience at court.

The Judiciary

Seven of the tales are concerned with Abū Zayd's appearance before a *qāḍī*, when he invariably takes the part of a vexatious litigant in the guise of the outraged innocent party. His object is his 'vindication' and compensation and he is generally successful in deluding the *qāḍī* with his eloquent pleading. In *Maqāma* 9 his indiscreet celebration within earshot of a court servant resulted in him being called back before the *qāḍī*, who sportingly laughed so much that his hat fell off. These amusing tales exemplify the tilting at authority by the common man but, more seriously, they also offer a real insight into legal rights, the nature and punishment of offences, and so on.

5. The official 'filling Abū Zayd's mouth with pearls'.

Maqāma 37 unfolds as the astute al-Ḥārith pays a visit to the local *qāḍī*, whom he has assiduously courted during his business trips to Ṣa'da, in Yemen. This made sound business sense, would allow him to establish his personal credentials and would stand him in good stead in the event of a dispute with another merchant. One should also remember that there are four different schools of law in Islam, and there may have been variations in the interpretation of civil cases.

The artist of the St Petersburg manuscript has produced a very comprehensive court scene (Plate 8) and the text immediately above the miniature reads:

> I used constantly to assist at the courts of litigation and to decide between the aggressors and the aggrieved. Now the *qāḍī* was sitting to administer justice on a day of general concourse and gathering of people, when lo! there came in an old man in threadbare garb . . .

It continues below:

> . . . with limbs apparently tremulous [from age], who regarded the crowd with a discriminating look, and then stated that he had a most intractable opponent; and in less time than a spark shines, or one points with a finger, a youth was brought in, who seemed [bold] as a lion. And the old man then said, 'May God help thee, O *qāḍī*, and save thee from the guilt of conniving [at wrong]!'

At centre stage the *qāḍī* and Abū Zayd are obviously engaged in serious dialogue. Abū Zayd makes his point concerning the recalcitrance of his son with a stab of the hand, while the *qāḍī* sits rather impassively. His outstretched palm suggests that he is sympathetically conceding a point to the plaintiff; the text reveals him as one who 'regarded [the plaintiff's] complaint as a serious matter' and gave it as his opinion that 'disobedience in children is as painful as bereavement of them, and perhaps it would be preferable to be entirely childless'. Our hero stands confidently to plead his case, far from intimidated by the sombre *qāḍī*; indeed, the caption has already shown him as extremely impertinent in impugning the *qāḍī*'s integrity. His clothing is dark, but not 'threadbare'.

The episode unfolds within a tripartite architectural framework; the building is spacious and fairly ornate. A draped curtain to the left suggests an ante-room where Abū Zayd's son has been waiting before being summoned by the court usher. The two small ribbed domes with clerestory windows are grey, and so are probably lead-covered. They are set over the smaller side-chambers, and a wrought metal balustrade surmounts the central, undomed area. This crenellation, which resembles pierced metalwork, serves to highlight the main action, which is further emphasized by a heavily scroll-patterned curtain forming an 'archway'. The curtain can apparently be pulled down by the brass ring at the centre to close off the area when the court is not sitting. Perhaps the chamber serves a variety of purposes.

Inset above the carved wooden architraves of the ante-rooms are stucco panels, which are probably perforated to provide air-flow. A yellow brick floor, set in a vertical bond, provides a clear base-line. As a similar format is also employed on page 256, it may indicate an element of planning in the setting, which can be adapted to a variety of functions required by the text.

There is nothing in this scene, such as 'Abbāsid or religious flags, to suggest that it takes place in a state institution. One may therefore assume that power is vested in the individual, namely the *qāḍī*. We need to identify those elements which will confirm that he presides in a judicial function, in whatever type of building. The *qāḍī* sits on a carved wooden bench with turned wood decoration, with a large bolster at his back. Various renderings of this type of bench can be seen in this artist's schoolroom, as well as in the Paris and Istanbul manuscripts, and it seems therefore to be a standard type. *Qāḍīs* with large pointed bolsters at their back also occur elsewhere. Very similar figures and cushions—which seem to have a Byzantine provenance—appear in the Dioscorides *De Materia Medica* manuscript of 1224 in the Freer Gallery, Washington. Curiously, considering evidence of its Byzantine influences, large pointed bolsters standing on end do not seem to occur in the BN 6094 *Maqāmāt*.

The *qāḍī* wears a white robe and trousers, and over his turban his black shawl (*ṭaylasān*) falls down around his shoulders. In this *Maqāma* the illustrations for BN 5847 and 3929 also portray a black shawl, although it is more usually shown as white. Abū Yūsuf, the distinguished jurist in al-Rashīd's era who was the first to be designated chief *qāḍī*, ordered theologians to wear a black turban with the *ṭaylasān*. That conferred on them a distinctive head-dress, while black signified allegiance to the 'Abbāsid dynasty.

Niẓām al-Mulk's *Book of Government or Rules for Kings* tells of one, Abū 'Abdallāh, who 'went to one of the towns of the Banū Aghlab where he put on a hood and lived as an honourable person [*'adl*]', which is an Islamic legal term for a person of good reputation whose testimony is assumed to be true.[38] The wearing of a shawl does not seem, therefore, to have been the prerogative of one particular professional group; rather, it indicates a person of good education and some social standing, engaged professionally in the practice or study of the law or ritual of Islam. This is borne out by the fact that the preacher in *Maqāma* 28 in BN 6094 also wears a black shawl.

Further confirmation is found in the fact that in Ṣalāḥ al-Dīn's time, around the end of the twelfth century, the preacher in the Cairo mosque was described as being dressed '*'alā' rasmi al-'abbāsiyya*' (after the fashion of the 'Abbāsids): he wore a black robe with black linen hood, a black turban and carried a sword. The *qāḍī*, therefore, represents a member of the social class called 'hood-wearers' (*arbāb al-ṭayālisa*). *Ṭaylasān* is also cognate with the Hebrew *tallith*, which the *Talmud Dictionary* describes as 'the cloak of honour, the scholar's or officer's distinction'; thus the hood or cloak was a sign of distinction in Eastern societies.[39]

The *ṭaylasān* does not originally appear to have been an Arab headdress. *Ṭaylasān* is not even an Arabic word, but a foreign borrowing. Both the *Tāj al-'arūs* and the *Muḥkam* dictionaries describe it as 'a certain article of apparel worn by the *'ajam* [Persians]', while elsewhere its description appears to vary according to period, fashion and country. However, al-Ṭabarī notes that a humble clerk in the Baghdad Palace wore a *ṭaylasān* and there is a well-known tale concerning Isḥāq al-Mawṣilī, a singer at al-Ma'mūn's court, who wore one.[40] It seems that it came to be associated with distinction at a comparatively late period, while at an earlier time it was a more popular form of headdress.

An early twelfth-century record of a probate sale from the Cairo *Geniza*, where Hebrew papers are stored, quotes the price of a *ṭaylasān* as 1 *dīnār*, and a merchant's bills for the period 1230–35 reveal that such shawls then cost 7 *dīnārs* each in Egypt. According to al-Jāḥiẓ, the best shawls were 'the Ṭabarī Ruyānī kind, then those of Āmul, then the Egyptian kind, then the Qūmis kind', but those made of half silk (*mulḥam*) from Nishapur were also held in high regard.[41]

Beneath his head-shawl, the *qāḍī* wears a white turban (*'imāma*). A turban could be made of a great length of material, and its donning might be construed as a badge of the Muslim, for a Prophetic Tradition runs, 'The difference between a Muslim and an infidel is the wearing of a turban on the cap.' Ibn al-Jawzī and Abū al-Faraj al-Iṣfahānī stress that the *'imāma* was the main distinctive dress of a male. Al-Jāḥiẓ describes it as 'a shield on the battlefield, a net in the summer; an outer garment [*dithār*] in the winter, and an honour in the assembly, a protector in vicissitudes, and an increase in the stature of a man'.[42]

It was obligatory to wear the turban outdoors, except on occasions of condolence or while on the pilgrimage, while government servants had to wear (black) turbans in their offices at all times. According to the *Rules and Regulations of the Court*, this was official etiquette, and any breach could lead to humiliation or even to corporal punishment. An account in the *Book of Government or Rules for Kings* reveals the ultimate humiliation meted out by 'Aḍūd al-Dawla, who 'ordered the great chamberlain to go and bring the *qāḍī* of the city bareheaded before him, with his turban round his neck'.[43]

This confirms that the turban was also recognized as a badge of rank. There is no sign in this miniature of the tall headdress known as *qalansuwa*, which in al-Kindī's day, the ninth century, was regarded by *qāḍīs* and legists as their perquisite and badge of office. By the thirteenth century the *qāḍī* was known as the *ṣāḥib al-'imāma* or *rabb al-'imāma*, in other words, 'the turban-wearer', or as the *ṣāḥib dastar* in Persia.[44] Another account tells how Abū Yūsuf, the Ḥanafi jurist, was something of a dandy. He was on extremely familiar terms with Hārūn al-Rashīd and one day, when the caliph saw him, he was moved to quote the poet Ibn Mayyāda:

With a travelling cloak wound round him,
He was brought by a mare
With scant hair on her forehead,
Tossing a unique personality.

On his death in *c.* 798, this same Abū Yūsuf left 200 pairs of silk trousers, each with Armenian braiding valued at 1 *dīnār*.[45]

Al-Tanūkhī tells of a certain *qāḍī* in Basra who was said every evening 'to leave his residence in Aḥnaf Square wearing breeches, with a light cloak on his back, and sandals of Git on his feet, and with a fan in his hand'.[46] In spite of the fact that Islamic law is grounded in the Qur'ān, these examples seem to illustrate something of a preoccupation with appearance and worldly matters on the part of jurists.

The *qāḍī*'s white robe and trousers in the illustration appear to be of a fine, diaphanous material. One cannot see if he wears shoes or sandals, but it is likely that he wore a type of shoe known as *suqmān*. All the characters, who appear to be Arabs, wear turbans (one of which has a long tail) and the standard type of robe with *ṭirāz* and wide sleeves. Yāqūt describes sleeves during the 'Abbāsid era as wide enough to double as pockets; indeed, it seems that too narrow a sleeve, like too short a coat, could be interpreted as reprehensible poverty or meanness on the part of the wearer. According to al-Maqrīzī, a certain chief *qāḍī* in Egypt reportedly carried a discourse in his sleeve which he had written out on flat sheets of paper to be delivered at a festival.[47] The illustration may, then, give a true representation of contemporary costume and the clerk's report could fit unfolded into his sleeve.

Abū Zayd's first recourse in a civil dispute was to take his complaint to the *qāḍī*. He appears to be following custom in presenting his own plaint orally: in the court of the *qāḍī*, only the plaintiff adduced evidence and questioned witnesses. (This was the theory; in practice, local custom and law seem to have prevailed.) The *qāḍī* delivers his judgment in the presence of the witnesses, as laid down; should this case have proved very difficult, he would have done so in the presence of learned lawyers with whom he could consult.[48] The *qāḍī* was supposed to sit in an open, spacious place and thus be accessible to all, as shown in the illustration. The *Book of Songs* reveals the chief mosque as a public place and open to all the community. The *qāḍīs* originally sat here, leaning against a pillar, perhaps because court work was to be conducted with the maximum publicity. An official witness who acted as deputy to al-Tanūkhī's father reports a feud between the censor, al-Kawākibī, and the *qāḍī*, Abū al-Ḥasan ibn 'Alī al-Sarrāj. Al-Kawākibī unexpectedly confronted the *qāḍī*:

> who had taken to sitting in the mosque only twice a week. Taking up his station at the gate with his force, he bade them tell the *qāḍī* that he was not entitled to continue sitting in his house. 'Come forth . . . to the mosque, where you will be within reach of the strong and the weak, as you are instructed in your deed of investiture.'[49]

In the early days, however, *qāḍīs* could hear cases at home, with the parties to the dispute conducting their business standing before him. It was apparently some time later that the practice of sitting in a row before the *qāḍī* was introduced, as can be seen from the secondary characters in the illustration. In the mid-ninth century, orthodox reaction sought to prohibit the use of the mosque as a courtroom, on the grounds of desecration, but the prohibition was ineffectual. There is nothing in this miniature to suggest that the scene is enacted in a mosque, although if it were a private house it is certainly an elaborate one.

It is likely that a ticket (*riqqa*) bearing the names of both plaintiff and defendant (and those of their respective fathers) has been used to call out Abū Zayd's case. Such tickets were collected by the clerk of the court (*kātib*) before the court convened. Al-Ḥaṣṣāf reports in the ninth century that a *qāḍī* could, on average, dispose of some 50 cases a day. Like their predecessors, *qāḍīs* in the Saljūq period charged fees for the drafting of legal documents. Textbooks appear to make no mention of fees beyond stipulating that they were paid, but some form of emolument was probably paid by the successful party.[50]

Despite receiving salaries, being accorded a special form of dress and acquiring land fiefs, *qāḍīs* did not necessarily command the respect of the jurists and their appointment may have posed a moral dilemma for some. Religious scruples seem to have prevented certain candidates from sitting in judgment over their fellow men. Al-Samarqandī writes in the tenth century, 'On the question of the acceptance of a judicial post there is no unanimity of opinion. Some maintain that it should not be accepted; while others that it may be, provided it has not been sought or striven for.'[51]

Al-Tanūkhī throws light on the appointment of *qāḍīs* when he describes how 'Abdullāh ibn Aḥmad ibn Dāsah related the following tale, on the authority of Abū al-Ḥusayn:

> When I was grown up the *qāḍī* Abū Ḥāzim wrote to my father, saying, 'I am informed that you have a grown-up son who is a student, etc. (his expressions were very complimentary), so send him to me to be invested with the *qāḍī*-ship.' My father said to me, 'What say you to this?' I said, 'Please send me, as you see how straitened our circumstances are, and possibly I may get a salary which will keep me in comfort.'

The father said that his son should not go, however, 'for offices come to an end, whereas integrity endures'.[52] One savant even feigned mental incompetence to avoid his appointment. For reasons of conscience, some *qāḍīs* also refused either to draw a salary or to accept money from the parties with whom they had dealings.

Al-Tanūkhī himself, who presided over several Mesopotamian districts as a *qāḍī* and was also superintendent of the Baghdad mint, received 'only 60 *dīnārs* a month as pay' for the combined posts, according to Yāqūt. Nāṣir-i Khusraw, the Persian traveller, tells us that a chief *qāḍī* of Fatimid Egypt drew a monthly salary of 2,000 *dīnārs*; apparently, he managed to supplement this.[53] These examples suggest that becoming a *qāḍī* was an unattractive prospect for some people. Perhaps because of this reluctance to take up the post, other less scrupulous people were recruited. For instance, al-Tanūkhī's account of an exemplary *qāḍī* hints at possible judicial corruption elsewhere. He tells us that after Abū Umayya al-Akhwaṣ, who was of 'obscure origin', was appointed a *qāḍī* in Basra, he:

> proceeded to his province and was anxious to conceal his personal deficiencies and want of knowledge, and further to display some good quality; so he maintained strict integrity in matters of display, took no bribes, was strictly honourable, and confined his takings to his official income and the gifts bestowed on him by Ibn al-Furāt.[54]

Nor did the appointment guarantee personal immunity for the incumbent: the *Book of Curious and Entertaining Information* records that the first *qāḍī* to be executed in Islam was Abū al-Muthanna, killed in the early tenth century by the restored caliph al-Muqtadir for having paid homage to Ibn al-Mu'tazz. By that period, *qāḍīs* were usually accountable to the chief *qāḍī* in Baghdad,[55] to whom cases outside the jurisdiction of Abū Zayd's *qāḍī* would presumably have been referred. According to Ibn Baṭṭūṭa, each of the four schools of Islamic jurisprudence usually had its own supreme *qāḍī*.

The figure at the right-hand side on a level with the *qāḍī* must be al-Ḥārith, in his role of occasional assistant at court and a figure of some authority, as the text makes clear. Perhaps this fact is being stressed by his sitting at the same height as the *qāḍī*. The figure at the left must be Abū Zayd's son, shown as a fully grown man. His arm and one leg are draped around the framework, which may be a compositional device to suggest an element of depth. Although it could be interpreted as a sign of insouciance on the part of a youth 'bold as a lion', the former interpretation is the more likely, for we have already considered this convention in *Maqāma* 38, on page 56, in the court of the governor of Merv in this same manuscript (Plate 3).

In the centre foreground, a court clerk is busily recording the proceedings with a pen. Arab historians generally recognize the family of the ninth-century vizier Yaḥya ibn Khālid as the founders of the class known as the 'people of the pen' (*ahl al-qalam*). The art of the pen is widely esteemed in Muslim society. Mention of the *qalam* occurs in *sūras* 68 and 96; it recalls the earliest Qur'ānic revelation and also serves to stress the prophethood of Muḥammad. Prescribed qualities for secretaries (*kuttāb*) included the avoidance of prolixity and repetition; concise writing was praised. Al-Ghazālī relates an anecdote concerning the second caliph 'Umar, who returned to a secretary a letter where the *s* in the *basmallāh* ('In the name of God') was not legible. 'Umar said, 'First make the *s* of the *basmallāh* legible, then you may return to your post.'

Pens were cut from reeds and slanted. According to al-Ghazālī and al-Ṣūlī, the slant ran from right to left for the writing of Arabic, Persian and Hebrew and from left to right for Greek. Al-Barmakī describes the best pens as being 'neither thin nor thick, and narrow in diameter and straight'. The reed was cut on an extremely hard surface with a knife whose blade was shaped like a crane's bill.[56]

A large brass or bronze ink-well (*maḥbara*) with a domed lid rests on the *qāḍī*'s bench, just above the clerk. It conforms in material and dimensions to types which were popular in Persia and Mesopotamia in the twelfth century. The ink-well in the illustration is decorated, and it may be incised and inlaid with silver and copper. Ink-wells also appear in BN 5847 (Illust. 16) and BL 1200 on folios 122v and 43r respectively, although these are unlike the example shown here and have flat tops. The ink-well of the Cairo chief *qāḍī* referred to above was silver and came from the 'citadel treasury';[57] the material obviously reflected his senior status.

According to Ibn al-Ṣābī', an incorruptible usher also appears to have been an indispensable figure in court, together with a trustworthy deputy for work that the *qāḍī* personally could not undertake. Such people apparently do not figure in the illustration. The two other seated men may be court officials, such as witnesses or assessors. They are facing each other and are perhaps quietly discussing points of law. Al-Kindī informs us that before al-Manṣūr's time:

> only witnesses known to be of good repute were accepted. Others were either openly rejected or, in case they were absolutely unknown, inquiries were made regarding them from their neighbours. But now, as there is such a lot of false swearing, secret inquiries are made regarding the witnesses; that is to say, a list of men fit to be called as witnesses is prepared. The result is that not reliability but inclusion in the prepared list is now the passport to the witness-box; the word 'witness' [*shāhid*] signifying such a definite individual.[58]

This practice of drawing up an official list of witnesses by a *qāḍī* has continued to the present day. A fixed number of assessors is then chosen by the *qāḍī* from the witness list, to assist him in his work. Such transformation of witnesses, who were originally a band of respectable and trustworthy men, into a permanent body of officials took place in the tenth century. Mez suggests that witnesses may be 'the resurrected notaries of the pre-Islamic empire'. An eleventh-century diary account describes the procedure:

> On Tuesday, the second day of the month, the Shaykh Abū al-Ḥasan ibn al-Shuhūrī took the oath as a notary [*shāhid*] at the place of the chief *qāḍī* [*qāḍī al-quḍāt*] Abū 'Abdallāh al-Dāmghānī, together with Ibn al-Juhrumī and Ibn Aḥmad al-Zanjānī.[59]

This process may have arisen from the needs of the burgeoning mercantile class, for the prudent merchant would obviously choose the best-known, approved candidates for notarial confirmation of his business documents. However, as the incident illustrated occurs on 'a day of general concourse and gathering of people', the two other seated figures may simply be people awaiting their turn to present their cases.

The scene conforms generally to the description of the chief *qāḍī*'s court and his entourage in Cairo, where an account describes him sitting on a dais with a silken cushion, with his assessors ranged according to seniority, and surrounded by court servants and clerks. Buchtal has pointed out the similarity between the pictorial representation of *qāḍī* scenes and certain miniatures of judgment scenes in Syriac manuscripts, as regards both human types and composition. In this regard, one might also compare judgment scenes in the contemporary Paris *Kalīla wa Dimna*.[60]

Despite the wealth of architectural features, there is no distraction from the human drama being enacted. Indeed, the architecture is employed to dramatic effect and complemented by eloquent hand and body gestures and facial expressions. There is more than a suggestion here of the shadow play (*khayāl al-ẓill*). The St Petersburg illustration, therefore, with its *qāḍī* in prescribed dress, its plaintiff and defendant, witnesses and scribe, might be construed as a typical lawcourt scene that would be easily recognized by a Muslim audience. Here, the substance of the 'case' is a pretext on the author's part for describing a scene set before a *qāḍī* because a complaint regarding a recalcitrant son would hardly merit a *qāḍī*'s opinion (*fatwa*). There is evidently satirical intent on the part of al-Ḥarīrī (which would have led to criticism of him in certain quarters), for when Abū Zayd and his son speed away with cash from the *qāḍī*, the father says, 'Let him whom his . . . fortune has treated ill repair to Ṣa'da town and her *qāḍī*. His bounty shames the bounteous that went before; his justice baffles those who come after.'

We shall now turn to the treatment of *Maqāma* 37 in BN 3929. The three lines of Arabic above tell of a man who:

> regarded the crowd with a discriminating look, and then stated that he had a most untractable opponent, and in less time than a spark shines, or one

6. The youth brought to the qāḍī of Ṣa'da.

points with a finger, a youth was brought in, who seemed [bold] as a lion.

This is the same point in the text as that chosen by the St Petersburg illustrator. Following his usual practice, the artist has a large caption in gold Thulūth script running down the right-hand side of the page, which reads, 'A picture of the *qāḍī* and the youth [who] had been brought in'.

We have here a variation of a throne, with the *qāḍī* sitting on a patterned cushion. Abū Zayd and his son are once more acting out their quarrel before him. The *qāḍī* wears white robes and a white turban, with his black head covering falling down over his shoulders. There are no architectural features and it is the shawl which confirms that the seated figure is a *qāḍī*, although he would be recognizable as a person of substance by his pose, which implies authority. He seems to have the requisite presence and gravity of mien to recall a famous predecessor, al-Māwardī, who died in the mid-eleventh century.

The two figures at the left-hand side are obviously al-Ḥārith and Abū Zayd, who are shown as Arabs, but the son is oriental-looking and has pigtails. Once again we have the adaptation of a standard Eastern enthronement scene, with the substitution of an Arab *qāḍī* for the ruler and the retention of the foreign page-boy doubling as a young man.

Yet another lawcourt scene occurs in the Istanbul manuscript, where Abū Zayd and his wife air their matrimonial grievances in *Maqāma* 45 (Plate 9). She accuses him of maltreating her and of withholding conjugal rights; Abū Zayd pleads extreme poverty and the inability to provide for any children of the union. This is a further ruse to obtain charity from the *qāḍī* and is a successful follow-up to their tricks in *Maqāma* 9. The text runs:

> . . . [when] there had appealed to him a worn wight in worn raiment and a fair one in faded finery. The old man was minded to speak and explain the object of his suit, but the wench cut short his peroration and checked his bark . . . Then she removed from her face the flap of kerchief and indited with the tongue of an impudent shrew.

Although the reproduction is unclear due to defacement by iconoclasts, one can make out the *qāḍī* seated on a squat, carved wooden throne with heavy turned legs, listening attentively to the plaintiff and defendant. He wears a light head-shawl and appears to be sitting on a cushion on a circular carpet with a central band of cruciform design. Parallels for this type of seat and its coverings occur elsewhere in *Maqāmāt* manuscripts, in Syriac manuscript illustrations (with slight variations) and in Sa'd al-Dīn Varāvīnī's *Book of Marzūbān [Marzūbān-nāma]* manuscript in Istanbul, dated 1299. Ibn Baṭṭūṭa's *Travels in Asia and Africa* confirms that figures of authority used a similar seat, for on a visit to Baghdad in 1327, he describes a professor of law at al-Mustanṣiriyya College as 'seated under a small wooden cupola on a chair covered by a carpet, speaking with much sedateness and gravity of mien, he being clothed in black and wearing a turban'.

The architectural features are standard and the setting is less elaborate than elsewhere in this manuscript. The lawcourt is presumably a sizeable building since there are three wind-towers. An interesting addition is the drape hanging from the ceiling at centre stage, which echoes the carpet in its semicircular shape. This seems to be a version of the canvas or felt *khaysh*, reported by al-Ṭabarī as in general use in 'Abbāsid times for cooling by evaporation. It was described by the poet Ibn al-Nadīm thus:

> The *khaysh* was made wet inside the dome, which called forth winter and removed the heat of summer; and the cord caused drops of water to fall from it on the ground as if pearls were being scattered. If the *khaysh* were set in hell, its coolness would certainly overcome the burning heat of the fire.

The *Book of Curious and Entertaining Information* reports that the *khaysh* was first introduced for al-Manṣūr. According to the same source, an unnamed poet cursed Iṣfahān by satirizing that city in the following terms: 'When I was there in summer, I had to sell my framework of canvas sheeting for keeping cool (and in one of the winter months I pawned my brazier).'[61]

Al-Muqadassī's late tenth-century account throws further light on the possibly non-Islamic origin of the *khaysh*, for we read that during preaching in Egypt a canvas awning was slung 'such as was done in the circus in Hellenic days'. He also records the use of the *khaysh* in Basra and Shīrāz.[62] The positioning of the contraption in the illustration (in an air current below the wind-tower) confirms that this is a *khaysh* used in a building constructed to permit through-ventilation. The three towers, then, may not be mere architectural whim or artistic licence. Wind-towers are a feature of certain Middle Eastern houses to this day.

A scroll pattern can clearly be seen on the *khaysh*; perhaps it represents a finer, decorative drape over the plain felt or canvas fabric, for Arabic literature mentions coloured gauze which draped the felt. This feature also figures prominently in the 23rd tale of this Istanbul manuscript. Al-Sharīshī describes in his commentary on the *Maqāmāt* how rose-water, as an alternative to plain water, was sometimes used to dispense fragrance. A very similar decorated drape with a leafy scroll pattern occurs on a Persian polychrome plate; this may be a *khaysh*, or it may represent one of several conventions common to painters of pottery and manuscript miniaturists, for example wavy pools, schematized trees and slender foliated branches.[63]

Al-Ḥārith sits patiently, observing yet another ruse by Abū Zayd and his wife. Abū Zayd tries to make his point eloquently, but his wife gestures brazenly to the *qāḍī*. Her arms outstretched to plead her case, she cries, 'So bid him show me henceforth sweet kindliness, or make him drink the bitter draught of divorce.'

Despite being described in the text as 'a worn wight in worn raiment and a

7. A complicated court-room drama.

fair one in faded finery', the pair appear to be clad in patterned bourgeois clothing, like al-Ḥārith; swirling folds are delineated. Again, one must question whether this is feasible for a couple living on the margins of society or whether these are features of composition and aesthetics. The men wear sandals (*ni'āl*), while the woman has boots. Women's footwear was usually made of coloured leather and was similar in shape to men's fine light boots.

Finally, we shall turn to the BL 1200 illustration of a *qāḍī* in *Maqāma* 8, where Abū Zayd and his son play out an exceedingly complicated drama. There has been a long preamble by the pair in their wrangle over a slave-girl. At this juncture the *qāḍī*, his patience exhausted, instructs them peremptorily, 'Now either explain or depart.' We have here a simple judgment scene. There are no architectural elements and the *qāḍī* sits on the rug-draped throne with heavy, turned legs which is a standard fitment in interior scenes in this manuscript; on this occasion the carpet is rectangular. With his long white head-shawl over his dark turban and robe, he is more reminiscent of a biblical prophet than an Arab; this effect is heightened by the halo (which, again, has no religious significance). The two central figures must be Abū Zayd and his son, who is shown as a mature man; al-Ḥārith stands to the left. They wear the standard Arab robes over light trousers, the folds delicately delineated; only al-Ḥārith's sleeves bear *ṭirāz* bands. The ordinary leather sandal (*na'l*) is shown.

Both the text above the miniature and the head-shawl confirm that this is a lawcourt scene; the artist has repeated this format in other courtrooms in this manuscript. His governor of Merv in the 38th tale is depicted in the same manner, but there his turban replaces the *qāḍī*'s shawl (this is surely coincidental). Apart from Abū Zayd's pointing finger, the illustration seems wooden and lifeless; some of this can be attributed to the schematic rendering of the faces.

These few examples of illustrated tales give some insight into the Islamic world: on points of law, the function and dress of the judiciary, and their suitability or otherwise for high office. Two further judgment scenes, in *Maqāmāt* 9 and 40, are analysed in the section on women in the *Maqāmāt* (see Chapter 6) (Illust. 17 and Plate 17 respectively).

No individualized architectural form for a courtroom (or for the higher court presided over by the governor) emerges from this typical selection of *Maqāmāt* miniatures. The buildings depicted follow standard architectural conventions, but it is the other features, such as the text, captions, costume and furnishings, which demonstrate the authority vested in the incumbent in office and precisely define the setting.

Perfect justice, as posited in al-Ghazālī's *Counsel for Kings*, should be impartial. In the eyes of the law, the unknown litigant of no repute and the well-known litigant of high worldly rank and dignity are equal. The Prophet said, 'God on high created nothing finer on earth than justice. Justice is God's balance on earth, and any man who upholds this balance will be carried by Him to Paradise.'[64] It is heartening to see how the scales of justice favour the apparently impoverished Abū Zayd, who invariably receives a reward at the hands of the high and mighty, even if one cannot always approve of his motives. This, in turn, counterbalances the element of satire sometimes directed at figures of authority by both the author and the artists.

3

Trade

Trade is an honourable pursuit in Islam and the Prophet himself, his wife Khadīja and other early Muslim leaders were successful, well-travelled business people from the mercantile communities of Mecca and Medina. Although economic activities and the amassing of wealth and possessions are not in themselves reprehensible in Islam, ostentation and dubious conduct in business are to be avoided. Trade flourished in the great cities of the Muslim world from the ninth to the fourteenth century and there were large numbers of merchants, especially those trading in textiles. This may in part be attributable to the fact that in the Islamic world cushions, rugs and wall hangings were often used instead of furniture, while the royal courts generated much demand.

The mercantile bourgeoisie enjoyed a close relationship with the urban environment, and middle-class life revolved around the nexus of mosque and market (*sūq*). Thus it is fitting that a vital character in the *Maqāmāt* is a merchant. We do not learn of the narrator's particular branch of trade, but his journeys, his mode of travel and his business and legal contacts are revealed throughout the tales. Al-Ḥārith traverses the Syrian desert by camel caravan and on one occasion he embarks on a sea voyage; he travels to Egypt, Yemen and Persia; he meets fellow merchants in the Wāsiṭ caravanserai (*khān*); and he seeks a personal slave in the slave market. He contacts *qāḍīs* in his ports of call and is zealous in his worship. Like businessmen everywhere, al-Ḥārith periodically suffers a reversal of fortune and is down on his luck.

The author of the *Maqāmāt*, al-Ḥarīrī, had a mercantile background, possibly the silk trade. We do not know why he chose the occupation of merchant for al-Ḥārith, but the narrative is apparently a form of autobiography based on al-Ḥarīrī's own travels and encounters. This would be consistent with the long-established anecdotal genre in Arabic literature, add authenticity to the tales and lend appeal for a bourgeois audience. Further, al-Ḥarīrī was in a somewhat ambiguous position as a government servant and outright criticism of authority might have compromised his post.

Trade provided a great source for wealth in a city and was also a fertile breeding-ground for the cross-fertilization of ideas from diverse cultural and social strains. Although there is little visible expression of trade by way of 'real' architecture in the illustrations, it is highly significant that what does appear is concerned with mercantile activity, such as the *khān*, the legal tribunal, the stalls and the 'hole in the wall' booths of the *sūq*. It also illustrates the means and the leisure which successful business implies, such as the literary gathering in the public library, and al-Ḥārith and friends drinking wine *al fresco*. This suggests that the audience of the *Maqāmāt* was composed of a like-minded group, a highly literate and successful segment of society.

The Caravan

In *Maqāma* 4 al-Ḥārith is travelling to Damietta, in Egypt. He tells how 'We came to a spot with dewy hillocks, and a fresh breeze, which we therefore chose as a place for the camels to rest and to repose ourselves.' The travellers overhear two men discussing one's duty towards ones fellows. Al-Ḥārith is entranced by the rhetoric of the older man, despite his display of selfishness and the cynicism of the wordly-wise.

The BN 5847 illustration is apt, and al-Wāsiṭī has placed it near the beginning of the tale, at Abū Zayd's reply to his son (Plate 10). His considered advice is carefully set out in five lines above the painting, but the artist has curiously shown the group asleep on a small hill while the camels rest in a hollow. Neither al-Ḥārith nor the son is identifiable, but an innocent and vulnerable-looking bareheaded old man sleeps blissfully against a rolled carpet at the right hand side and this is surely Abū Zayd. The contrast between this picture of guilelessness and the consternation of the duped merchants in al-Wāsiṭī's wonderful endpiece illustrates neatly the 'sting in the tail' aspect of Abū Zayd's behaviour, and seems deliberate on the artist's part.

The travellers seem comfortable among their assorted merchandise and plump cushions. Their packages and bales are all of a size; this would make them easily manageable and allow the camels' loads to be well balanced. In *Maqāma* 12 there is a reference to 'the corded and the sealed', that is, the goods which were corded in bales or sealed up in boxes. Usāma ibn Munqidh's *Memoirs* describe how, on an expedition connected with the campaigns against the Franks in the early twelfth century, 'Whenever I wanted to stop, I would put the bags in the centre of the rug, fold its end around them, spread another rug on top and sleep over the bags.[1] While this afforded the traveller some degree of comfort, in this instance it would also help protect a valuable cargo.

Large bales of shop merchandise are being carried off by thieves in the BN

3465 *Kalīla wa Dimna* manuscript. All these are sausage-shaped packages which are easily borne by one man, and they could presumably be packed and carried by pack animals in a type of litter. Similar bales and packages occur in the caravan scene where the Prophet is being anointed in the Edinburgh University *Universal History*, of the vizier Rashīd al-Dīn, dated 1306.[2] This is therefore an authentic and rather unusual picture of a merchant caravan at rest. It lacks the elements of the tending of the fire for the cook, the travellers' tents, the litters in which the group travelled by day, and other genre elements which feature in the St Petersburg and works of the later Persian schools of painting. Some of these have been discussed at some length in the context of the pilgrimage, and travelling by camel features on ivory, wood and metalwork.[3] The *Biographical Dictionary* tells how Ṣāḥib ibn ʻAbbād, who died in 995, turned down the post of wazīr to Nūḥ ibn Manṣūr, on the grounds (among others) that 'it would require four hundred camels' to transport his books alone.[4]

Three camels crouch down in the hollow of the hillock, the 'resting place for the white camels' of the text, but only one conforms to that description, and the others are darker. It is unlikely that they would go down for the night with their saddles in place for they, too, deserve their rest. Their trappings include saddles with two pairs of V-shaped carved wooden legs which sit astride the hump; these saddles are covered in bold patterned textiles, and one very fancy under-blanket is visible. In *Maqāma* 22 there is a reference to a 'cushion saddle' *[waliyya]*, which was a cushion placed on the back of the camel, under the saddle. Similar heavy patterns are found throughout the *Maqāmāt* manuscripts in general, as well as other contemporary art works.[5]

There is a suggestion in the St Petersburg illustration that the camels might have walked in pairs, one behind the other, with ropes or poles passing through rings attached to the camel-trappings, but al-Wāsiṭī has not shown them. The camel herd lies down beside his beasts, which could not have been too pleasant, but his charges are valuable in every sense, and their lives depended on them. His long wide sleeve curled over his head reminds one of the poses of Ṣūfīs in Persian miniatures.

It is surprising that no tents are shown, because other *Maqāmāt* illustrators produced rather splendid examples throughout the tales. By day the sun is baking hot, but at night there is a very dramatic drop in temperature, with a heavy dew. It is unlikely, then, that this group slept out in the open, for their clothes and cargo would be soaking. Ibn Jubayr's *Travels* describes the pilgrim caravan of the governor of Iraq in 1183 as 'beautiful to look upon and superbly provided, with large handsome tents and erections, and wonderful pavilions and awnings, and of an aspect such that I have never seen more remarkable.' It was a piece of 'regal splendour' and 'all this erection was held firm by thick linen cords with pegs driven [into the ground] and the whole was arranged with remarkable construction.'[6] Even the less elaborate tents of a merchant caravan would conform in structure, although obviously not in sumptuousness of textiles, to provide maximum comfort for people who spent much of their time on arduous travel. Layers of variegated textiles were employed. It may be that the tops were specially woven in one piece and the sides came separately; interior hangings would bridge gaps and act as draught-proof insulation. By day the thick walls would keep out light and heat. Ibn Taghribirdī's *Chronicles of Egypt [Ḥawādith al-duhūr fī mada al-ayyām wa al-shuhūr]* mention a Tent Market (*sūq al-khiyām*) in the north-east quarter of Cairo in the fifteenth century. Andrews' unpublished thesis on the dwellings of nomads in Central Asia in the present day, and he gives a fascinating account of tent types and their construction;[7] this seems to hold as well for the thirteenth century *Maqāmāt* and other tents, where the same basic priorities would have to be considered, that is, compatibility with the natural environment and portability, and comfortable shelter.[8]

Ibn Khallikān quotes the ninth-century poet Muslim ibn al-Walīd al-Anṣārī, whose advice for the weary traveller is apposite: 'Let not the longing of your soul for family and home prevent your enjoying an easy life in comfort; in every country where you choose to dwell, you will find a family and [friendly] neighbours in place of those you left behind.'

It is not clear who organised a caravan, but it is likely that people were contracted to do so, for the hire system was widespread in the Islamic world; people could rent houses, water cisterns, even clothing, and the *Book of Songs* reveals that carpets could be hired for festive occasions.[9] I have personal knowledge of this practice today in the Arabian Gulf. Perhaps the organisers were middle-men who provided a service of animals, accommodation and food, made arrangements with the tribesmen whose territories they passed through for safe conduct and the like, and charged a fee.

Tents occur elsewhere in the *Maqāmāt* illustrations. The most attractive type of domestic tent which is not made from animal hair appears in the Istanbul manuscript in *Maqāma* 26, which we saw in the section on Arab governors. Other examples are a pointed, rectangular shape in BN 5847, a rounded tent in the St Petersburg manuscript and an elaborate version with slightly sloping sides in BN 6094. Variations of tents also occur in the contemporary Istanbul *Romance of Warqa and Gulshāh* manuscript. The ridge tents of the forces of Buwayhid Majd al-Dawla are found in the later Edinburgh Rashīd al-Dīn manuscript, and curved top tents with sloping sides appear at the pre-Islamic Arabian fair illustrated in the Edinburgh al-Bīrūnī's *Chronology of Ancient Peoples*.

Agents were certainly appointed to transact business. Miskawayh's *The Experiences of the Nations [Tajārib al-umām]* reports that Prince Bakhtiyār became estranged from 'Aḍūd al-Dawla because he forbade 'the agent of the latter in Baghdad to purchase horses and commodities which he was in the habit of ordering and had been permitted to obtain'. In the *Book of the Dynasties of Islam*, al-Dhahabī reports that in 1069 or 1070 merchants were engaged to transport the personal effects of the Fatimid caliph of Egypt, al-Mustanṣir bi Allāh. The goods were pillaged by military slaves and sold to pay for food during a famine. The boxes were overflowing with some 70,000 brocade robes, 11,000 military vests and 20,000 swords encrusted with precious gems or gold. In the same period, Nāṣir-i Khusraw received a blank letter of credit from Aswān addressed to his agent (*wakīl*) in 'Aydhāb. It read, 'Give Nāṣir all that he may demand, obtain a receipt from him and debit the sum to me.'[10]

The Karkh quarter of Baghdad included an area for the hire of beasts of burden, principally camels, horses and donkeys. The usual means of transport for people was camels and horses; donkeys were presumably reserved for carrying merchandise. Given the degree of planning of the markets, and Ibn Taghrībirdī's report that the tent market in fifteenth-century Cairo was in the vicinity of the horse market (*sūq al-khayl*) and the farriers' oratory (*muṣallā al-bayāṭira*), it is likely that whoever organized a caravan would easily find his requirements in the market-place.

Kai' Kā'ūs' advice to merchants in the *Book of Qābūs [Qābūs-nāma]* on the calculation of their profit margins is relevant to al-Ḥārith: 'If on dry land an accident occurs through which your goods are lost, there is a chance that your life will be saved; whereas at sea there is peril to both; [and] you may find a replacement for your goods, but not for your life.'[11] In other words, the imported merchandise had to be priced high enough to provide a form of life insurance. The element of danger implicit in travelling reinforces the apparent need at that time for a talisman for the voyage to Oman in *Maqāma* 39, as we shall see (Chapter 6), as well as for the well-documented hazardous desert crossing in *Maqāma* 12. Abū Zayd was only too happy to supply both—at a price.

There seems to have been some degree of interdependence between rulers and merchants. By the end of the tenth century the bourgeoisie was able to assert itself as a powerful force in the socio-economic sphere of the Islamic world, and by the eleventh century it reached its zenith. It is clear that on occasion there was government intervention in the provision of a safe passage. This was not necessarily altruistic on the part of the rulers, for they needed to secure the frontiers and establish customs posts to levy import duties. Niẓām al-Mulk's *Book of Government or Rules for Kings* reports that early in the eleventh century there was an enormous gathering of merchants in Rayy. Maḥmūd, the Ghaznavid sultan, 'dispatched them with a prince and 150 horsemen as escort' and reassured them, 'Do not be anxious, for I am sending some troops in your tracks.'[12]

Al-Ḥārith and his companions rewarded Abū Zayd and his son handsomely for delighting them with their eloquence. The pair made off swiftly on a pretext and the merchants foolishly waited for some time for their return. Al-Ḥārith eventually discovered a message on his camel-saddle which contained a pious allusion to etiquette and was Abū Zayd's justification for his behaviour.

The Khān

Maqāma 29 is set in a merchants' caravanserai in Wāsiṭ (Plate 11), where al-Ḥārith had suffered a reversal of fortune in trade. He set the scene by relating how he stopped at a *khān* in Wāsiṭ 'frequented by a jumble from every land and a medley of travellers'. Because of his reduced circumstances, he foolishly agreed to Abū Zayd's plan to act as his marriage broker in an alliance with a wealthy but unknown bride. Abū Zayd assured al-Ḥārith that he would deliver a splendid wedding speech in praise of the 'groom' which would greatly impress the other merchants (and presumably encourage their generosity).

Such were Abū Zayd's oratorical powers and al-Ḥārith's love for his old friend that he relished this plan and enthused naively, 'Now he roused my spirits more by the description of the address to be indited than of the bride to be displayed.' Abū Zayd invited the 'wedding guests' to his room, where he consulted his astrolabe and almanac and made elaborate calculations as to the auspiciousness of day and time. Al-Ḥārith, who has invariably given the impression of being a decent and pious man, would have done well to ponder the words of al-Zamakhsharī, who concludes in his commentary on verses 25 and 26 of *sūra* 72:

> He does not reveal what is concealed but to him whom He is pleased with . . . That entails the abolishment of divination and astrology because the divinators and the astrologers are very far from His approval.[13]

Abū Zayd offered sweetmeats to the gathering and set out 'a feast to be remembered for aye'. This turned out to be prophetic in more ways than one.

The text at al-Wāsiṭī's illustration has al-Ḥārith describing how, after Abū Zayd has bagged what he has chosen and tied it in bundles 'and tucked up his sleeves and girded himself, he accosted me as accosts one who has donned impudence and arrayed himself with the garb of sincere friendship, saying, 'Hast thou a mind to accompany me to the swamplands *[baṭīḥa]* so that I may wed thee to another fair one?' Al-Ḥārith angrily swears by Allāh that he will not go with him, but Abū Zayd merely 'smiled at my speech and stepped forward to embrace me', at which al-Ḥārith 'turned aside from him in outrage'.

Abū Zayd's son stands at the left-hand side of al-Wāsiṭī's painting. His father is passing a package to him over the recumbent figures of five men, who illustrate literally the Qur'ānic allusion in the text to verses 109 and 110 of *sūra* 17: 'prone upon their faces . . . like the roots of rotten palm-trees'. The horrified al-Ḥārith (who is not shown) has dissociated himself from this scene, realizing that the sweetmeats on trays of *khalanj* wood have been doctored with seeds of the henbane plant (*banj*). There seems to be some confusion between the terms *banj* and hashish. Strictly speaking, *banj* was obtained from the hyoscyamus or henbane plant, and hashish from the *cannabis sativa* or hemp plant; however, the terms appear to have been interchangeable. The use of *banj* to stupefy potential victims was well known among the Banū Sāsān or criminal underclasses of 'beggar princes', of whom Abū Zayd claims to be one. Chapter 5 of Ibn Ghānim al-Maqdisī's thirteenth-century *Disclosure of the Secrets [Kashf al-asrār]*, reveals that one of the current practices was to:

> mix together a concoction of one part each of the seed of black Indian hemp, wax from the ear [*wasakh al-udhn*] and squills [*baṣal al-fār*] and then they put the resultant substance into any kind of food whatsoever. The person eating it goes to sleep immediately.[14]

At the popular level of the *Arabian Nights [Alf layla wa layla]*, one reads in 'The Tale of the Second Eunuch', Kāfūr, how a caliph's wife, Zubayda, instructed a slave-girl to drug her mistress, Quṭ al-Qulūb, either by placing *banj* in her nostrils while asleep or by putting it into a drink. Abū Dulaf does not criticize the beggar chiefs who stupefied their young apprentices with drugged food or wine and then committed homosexual assaults on them. The Mamlūk poet Abū al-Fatḥ ibn Sayyid al-Nās wryly reports that Ṣūfīs of that period were characterized by their 'copulating with pretty boys, drinking wine, eating hashish, dancing, singing and pimping'.[15]

Ibn Munqidh's *Memoirs* mention henbane growing in a thicket 'on a mountainside'; this suggests that it grew wild and was freely available. There is an illustration of the *banj* plant in a fourteenth-century manual of herbs by al-'Umarī, where it is used as a pain-killer. Common folk might have learned of its properties through the shadow play, where the druggist 'Usayla al-Ma'ājini ('Little Drop of Honey') concocted therapeutic remedies; the term *ma'ājin* applied equally to narcotics such as opium and hashish. Although many condemn the use of *banj*, Ṣafī al-Dīn's *Collected Writings [Dīwān]* appear to advocate its use. He seeks to justify this by saying that it is neither specifically condemned by the law nor unanimously denounced by consensus (*ijmā'*). Something of this ambiguity towards drug abuse can be gleaned from a report by Ibn Iyās, who reports that in Egypt in 1266 the orthodox sultan Baybars ordered that the levy on hashish was to be suppressed and the drug burned instead.[16]

Drugs could apparently be obtained with comparative ease. A twelfth-century report by Ibn 'Abdūn on the ordinances of the Seville market recommends that:

> Only a skilled physician should sell potions and electuaries and mix drugs. These things should not be bought from the grocer, or the apothecary, whose only concern is to take money without knowledge. They spoil the prescriptions and kill the sick, for they mix medicines which are unknown and of contrary effect.[17]

Abū Zayd's talents therefore seem boundless. His unprincipled behaviour is a reflection of a fairly widespread use and abuse of narcotics in medieval Muslim society. With hindsight, the worldly visiting merchants should have been more wary of their travelling companions, for the *Book of the Dynasties of Islam* reports that in 1234 or 1235 the Ayyūbid sultan al-Ashraf constructed a mosque in Damascus on the site of a *khān* 'reserved for debauchery and drunkenness' in the quarter of 'Uqayba.[18]

Al-Wāsiṭī's *khān* is a substantial, brick-built three-storeyed building. It is likely to have been near the Tigris, since *Route IV* of Ḥamd Allāh Mustawfī al-Qazwīnī's *The Recreation of Hearts [Nuzhat al-qulūb]* makes it clear that Wāsiṭ was strategically placed for trade[19] and al-Ḥārith describes in a vivid metaphor how he had stopped over 'with the alighting of the fish on the dry land'. Most of the twelfth- to fourteenth-century *khāns* in Iraq are badly damaged or have disappeared, although one twelfth-century fortified *khān* has been identified in the area north-west of Mosul.

Al-Wāsiṭī's *khān* is an urban caravanserai in a large commercial trading centre. While security would have been important, there was no need for the heavy fortifications required on a desolate overland trade route. It is an adaptation of a rather large house form, for it was a lodging house with a central courtyard for the foreign merchants who plied the caravan routes.

A carved wooden ventilation shaft is set into the vaulted roof. At the left of the top storey there is a small secure 'tower' with a fixed air vent and a wooden door; its purpose is unknown, and the exterior is much rougher than the carefully executed main building. Good ventilation would be a prerequisite in the prevailing climate, especially when animals were stabled so near the human quarters. Letters among the Cairo *Geniza* documents confirm this; they frequently contained requests from travellers for private lodgings, as some people found the noise and smell of the pack animals overpowering.[20] Ventilation, therefore, would be a prime concern of the architect, together with the practical considerations of loading and unloading and security.

To the right of the roof elevation there is what appears to be a bluish-grey *miḥrāb* wall with very faint epigraphy; it perhaps represents a place where a traveller could escape from the noise and bustle downstairs to pray quietly. Six columns run the length of the first-floor gallery; they are bluish in colour and may be of the indigenous Iraqi marble. Marble was widely used for decorative purposes and for the fabric of contemporary buildings in northern Iraq; however, it was used less frequently elsewhere in Iraq, on the grounds of expense. If the columns in this *khān* are marble, it is possible that al-Wāsiṭī's model for the building was endowed as a pious foundation (*waqf*) by an influential, wealthy person, with the income derived from trading being given for charitable causes. For example, the income from the Mirjāniyya *khān*, which was completed in 1359, together with the income from six other *khāns*, wine-presses, adjoining shops and other sources of revenue, contributed towards the

6. *The* amīr *listens intently to an eloquent sermon.*

7. A scene in an unidentified government office.

8. Abū Zayd and his son before a judge.

ترامع البله بالبلاغ بالرؤذان جمال في اسمار يفسر الشيخ بالكلام
وتبيان المرام فمنعته الفتاة من الافصاح وخمسانه

ثم نضت عنها فضلة الوشاح وأنشد عن النساح
بلسان السليطة الوقاح

9. An 'impudent shrew' in the Ramla court.

10. The caravan at rest among 'dewy hillocks'.

upkeep of the Mirjāniyya religious school (*madrasa*). In addition to dues and taxes levied on the population, the caliph derived revenues from his *mustaghallāt*, the caravanserais and markets administered by a specialist department known as the *dīwān al-'aqār*.[21]

Since time was of the essence to a merchant, al-Ḥārith's sojourn would be fairly brief. Although a *khān* formed part of a profit-orientated activity and would presumably therefore not be over-ostentatious, it would certainly be comfortable. Syrian caravanserais were apparently the poorest. In 1203 Yāqūt mentions a stone Ayyūbid *khān* between Homs and Damascus, where the road to Palmyra branched off. It was situated in 'a pleasant village with a famous spring, always equally cold'.[22]

The columns in the illustration have bell-shaped capitals and bear a decorative frieze in a different medium. Contemporary bell-shaped capitals elsewhere in the Islamic world have already been discussed at length, and the ones shown are evidently authentic. The balustrade at first-floor level is made from carved red wood and the balusters are identical to those in al-Wāsiṭī's Banū Ḥarām mosque in Basra in *Maqāma* 48. The area below the gallery is framed by a very large pair of bluish-grey spandrels; deeply carved with an arabesque leaf scroll pattern, they echo the semicircular arches of the lower doorways. In the Baghdad area the rounded archway seems to have been mainly confined to the windows of certain buildings.

There are five rooms upstairs and five below, all with heavy wooden doors with iron reinforcement bands for security and round metal handles. The panels of the door at the top left-hand side are carved, but this feature is not clear on the other doors. Mulberry wood (*tūth*) seems to have been the preferred material for doors, although a red wood has been used for two downstairs doors in this *khān*. Methods of construction included posts and panels or single leaves. Nails, glue and decorative ironwork were used to join the parts, and the wood might be carved or inlaid. The five downstairs doors are rounded and larger than the five pointed doors on the upper storey. The larger dimensions would facilitate the entry of pack animals and their burdens into the lower storerooms, while the smaller upper chambers admitted the travellers and their personal belongings and more portable valuables.

Ibn Jubayr's *Travels* tell how at a *khān* at Acre in 1184 the merchants deposited their baggages (presumably downstairs) and 'lodged in the upper storey'. All the doors in the illustration appear to have two leaves, as indicated by the two large rings or handles on either side. This is more obvious in the BN 3929 illustration.

The *khān* was part of a commercial hierarchy which was located according to the needs of particular groups of merchants and artisans. As well as providing lodgings for visiting traders, it was used to store the products of neighbouring workshops. A syndicate of merchants, presided over by the chief merchant (*ra'īs al-tujjār*), was formed to supervise commercial transactions, to arbitrate in disputes and perhaps also to establish a standard rate for commodities. Ordinary members of a syndicate were called trustees (*umanā'*). A superintendent (*muḥtasib*) with very wide powers looked after the day-to-day running of the market; among his duties was the punishment of traders who cheated in weights and measures.

In general, the mercantile community seems to have enjoyed a large measure of autonomy, and higher authority appears only to have intervened in the matter of tax collection. Although customs duty is forbidden according to the Sharī'a, the jurists circumvented this by including duty in the obligatory alms tax (*zakāt*) and customs offices seem to have been prevalent. Muslim merchants paid 2 1/2 per cent tax and non-Muslim merchants 5 per cent, while foreigners had 10 per cent dues levied on their goods.[23] A merchant was supposed to have free passage across a frontier for one year, paying customs dues on only one occasion, but there seems to have been a 10 per cent tax levied on all the cash carried; this was the theory, but tariffs apparently varied widely. Commenting on the complicated customs system at Fārs in an earlier period, al-Muqaddasī says, 'Ask not about the multiplicity and oppressiveness of its taxes.' Basra, in particular, was notorious for interference and searches in later times, so the caliph 'Umar's ruling that no merchant's goods should be searched had obviously long been disregarded. In 1184 Ibn Jubayr's party arrived at Acre, where they were accompanied to the customs house, which was:

> a *khān* prepared to accommodate the caravan. Before the door are stone benches, spread with carpets, where are the Christian clerks of the Customs with their ebony ink-stands ornamented with gold. All the customs dues go to the registrar [*ṣāḥib al-dīwān*], who holds a contract to farm the customs.

Ordinary travellers with no merchandise were also searched, but 'all this was done with civility and respect, and without harshness and unfairness'.

All the manuscripts without exception show a building of monumental proportions on two storeys, an exterior, and rooms giving on to a balcony. The famous Jala'irid Khān Mirjān in Baghdad was built by the governor of Baghdad, Amīn al-Dīn Mirjān, in 1359. A large two-storey rectangle constructed of brick, its projecting entrance was centrally situated on the north side and was dominated by a pointed arch (*īwān*). The large internal courtyard (*ṣaḥn*) was roofed in and, for this reason, Khān Mirjān was known as a 'covered *khān*'. The roof was carried on 8 solid, pointed arches of about 2 metres wide and was 14 metres high.[24] Angled roof vents provided lighting and ventilation in every direction. In all, there were 58 rooms of various sizes. Assuming that al-Wāsiṭī's illustration is fairly typical and that the courtyard is square, his *khān* would have some 40 rooms. Rentals for rooms may have varied according to size, for the impoverished al-Ḥārith secludes himself in a chamber, 'not paying an excess of rent'. Perhaps the little room with the fixed air vent on the top storey was classed as superior accommodation and cost more because it had access to the roof and was well away from the pack animals.

Once more, it appears that al-Wāsiṭī has exerted artistic licence by showing the drugged 'wedding guests' downstairs in the courtyard whereas the text clearly says that the merchants entered Abū Zayd's room. One might reasonably expect this scene to take place upstairs, because the guests' quarters were always set above the animals at courtyard level. Close examination of the miniature shows that the action is 'framed' by the two large spandrels to indicate the courtyard space; al-Wāsiṭī has therefore superimposed the scene enacted in Abū Zayd's (upper) room upon the general features of the *khān* as viewed from the courtyard. Confirmation of this may lie in the absence of columns at ground-floor level to support the gallery.

A *ḥadīth* says:

> The most worthy earnings are those of the merchants, who if they are spoken to, do not lie, if they are trusted, do not betray, if they promise, do not fail, if they buy, do not condemn, if they sell, do not extol, if they owe, do not delay, and if they are owed, do not press.[25]

Unfortunately for al-Ḥārith and his companions, their trust on this occasion is sadly misplaced. Our rogue hero plumbs new depths of hypocrisy as he coolly arrays himself 'with the garb of sincere friendship' and the artist has provided a very apt illustration of Abū Zayd's perfidy.

While travelling in May and June of 1184, Ibn Jubayr describes the inn (*qayṣariyya*) for the merchants in Mosul:

> [It is] like a large *khān*, and is bolted with iron doors and surrounded by shops and houses one over the other. It is decorated throughout in a splendid manner, and of an architectural elegance that has no like, for I have never in any land seen a *qayṣariyya* to compare with it.

The *qāḍī* Abū Bakr Aḥmad ibn Sayyār tells how a certain benighted traveller had to stay overnight in a deserted *khān* in a thicket. There was a staircase, so the building must have had at least two storeys.[26]

Caravanserais opened at around 9 o'clock in the morning and closed at 6 in the evening, and this artist implies something of the hustle and bustle. Since time was of the essence to a merchant, his sojourn in the *khān* would have been fairly brief.

There is no sign of the so-called 'Greek' locks which al-Muqaddasī had seen.[27] If this is so, then the doors must have had two leaves, which opened inwards. It is not possible from the reproduction to say if these are 'iron' doors like those of the Mosul *khān* described by Ibn Jubayr.

Large doors obviously need substantial fittings. In one of Badīʻ al-Zamān al-Hamadhānī's earlier *Maqāmāt,* a boastful merchant told a guest that his door handle had been purchased from a famous shop; it contained 6 pounds of copper and cost 3 *dīnārs* in Mu'izz al-Dawla's currency. The fitments in a *khān* would be concerned with security, and here they are probably iron. Iron nails with ornamental heads were used, both for utility and as decoration; contemporary Baghdadi examples appear on the door of the al-'Amādiyya mosque. They apparently reinforce a joint and take the form of an eight-petalled rosette, a common motif on applied decoration at that time. Decorative nails formed a geometric motif on a door commissioned by Badr al-Dīn Lu'lu' in 1246, and they are still used today.[28] This type of urban *khān* would be relatively secure within a city's own defensive system, such as Baghdad's massive walls and huge gates.

While there might be dozens of *khāns* in a medium-sized town, cities such as Baghdad or Old Cairo boasted hundreds of these establishments. The *Chronicles of Egypt* tell us that the Masrūr caravanserai was situated in the north-eastern quarter of Cairo; they also mention the rice caravanserai (*funduq al-aruzz*), as well as the Tanbadhī caravanserai on the shores of the Nile. The term *qayṣariyya* for *khān* was apparently confined to Arab countries that had earlier been subject to the Byzantines such as Egypt, Syria and Morocco. *Qayṣariyya* might indicate a market building specially licensed by Caesar in return for a fixed fee. Ibn Jubayr's *Travels* extols the wonders of the *qayṣariyya* in Aleppo, Syria: 'a walled-in garden in its freshness and beauty, flanked, as it is, by the venerated mosque. He who sits in it yearns for no other sight even were it paradisaical'.[29]

The importance of the *khān* to the mercantile class, who may have been patrons as well as readers of these manuscripts, may be gauged by the fact that most of the manuscripts illustrate such a building. *Maqāmāt* illustrations have large and fairly imposing edifices, with dimensions and features that appear in contemporary architecture, and they seem to represent a typical *khān* of the day in function and form.

The Slave Market

Maqāma 34 relates how al-Ḥārith, following the death of his personal slave, sought to purchase a replacement from the slave market (*sūq al-raqīq*) in the Yemeni town of Zabīd. Al-Ḥārith tells how he had owned a slave since he was a youth and had trained him:

> until he had perfected his right conduct, and he was fully familiar with my ways, and knew how to draw forth my goodwill, so as not to over-step my intentions, nor to be remiss in [carrying out] my wishes. Therefore needs his good services had won him my heart, and I singled him out [as my companion] in my stay and travel. But pernicious fate made away with him

when we had reached Zabīd, and when 'the sole of his foot was turned up', and his voice had waxed still.

Al-Ḥārith's grief is patently heartfelt, even one year after the young man's death, and demonstrates the strong bond that could exist between slave and master. The *Biographical Dictionary* quotes Abū Isḥāq's verses on his slave:

Your face is so [handsome] that my hand seems to have sketched its outline, but your words [are false] and have fatigued my hopes. [However, he continues:] Were you not mine I should purchase you with all my wealth! Did I not possess you, I should give my life to obtain you.

In the middle of the tenth century a Turkish slave-boy belonging to Prince Bakhtiyār was taken prisoner at the battle of Aḥwāz. According to Miskawayh's *The Experiences of the Nations*, 'Towards this lad, whose name was Baytakin, [the prince] had not previously displayed any attachment or affection; but now he went mad over his loss and could bear with fortitude all other losses save this.'[30]

We know that al-Ḥārith's slave was in 'the full vigour of life' (*ashūdd*), which the Arabs reckoned to be from 15 to 40 years of age. In his *Travels in Asia and Africa*, Ibn Baṭṭūṭa relates a visit he made in 1333 to the sultan of Bīrgī at his residence, where:

we found about twenty of his servants of striking beautiful appearance and dressed in silk garments. Their hair was parted and hanging down, and their colour was a radiant white tinged with red. 'Who', I asked the jurist, 'are these beautiful forms?' 'These', he replied, 'are Greek pages.'

This account recalls in form and content the reaction of the Egyptian women to the biblical Joseph (Yūsuf) in *sūra* 12.

In the first half of the eleventh century, the Christian doctor Ibn Buṭlān wrote a useful guide to the art of making a sound purchase of a slave, listing the superior qualities of slaves from various regions. At the market, slaves were classified according to religion, race and attainments. For example, the white slaves were mainly Armenians, Berbers and Greeks, while Abyssinians were very good cooks and could be cheaply acquired. Ṭāhir ibn 'Abdallāh ibn Ṭāhir instructed his agents, 'If you ever come across a Tukhāristān draught horse, a Bardh'a mule, an Egyptian ass or a Samarqand slave, then buy it immediately, and don't bother referring back to me for a decision.'[31] Al-Ḥārith's slave is evidently a 'white slave'.

The importance of slaves in commerce can be inferred from the remarks of one Ibn Riḍwān ibn 'Aqīl, who said that he employed the most agile of strong, cunning youths for hoarding and selling. A slave could rise to a position of prominence. For example, the greatest of the Eastern Muslim geographers,

8. The slave market.

Yāqūt, was of Greek parentage and was bought in Baghdad by a merchant from Ḥamā. He was given a good education and then employed as a travelling clerk with his master before being manumitted. This training accords well with the counsel given in the *Book of Qābūs* regarding employees, which runs:

> Keep a complete tally of all your profit and loss, and have all written down in your own hand to protect yourself from oversight and error. Furthermore, always keep a reckoning with your slaves and those about you.[32]

Le Strange mentions a square called Raḥba Suwayd, named after the fief of a freed slave of al-Manṣūr. An eleventh-century papyrus document concerning manumission provides the name and a full description of the slave, expresses the master's thanks for his services and is signed and witnessed.[33]

Not all masters treated their slaves well, however, and some slaves absconded. Another eleventh-century legal document advises, 'If a slave runs away and a man restores him to his master from a distance of three days' journey or more, the finder can claim a reward of 40 *dirhams* from the owner.' The reward varied according to the distance from the master's home and was also, presumably, based on the original purchase price. This document also stipulates, 'If a runaway slave has been given as pledge for a debt, the reward is due from the pledge-holder.'[34]

A poet mused in Niẓām al-Mulk's *Book of Government or Rules for Kings* that: 'One obedient slave is better than 300 sons; for the latter desire their father's death, the former his master's glory.'[35]

Al-Wāsiṭī's painting, which is in the correct place in the tale, is framed by two lines of text above and two lines below, which convey well the element of bargaining in a *sūq*:

> Now I thought he would look askance at me and demand from me a high sum, but he did not soar whither I had soared, nor held he on to that to which I held on, nay, on the contrary he said, 'Here is the boy! If the price is low and his keep but slight, his master thinks himself blessed in him and loves him all the better for it, and I wish above all to make thee fond of the lad by lightening to thee the price for him; so weigh out 200 *dirhams* if thou wilt, and be thankful to me as long as thou livest.' So I paid him the amount at once, as the lawful price is paid in a cheap bargain (and it occurred not to my mind that everyone who sells cheap makes one pay dear).

This slave market is a simply framed building of two storeys of strut-and-post construction, with what may be a woven matting roof. It is the most basic, open-shed type of building to be seen in any market-place, even today. It may represent a permanent structure situated in one of the large markets held on the same day every week. Al-Ya'qūbī mentions a Sāmarrā slave market in the ninth century which consisted of a quadrangle intersected by alley-ways, and perhaps this stall was one of many. It was considered degrading for a good class of slave to be sold publicly,[36] so one wonders at al-Ḥārith's naivety in the market-place. It is likely that a sophisticated metropolitan readership would be well aware of the nuances of the text. Al-Wāsiṭī's *sūq* seems to reflect a contemporary scene.

Al-Ḥārith is the figure at the right-hand foreground, while we know that the man in the face veil is Abū Zayd; they are both in Arab clothes. The boy is of straight build and good appearance. During his farewell pilgrimage, the Prophet preached a sermon containing the following injunction from *sūra* 16: 'And your slaves! See that ye feed them with such food as ye eat yourselves, and clothe them with the like clothing as ye wear yourselves.'

Abū Zayd has (significantly, as we shall see) dressed the boy in Arab clothes and a turban. Al-Ḥārith is so captivated by the lad that a quotation from *sūra* 12 immediately springs to mind: 'This is not a young man, but forsooth an honoured angel.' Al-Ḥārith also fails to note the significance of the boy's turban, for Prophetic tradition has it that 'the difference between a Muslim and an infidel is the wearing of a turban on the cap'. Unfortunately, al-Ḥārith is so keen to strike a speedy bargain that he disregards the context of this verse, the story of Yūsuf, who is, of course, a free man.

Once again, al-Ḥārith is shown not merely as naive, but as ridiculously so. It should be remembered, however, that throughout the 50 tales al-Ḥārith needs to be taken in by Abū Zayd or there would be no dénouement and no moral summing up—this use of al-Ḥārith would have become apparent to the enlightened reader who persevered with a difficult text and savoured the literary devices.

Although there are injunctions in the *aḥādīth* (pl. of *ḥadīth)* against both the keeping of male Muslims in captivity and the showing of favouritism to Muslim slaves, Muslims could not, strictly speaking, be reduced to slavery, although they could be born into servitude.[37] In the eleventh century Ibn Randaqa al-Ṭurṭūshī related how the vizier Niẓām al-Mulk advised Sultan Mālikshāh that if a page in military service were a young Turk, he would sell for more than 30 *dīnārs*. This price seems to accord with that quoted in contemporary Egyptian texts, which suggests that this was the going rate throughout the area at that time. This is borne out by an account in the *Arabian Nights* in which some 50 *dīnārs* are paid in Kūfa for a woman and her beautiful daughter. The whims of rulers could doubtless influence prices; al-Naṣr is reported to have paid 5,000 *dīnārs* for a 15-year-old youth of outstanding beauty. It seems that the keeping of slave-girls, as revealed in the pietist literature of the first five centuries of Islam, met with less resistance than any other luxury. This was possibly instrumental in the enormous expansion of the slave trade generally at that period.[38]

After the old man in the face veil has extolled the lad's many supposed virtues, a price is agreed of '200 *dirhams*': the *dirham* was silver currency, so al-Ḥārith thinks he has a bargain. He obviously expected to pay much more, since he carries gold and silver coins, 'the yellow and the white' of the text. Dealers were held in low esteem and generally distrusted, perhaps because they were well-practised in the art of making slaves marketable by increasing their allure and exaggerating their alleged virtues, as Abū Zayd does. Perceived defects obviously affected the price paid for a slave, and even Sultan Baybars, who was originally a slave, almost failed to find a buyer in the market. Although he was tall and ruddy and had blue eyes, a cataract diminished his value, and his seller achieved but a relatively modest price.[39]

Of the three men in the upper register, the one holding the scales is in charge of the money. He seems to have his thumb on the weighing pan, which may indicate both suspicions as to his honesty and an ironic confirmation of the generally held low opinion of slave dealers. Perhaps he is some sort of broker in overall superintendence of the market who receives a commission from the vendor or purchaser. The sale of slaves, like every other marketable item, would have been strictly regulated. Al-Wāsiṭī's scales have a calibration ring and a movable pointer just below the carrying ring or handle, but there is no visible means of transporting the balance. This would be important, to protect the accuracy of the mechanism. Neither money nor weights are visible; they may be in the brass scale-pans.

The Weights and Measures (*al-Awzān wa al maqādir*) is a special category of Islamic canon law, and the importance of weights in a major trading civilization loomed large. 'Abd al-Raḥmān al-Khāzin, al-Bīrūnī and 'Umar al-Khayyām all wrote treatises on weights and measures. Al-Bīrūnī's balance is illustrated in a Khāzinī manuscript: here the weights can be clearly seen stored one on top of the other in descending order, on a carrying base. This was lifted by a hooked metal rod; the weights must therefore have had a notch, measuring half their diameter, which slipped around the rod. Miskawayh's *The Experiences of the Nations* describes a set of scales which belonged to Abū 'Alī, the treasurer of al-Muṭī', as:

> an instrument like a balance, or rather the case for one, made of teak wood, with a beam like that of a balance; but no place for weight or pan, being carved out of the blocks like a reservoir with a cover made to fit it. It contained nothing.[40]

A pair of brass scales with two fairly deep bowls occurs in a late twelfth-century *Book of Antidotes* manuscript of the Baghdad School, BN 2964. These were used to weigh out the ingredients for drug prescriptions. Scales also frequently appear on metalwork in connection with the astrological symbol of Libra.[41]

Abū Zayd sets a riddle on the goldsmith's balance in *Maqāma* 42, part of which runs:

> One flighty and leaning with one half to one side, but no man of sense will upbraid him for either. He is always raised up on high as a just king is rightly exalted for aye in his station. Alike are to him both the pebble and nugget, though trust should in no wise be balanced with falsehood.

This balance appears in the Arabic text as *al-ṭayyār* and it has indeed connotations of a bird; it is a pleasing and apt metaphor. Al-Ghazālī also saw bird-like qualities in a balance. According to his *Fitting Conduct in Religion,* the merchant's scales:

> should be delicate and responsive, like a bird in flight, so that their balance will be absolutely just. The scale cords should be long and the scale balance points [where the scales are attached] of good quality.[42]

A financial transaction was not merely a case of exchanging the requisite number of coins. Fraud was practised by clipping genuine currency and making up its weight with quicksilver or antimony, and it follows that counterfeit coins had a definite, if modest, value. Clearly, the weights were also open to manipulation, hence the need for regulation. An early example of lack of public confidence in the economy is reported by Rashīd al-Dīn in his *Universal*

History: the late thirteenth-century Persian ruler, Gaykhātū, was inspired by Chinese paper money (*chao*) and he issued a decree that anyone refusing his currency would be executed. He was soon forced to rescind this measure, however, because the markets closed down and the people revolted.[43]

Slave dealing was subject to official regulation. A tenth-century edict in Baghdad enjoined the instant removal of all disreputable purchasers from the market-place, and we know that among the many duties of the chief of municipal police was superintendence of the slave market. Perhaps the vendors were licensed brokers who provided the purchasers with a receipt.

A purchase deed for a slave dated 1382 has been discovered in the precincts of the Dome of the Rock, although it has no obvious connection with Jerusalem. It bears an impressive red seal (*tamgha*) of a type more usually associated with Mongol documents, and is written and endorsed in a Persian style of handwriting.[44] The purchase deed would probably have carried full details of the slave's place and date of birth, religion, and the dates and purchase prices of named previous owners. Such a document would provide proof of purchase; it would also serve as a reference for the slave, so it would be advantageous to both master and servant as proof of provenance.

Three slaves in the lower-right foreground of the illustration are dark-skinned and appear to be African. They all wear a type of loose robe which the text later describes as *mi'rad*, or the garment in which a slave was displayed. Al-Wāsiṭī's Indian slaves outside the palace of the ruler in *Maqāma* 39 wear similar garments, and al-Wāsiṭī seems to have portrayed a typical transaction in the *sūq*.

However, it is possible that, despite the text, the artist chose to illustrate a scene within a slave merchant's house; we know that better-class slaves could be sold in private houses or through well-known dealers. These houses contained lower and upper rooms, with stalls for the slaves. In al-Manṣūr's time, his domestic slaves were accommodated in a barracks.

Al-Ya'qūbī notes that the lodgings of the chamberlain's pages in Baghdad were close to the Slave's House and that, in time, the surrounding suburb also took the name *dār al-raqīq* (slave market). Al-Baghdādī, writing in the eleventh century, confirms this; he also mentions a 'slave's quarter' (*qaṭī'at al-raqīq*) that formed part of the fief of a lady, Umm Ja'far. In the same period Ibn 'Aqīl notes that *dār al-raqīq* was a commodious quarter which contained 'many wonderful buildings'.[45]

Slaves were a highly visible feature of the urban scene and the miniatures demonstrate the deep bonds which were possible between slave and master. Unfortunately, a slave was often merely 'one commodity among many' (*sil'a min al-sila'*), as can be seen from the above quote concerning 'a Tukhāristān draught horse, a Bardh'a mule, an Egyptian ass or a Samarqand slave'.

4

Aspects of Urban Life

One of the earliest problems for the Muslims was the question of authority; who should have it and what kind of power should he exert? To ensure its own survival, the ruling class had to nurture its roots in the city, gain the approbation of the religious authorities and exact the necessary revenue from trade and industry to maintain the court apparatus. There were complex interactions between the various social groups within cities, and the city structure lent itself to the needs of rulers and their entourages, practitioners and scholars of religion and law, merchants and craftsmen, all of whom are in the *Maqāmāt*. Urban civilization was at some remove from that of the villages and deserts; it represented the bench-mark for the definition of non-urban cultural patterns and the rural inhabitants.

As already mentioned, the illustrations reveal little 'real' city architecture beyond the requisite elements of, say, pulpit or *miḥrāb* for a mosque. There are no *qāḍī*'s courts or palaces: the interest is directed towards the incumbent instead. The focus on the interplay between the characters reflects the nature of the literary genre, with its emphasis on language and speech. The architecture, which reflects the circumstances of the plot, is basically that of the urban mercantile environment, that is, the mosque and government buildings, the *sūq*, the imposing *khān* which exudes an impression of security and wealth, and the functional slave market. This points to an audience for the *Māqamāt* of like-minded city-dwellers who were aware of the literary context and would pick up the necessary cultural pointers of uniform, status, architectural features and so on.

The Cupper (Ḥajjāma)

Maqāma 47 finds al-Ḥārith in Ḥajr al-Yamāma, a city in the Ḥijāz to the east of Mecca. Al-Ḥārith says that he needs a cupping and that his blood is heated, although he gives no indication of the cause of the malady. Cupping was generally regarded as therapeutic and he would, of course, be tired and weary after his travels. Cuppers appear to have carried out treatment in private homes and, as al-Ḥārith is loath to visit the cupper's establishment, he sends his slave out to fetch the practitioner to his lodgings. Since the cupper is unable to call, al-Ḥārith reluctantly goes to the market-place.

All the artists depict the cupper's establishment as a small narrow booth in the suq. Al-Wāsiṭī's illustration in BN 5847 (Plate 12) shows an old man surrounded by a crowd who jostle to find out what is going on, while a bare-headed youth weeps and looks fearful. The old man gesticulates theatrically, and is evidently haranguing someone. The text reveals that the young man has been berated and accused of having no money to pay, and dismissed for snivelling. The spectators, like the cupper, are the usual well-dressed figures found throughout this work. They are evidently town-dwellers, and mostly Arabs. There is a variety of costumes, with the dark elaborate fabrics providing the necessary foil to the plain, semi-circular backdrop.

The shop itself reveals some of the tools of the cupper's trade; the lower shelf holds three large handled vessels, which do not seem to be glass. Above these are some small rolled-up packages which may be bandages, for it would be necessary for the practitioner to dress a wound if he practised scarification. It should be noted that the audience here in the *sūq* is exclusively male, and the dialogue itself is somewhat coarse. The lack of a female presence in the *sūq* would undoubtedly encourage a lively and raucous element, and al-Wāsiṭī suggests this. Other painters show the youth with his back bared, but this would probably not happen in a public place if women were likely to be around. However, nude or semi-nude people were depicted in medical manuscripts of the period, but with an air of decorum and passivity befitting the didactic nature of the literature. Women are generally absent from the manuscripts: where they do appear, it is only as accessories to Abū Zayd, not usually in a public place, and in response to the dictates of the text. At any rate, they evidently were not occupied in retail trade, although Herodotus notes women carrying on retail business in Egypt.[1]

One can understand the reluctance of the fastidious al-Ḥārith to be the subject of a gawping crowd and the target of the sharp tongue of a coarse fellow such as this cupper, especially when he turns out to be none other than Abū Zayd who is up to his usual tricks with his son as accomplice. There is also the question of confidence in the skills of the cupper, scrupulousness in matters of hygiene and so forth, as well as the natural squeamishness on the part of many people at invasive techniques which produce blood. No scalpels are evident here, but they appear in another prior illustration by al-Wāsiṭī, as well as in the other manuscripts. A certain Ibn al-Dukaynī was notorious in Baghdad for amusing himself in 'unsurpassed style', and 'if he felt the results of intoxication in the morning he would call for Dabīqī fabrics and have bandages for bleeding torn off them by hand, asserting that nothing would stop his headache but the sound of this music.'[2] The Egyptian town of Dabīq was famous for fine textiles.

The medieval *sūq* in Mesopotamia and Iran was a very long covered street approximately 15 metres wide. Its roof had multiple domes, pierced at the centre with a round opening of approximately 1 metre wide to provide light and ventilation. All the boutiques were of similar size; they had neither doors nor windows and were open to the street. Shopkeepers made them fast at nightfall by affixing a wooden shutter with rings, through which iron bars were padlocked in two places. The shops were two stairs up and sometimes had a mezzanine area which served as an office. Customers were offered stools, an element in the unhurried ritual of business transactions that is still evident in the Middle Eastern *sūq* today.[3] This little shop is therefore typical.

The cupping technique was called *ḥijāma*, and the cupping vessel *miḥjama*. Only the Istanbul manuscript painter has interpreted correctly the treatment prescribed in the text: the two 'neck veins' (*akhdā'ain*) are defined in the Siḥāḥ dictionary as 'the two concealed neck veins in the place of the cupping of the neck', which was under the occiput or back of the skull.

Abū Zayd himself refers to 'the cupping of the hind-part of thy neck'. 'Alī ibn Riḍwān's handwritten eleventh-century commentary on Galen's *On the Prevention of Bodily Ills in Egypt [Fī daf' maḍarr al-abdān fī Miṣr]* tells how he had been suffering from severe headaches caused by an 'overfilling [plethora] of the blood vessels of the head'. Galen appeared to him in a dream and prescribed 'cupping at the occipital protuberance'; this remedied the condition.[4] Cupping of the neck veins was also considered particularly efficacious in the treatment of melancholy.

Although the cups were graded according to disease and the age of the patient, Abū Zayd's vessels are of uniform size. Cups might be of glass; other materials used were copper, wood and horn. Only the fourteenth-century BL 22.114 *Maqāmāt* illustration shows a horn-shaped implement, where it is affixed to the outside of the cupper's booth and serves as a decorative appendage.

Cupping was performed on wet or dry skin, the object being to draw out blood from deep within the body to superficial tissues. Dry cupping could be practised with or without a flame. A tenth-century medical treatise by the greatest Arab surgeon, Abū al-Qāsim Khalaf ibn 'Abbās al-Zahrāwī, also shows cupping-cups and includes one illustration of a shelf for a candle.[5] When the glass was heated, the air trapped inside expanded and the resulting vacuum 'sucked' the blood to the surface of the skin. This action is summed up in the early tenth-century treatise on melancholy by Isḥāq ibn 'Imrān, who describes the concurrence of certain factors leading to an organ attracting illness 'as the cupping glass the blood'.[6] The implements and methods of cupping in the illustration therefore seem to be authentic.

Children might be cupped from upwards of 2 years of age, but cupping was not recommended for adults over 60; it seems to have had no beneficial effect on obese adults. Dry cupping was also believed to retard one's hair turning grey. With wet cupping, the cupper waited until the skin was withdrawn and had become dry before scarification; no lances are shown in the illustration. The cupper sometimes had a female assistant who was responsible for one of the specialist functions; she she was known as the *ṣān'ia*,[7] which specifically implies skill in the work of the hand or hands. It was recommended that thick skin be rubbed with an emollient such as camomile.

Cupping was one of the three principal methods of treating illness recommended by the Prophet.[8] This branch of early 'Prophetic medicine' (*al-ṭibb al-nabāwī* or *ṭibb al-nābī*) has retained its religious character and it formed the basis into which medical knowledge from other traditions was absorbed.[9] Discourse 12 of Part IV of 'Alī ibn Rabbān al-Ṭabarī's ninth-century medical treatise *The Paradise of Wisdom in Medicine [Firdaws al-ḥikma fī al-ṭibb]*, which was the first systematic work on Islamic medicine and made full use of Syrian and Greek sources as well as Sanskrit translations, mentions phlebotomy and cupping.[10] However, the work deals with very little anatomy or surgery. This seems to indicate an official reliance on non-invasive techniques in the early days of Islamic medicine, possibly in the light of the Prophet's prescriptions and prevailing medical expertise. Prior to that period, Arabic medical works had tended to treat surgery as the 'poor relation' of the medical sciences; it is likely that religious scruples played a part.

The terms 'cupper' and 'phlebotomist' are used synonymously at times; this is borne out by the text, where Abū Zayd harangues the onlookers in the following terms: 'If I possessed but food for one day, my hand would never touch the lancet or cupping-cup.' The practitioner was also known as *ṣāḥib al-mabāḍī' wa al-mawāsī*, that is, 'the man with lancets and razors', who was but one of a number of medical or paramedical specialists. In 'The Tale of the Second Eunuch' in the *Arabian Nights*, Kāfūr tells how his master had the bastinado administered to him until he was rendered senseless, when 'they brought the barber who docked me and gelded me and cauterized the wound'. These accounts confirm Ullmann's comment that surgery was 'left to cuppers and barbers'.[11] The scene here suggests a low-grade physician.

Whatever their titles, these paramedical practitioners apparently occupied a somewhat ambiguous social position.[12] The testimony of a cupper, like those of a pigeon-trainer and a bath attendant, as well as tanners, sweepers, weavers and others, was reprehensible (*makrūha*) to Muslim jurists, for reasons which are unclear. However, the extent to which this was interpreted appears to have varied according to local custom and practice (*'urf*). So, paradoxically, the cupper was not necessarily despised, and cupping was also recognized as a subsection of the highly honoured medical profession.

Aspiring doctors attempted to acquire surgical skills by practising bleeding. Cupping also seems to have had the seal of royal approval; the 'Feast of the

Cupping' (*faṣd*) was an important festival at the 'Abbāsid court, when gifts were given and a special feast prepared, and courtiers bearing presents came to congratulate the caliph and to wish him good health.[13] This probably took place at an important time of the year, perhaps a birthday, for there are clear indications that astrological calculations were used to determine the most appropriate time for cupping; in the case of a ruler, the court physicians and astrologers would consult with each other to ensure the good health and long life of their patron. The *Letter Concerning What the Physician Needs by Way of Astronomy [Risāla fī ma yaḥtāj al-ṭabīb min 'ilm al-falak]* by al-'Aynzarbī, who died in 1153 and was the personal physician to the Fatimid caliph al-Ẓāfir bi 'Amr Allāh, deals with the question of the degree of astrological knowledge required by doctors. It declares: 'Bleeding of the neck is unfavourable if the moon is in the sign of Taurus, [that of the back when the moon is in the sign of Leo].'[14] This attention to timing is confirmed elsewhere, where it is suggested that the best time for cupping was between 2 and 3 o'clock in the afternoon in the middle of the lunar month.

By the 47th tale, the conscientious reader will be aware that there is an element of play-acting in this dialogue between the 'cupper' and his customer within the circumscribed contours of the shop. The image calls to mind the shadow play, with the action of silhouette figures taking place in a confined space, the ribaldry and the characters crowding around. I have found no portrayals of a cupper in shadow-play illustrations, but a blood-letting instrument appears in the earliest al-Jazarī *Treatise on Automata* manuscript, dated 1206, which is in Istanbul, while a lawcourt scene in a Paris *Kalīla wa Dimna* manuscript is entitled 'The cupper [*al-muzayyin*] and his wife before the *qāḍī*'.[15] *Muzayyin* also means barber.

Al-Wāsiṭī has once more provided a comprehensive and amusing painting. Perhaps it is significant that the illustration on the adjoining page (which is not reproduced) shows the other half of this crowd, a motley and more coarse group of spectators which includes bedu and others from farther afield. They confirm the position of Baghdad as a thriving international metropolis, and could represent a humourous 'them and us' touch by the artist as a sop to the well-heeled readership, who were secure in society and able to afford precious clothing. A taste for elaborate garments had been a common indulgence since the earliest days of Islam; al-Shaybanī's *Treatise on Economic Ethics [Kitāb al-kasb]*, in the second half of the eighth century, attributes the following saying to the Prophet: 'When Allāh gives riches to a man, he wants it to be seen on him.'[16] One must also bear in mind that the painter would be mindful of his own audience, a solid middle-class readership who were flattered to see themselves mirrored in the tales.

BN 6094 also shows the cupper in the market-place before a crowd of people. Abū Zayd here fits the description of 'the man with lances and razors' for no cups are shown. The shop is orderly, with lances, tongs to hold a hot cupping glass, and a casket all neatly set out on shelves. Al-Ḥārith's request for a *shaykh* 'who cupped skilfully' sounds eminently sensible since Usāma ibn Munqidh, writing in the period of the Crusades, describes how he had witnessed 'manifestations of men's weakness of soul and faintness of heart, which I did not think possible among women' in connection with blood-letting.[17]

There is no source of heat, either by candle or stove, in al-Wāsiṭī's illustration, but there is a tiled stove in the BN 6094. It might be a borrowing from some such work as Ibn Ghānim al-Maqdisī's *Disclosure of the Secrets*,[18] as fire was an essential element in alchemy and the preparation of medications. For a medieval description of a Syrian city, we may turn to the peripatetic Ibn Jubayr, who describes Aleppo as:

> a town of rare beauty, with large markets arranged in long adjacent rows so that you pass from a row of shops of one craft into that of another until you have gone through all the urban industries. These markets are all roofed with wood, so that their occupants enjoy an ample shade, and all hold the gaze from their beauty, and halt in wonder those who are hurrying by.[19]

The physical layout of markets was (and is) a feature of the *sūq*. The urban mercantile context has been popularly treated in all the *Maqāmāt* manuscripts as a 'hole in the wall' type of shop. They show a single, separate building, similar to that in the early thirteenth-century *Kalīla wa Dimna* manuscript in Paris, where two thieves are seen making off with bales of merchandise. The St Petersburg *Maqāmāt* manuscript alone suggests a busy environment beyond the confines of the folio. Here one may recall the built-up *sūq* in the Istanbul *Romance of Warqa and Gulshāh*, which depicts a more realistic market-place of several shops in a row. However, it is inconceivable that its butcher, baker and apothecary would be side by side in a real *sūq*, and the illustration is a composite that is more decorative than accurate.

The markets at the founding of Baghdad, and later Sāmarrā, were carefully planned, with each trade or craft occupying its separate market or lane (*darb*). For instance, we know from al-Ya'qūbī that the great market in western Baghdad, al-Karkh, was 2 *farsakh* long by 1 *farsakh* wide (1 *farsakh* was approx. 5 km) and was divided into blocks for the various commodities.[20] Ibn 'Aqīl's description of eleventh-century Baghdad confirms this division and he mentions that 'the term *sūq* consisted not only of shops, but also of dwellings'. He goes on to say that in the market-places of al-Karkh and Bāb al-ṭāq, 'The perfumers did not mix with the merchants of greasy and other offensive odours; nor did the merchants of new articles mix with those of used articles.'[21] It is likely, then, that the cupper carried on his trade in an area shared with other paramedical practitioners, such as apothecaries.

The main text has a reference to the cost of a cupping session, and to an Arabic proverb. Al-Ḥārith takes pity on the berated cupper and gives him 2 *dirhams*, which presumably covers the cost of the youth's treatment. The impudent 'customer' says that the cupper is 'more bereft of customers than the cupper of Sābāṭ'. This was a proverbially foolish cupper who, to encourage customers, offered to cup some soldiers for 1 *dāniq*, which was an extremely small sum. Smaller coinage was graded on a sexagesimal system, where 6 *dāniq* equalled 1 *dirham*; it went down as far as 'barleycorns'. At the beginning of the tenth century there were 14 *dirhams* to the *dīnār*. (It is difficult to be precise concerning currency, as some rulers apparently were not averse to tampering with the gold and silver content.)

To appear busy, the cupper of Sābāṭ bled his own mother and so weakened her that she died. Only the London BL 1200 *Maqāmāt* artist has picked this point up; the dead mother and her son add a lighthearted touch to an otherwise predictable manuscript. This illustration seems to have been missed by others; without an understanding of the text, it would appear to be an irrelevance, although it would have been understood by the contemporary reader and was certainly familiar to whoever dictated the positioning of the illustrations.

The miniatures of the cupper's booth reveal a wealth of medical and paramedical information and demonstrate the importance of the cupper and his craft. As there is such uniformity in the depiction of the instruments, the application of cups and the cupper's booth or shop, it may be assumed that they represent a typical and easily recognizable scene in the medieval Middle Eastern marketplace. It appears from the illustrations and the text that at the popular level, cuppers who were not physicians were still practising not only when al-Ḥarīrī was writing, but some 100 years later, when these illustrations appeared.

The Library

Although the 2nd tale is called the *Maqāma* of Ḥulwān, a town in Iraq, the text makes it clear that the library is in Basra, as al-Ḥārith says:

> But when I had returned from abroad to my native town, I happened to be in its public library, the haunt of the literary, and the rendezvous of all, whether residents or travellers, when there came in a man in rags, with a short thick beard.

This unprepossessing stranger astounded the gathering by 'the stores of his mind' in his commentary upon the work of Abū 'Ubayda, an eminent eighth-century Arab bard, better known as the court poet, al-Buḥturī.

The moment illustrated in al-Wāsiṭī's manuscript represents Abū Zayd's attempt to convince the assembly that his verses are his own composition and that he is innocent of plagiarism. The four very concise lines of Arabic begin as follow: 'He said, "By Allāh, right is most worthy to be followed, and trust is most fitting to be listened to. Know, friends, that it is his who talks with you today."' Al-Ḥārith recounts:

> Now it was as though the company doubted of his fathering and were unwilling to give credit to his claim. And he perceived what had fallen into their thoughts, and was aware of their inward unbelief, and was afraid that blame might chance to him, or ill-fame reach him, so he quoted from the Qur'ān, 'Some suspicions are a sin.'

Al-Wāsiṭī has included the textual exegesis of a commentator in red zigzag lines down the right-hand side of the page. The commentary appears to be justifying his claim by quoting poetry in support of Abū Zayd, and the script seems to be in al-Wāsiṭī's hand. The commentary, of course, is not his.

Al-Ḥārith is probably the figure at the left-hand side; his appearance is consistent throughout the wide chronological span of the 50 tales in this manuscript. Abū Zayd is at the extreme right of the illustration, where he has 'sat down at the edge of the throng' in accordance with the text and is

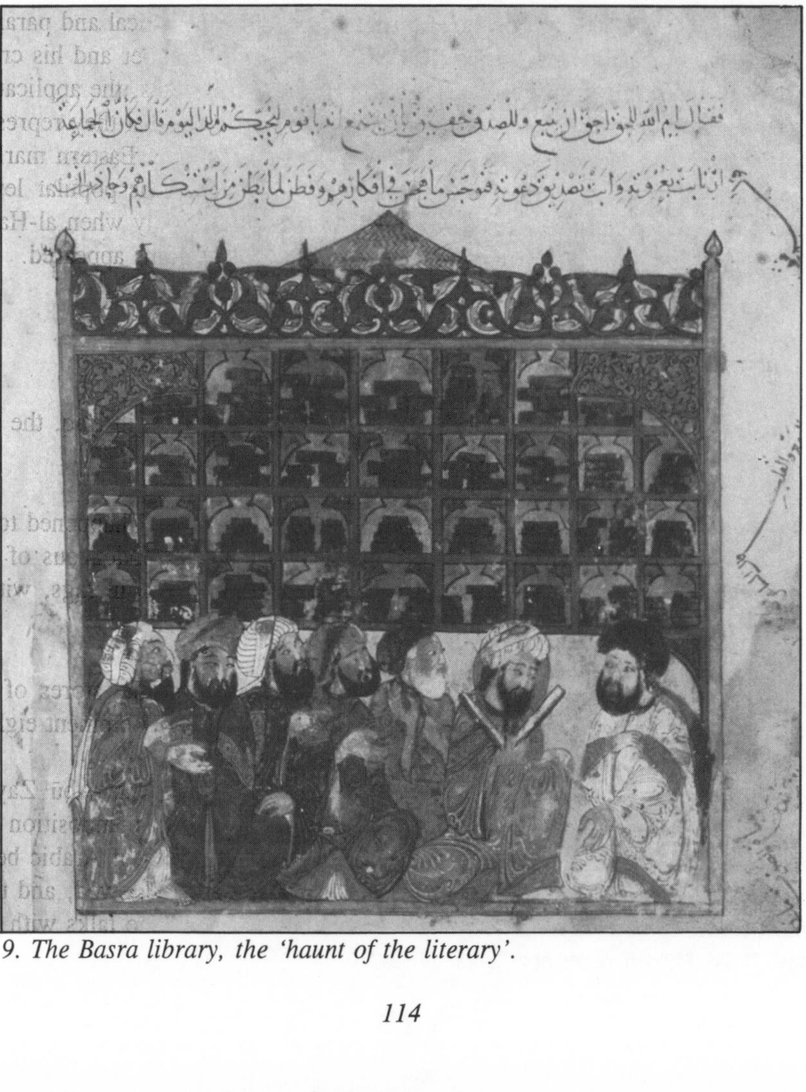

9. The Basra library, the 'haunt of the literary'.

consulting a man reading a book—this should be the volume of poetry by Abū 'Ubayda, upon which Abū Zayd has had the temerity to improve.

Abū Zayd is not of a 'squalid aspect', but he does have the requisite 'short thick beard'. One should bear in mind that this is one of the earliest tales, and Abū Zayd's beard is not yet white. Al-Wāsiṭī as scribe would have a good insight into Abū Zayd's defects as the tales progress, yet he invariably portrayed him in a kindly light, despite what he knew of his motivation and behaviour. This may imply that as his affinity with Abū Zayd grew, so did his portrayal of him as a character in his own right, and not as a mere 'type'; perhaps he even sought to gain more sympathy for his hero, as an old man. Of course, his role as scribe also allowed him an insight into the kindlier aspects of of Abū Zayd and his ultimate repentance. The other men are the standard, well-dressed bourgeois types one would expect to find in a prestigious city library, and their hand gestures indicate that they are indeed disputing Abū Zayd's claim to authorship of his commentary.

The human scene in the lower register brings to mind the 'author portrait' in form and content. This had a classical prototype, and one recalls the nine distinguished physicians of antiquity who hold books in the *Book of Antidotes*. There is a further parallel with that manuscript in the 'framing' of this group of scholars, which is now much expanded from the sage and student alone within a small niche that is found elsewhere in the *Book of Antidotes*. This convention also occurs in the contemporary *De Materia Medica* manuscript and is particularly striking in the BL 1200 work in *Maqāma* 29.[22] It is a device that was taken up later by Persian painters.

The author portrait persisted in Arab painting up to the end of the thirteenth century: the *Epistles of the Sincere Brethren* double frontispiece of 1287 is a particularly sophisticated example. The little-known manuscript in Istanbul, the *Book of Marzūbān*, depicts its author, Sa'd al-Dīn Varāvīnī, describing his work to a group of men. It is significant that the manuscript had been re-cast in Persian early in the thirteenth century. This critical work marks the turning-point of manuscript illustration in post-Mongol conquest Baghdad towards the new art of Iranian-Mongol painting.[23]

Finally, there is a further, more subtle element in common with the author portraits: the implicit notions of instruction, presentation and approbation. Al-Wāsiṭī's miniature is thus aptly sited under the caption which continues: '. . . it is on trial that men are to be honoured or despised'. Abū Zayd has confidently set himself up as an authority who will be challenged but will ultimately win the esteem of the assembly.

An interior scene is suggested by a decorative framework of ruled uprights with finials. A pair of very decorative spandrels indicate the entrance to this section of the library. They are deeply carved with tight floral whorls, looser variations of which are found on textiles and ceramics, and in manuscript painting and metalwork.[24] An additional component of depth is introduced by the upward-turned book in the foreground and the postures of the men, whose turbans are clearly in front of the bookshelves; the corbels of the shelves also emphasize depth.

Four rows of leather-bound volumes are stacked on their sides on a range of shelves. There is an attempt at perspective by means of enclosing each small compartment within simple spandrels. These are surely more decorative than practical, for they severely limit the number and size of volumes which can be stored, and this implies that libraries were huge buildings. In late tenth-century Cairo the palace library of the second Fatimid ruler al-ʻAzīz housed 40 collections of books, in other words 40 rooms of books; the 'ancient sciences' alone were represented by 18,000 volumes. Identical niches appear in the St Petersburg library illustration; there the books are also stored flat on their sides, one above the other. A remarkably consistent library is provided in BL 1200 (Illust. 10). This same type of shelving and stacking of volumes occurs in the illustration of an astronomers' library in a sixteenth-century *Book of the King of Kings [Shāhanshāhi-nāma]* manuscript in Istanbul by Aḥmad-i Tabrīzī, and the practice continues up to the present day.[25]

It is not possible here to see if book titles are inscribed on the leather covers, but there must have been some indicator of each of the works on a shelf and of its category and contents. BN 3929 has some book titles where the word *dīwān* (collected works) is clearly legible. This alludes to the poetry books required by the text, so they should include the name of Abū ʻUbayda. It is likely that this setting is the Arabic philology and poetry room in the Basra public library, because when the philosopher Ibn Sīnā (known to the West as Avicenna) was summoned as a doctor to attend the Sāmānid prince Nūḥ, he asked permission to use his library in Bukhārā and he mentions such a department there.[26] Catalogues were shelved in each department according to subject-matter. Volumes were laid flat on shelves in wood-veneered cupboards which were approx. 2.7 m wide by 1.8 m long; wooden doors folded downwards, but these are not illustrated.[27] These valuable volumes are not chained.

The crenellated frieze of al-Wāsiṭī's elaborate building resembles that noted in the illustration in the St Petersburg manuscript of the governor of Merv's palace. It too features an abstract floral motif of leaves. Further examples are found on architecture in contemporary Iraq.[28] The pyramid-shaped roof is apparently made of woven matting laid in a chevron pattern, suggesting that a further covered area lies behind this section of the library. Similar roofs are seen elsewhere in the *Maqāmāt*. Al-Wāsiṭī's miniature conforms to al-Muqaddasī's description of a large ante-room in a library leading on to a long arched hall with rooms on all sides, where scholars from all disciplines could converse in peace. An account by Miskawayh confirms this: "Aḍūd al-Dawla had a room built adjoining his own suite in his palace library at Shīrāz which was reserved for very high-level scholarly discussions and held away from the common people.'[29] No windows are shown, and one wonders what form of illumination was used, since libraries would be a potential fire hazard, particularly in a very hot, dry climate. Ibn ʻAqīl speaks in the past tense of a library in the Karkh

10. Abū Zayd astounds the littérateurs.

area of Baghdad which was famous in its day but burned down in the mid-eleventh century.[30]

Al-Wāsiṭī's library is obviously a substantial and fairly elaborate building of some importance in a town that was famed as a seat of scholarship. The group of scholars reflects the esteem in which learning was held at that time. Perhaps the generosity of a benefactor is also demonstrated. The practice of endowing a library is confirmed in Ibn Khallikān's *Biographical Dictionary*. It reports that al-Khaṭīb, who died in 1071, ordered (among other bequests) that all his books should be used as an endowment (*waqf*) for the use of Muslims.[31]

In 1233 the caliph al-Mustanṣir built a cosmopolitan library in Baghdad where hundreds of librarians looked after hundreds of thousands of books. Yāqūt writes in praise of a library in Merv where he worked for 3 years and he mentions that Merv had 10 wealthy libraries; these included 2 in the mosque, with the others being attached to colleges (*madāris*). As a distinguished writer, he was allowed to take out 200 volumes without leaving a pledge. The cost of borrowing was about 1 *dīnār* per volume.[32] As this was an enormous sum at that time, only the wealthiest people could have afforded to frequent the libraries. Indeed, there is everything in al-Wāsiṭī's portrait to suggest that this was so.

It is not clear why Pauty should describe this library as 'a bookseller's'.[33] One must assume that he did not read the Arabic text, namely *dār kutubihā*, which translates freely as 'the house of its books', the *ha* (its) referring to the city (*madīna*) of Basra. It is true that the relative cheapness of paper made literary works available to an ever-wider public, and bookshops flourished as centres for littérateurs and calligraphers. In the tenth century one Baghdad street, *sūq al-warrāqīn*, boasted 100 booksellers. Their shops, and those of the paper-sellers, occupied both sides of the roadway from the Ḥarrānī archway to the New Bridge over the Saraṭ canal in Baghdad in the 'Abbāsid period. The *Biographical Dictionary* mentions an Egyptian bookseller who died in 1210 who:

> used to sit in the vestibule of his house for the purpose of exercising his profession, offering books for sale to men of rank and learning . . . They were accustomed to assemble there every Sunday and Wednesday, and remain till the hours of sale were over.[34]

However, it is obvious that al-Wāsiṭī is depicting a library.

We have no way of knowing how much al-Wāsiṭī was paid, either as artist or scribe. Since he was both copyist and illustrator, he was presumably doubly rewarded for his talents, especially as he had sufficient status to sign the manuscript as his own work. When the calligrapher 'Umar ibn Ḥasan al-Khaṭṭāṭ died in 1157, his writing implements, which included ink-wells, pencils and knives, were sold for 900 *amīri dīnārs*, yet Ibn 'Aqīl, who died early in the twelfth century, complained of his poverty-stricken circumstances as a copyist.[35]

Two accounts demonstrate the importance of books to some readers. In a medical treatise on depression from the early tenth century, Isḥāq ibn 'Imrān writes, 'So the loss of a beloved child or of an irreplaceable library can release such sadness and dejection that melancholy is the result.' Muḥammad ibn 'Alī ibn al-Ṭiqṭāqā, writing at the beginning of the thirteenth century in *On the Systems of Government and the Muslim Dynasties [al-Fakhrī fī ādāb al-sulṭāniyya]*, relates how 'a certain caliph sent for a certain scholar', who was late. The ruler pardoned his tardiness when the scholar, who had been engrossed in reading, said of his books:

> We have companions of whose talk we do not tire, trusty and trusted, whether absent or here to see. They enrich us from their knowledge with knowledge of the past, counsel, education, honour and dignity. If you say they are dead, you are not wrong, and if you say they are alive you do not lie.[36]

There is a subtle interplay between the Arabic of the text and al-Wāsiṭī's visual interpretation. Al-Muqaddasī refers to a library in Shīrāz as *khizānat al-kutub* (treasury of books); the root meaning of *khizāna* has connotations of treasure, so we have both a visual treasury of precious and much-loved volumes, and the storehouse or hoarding of linguistic treasures in Abū Zayd's mind.

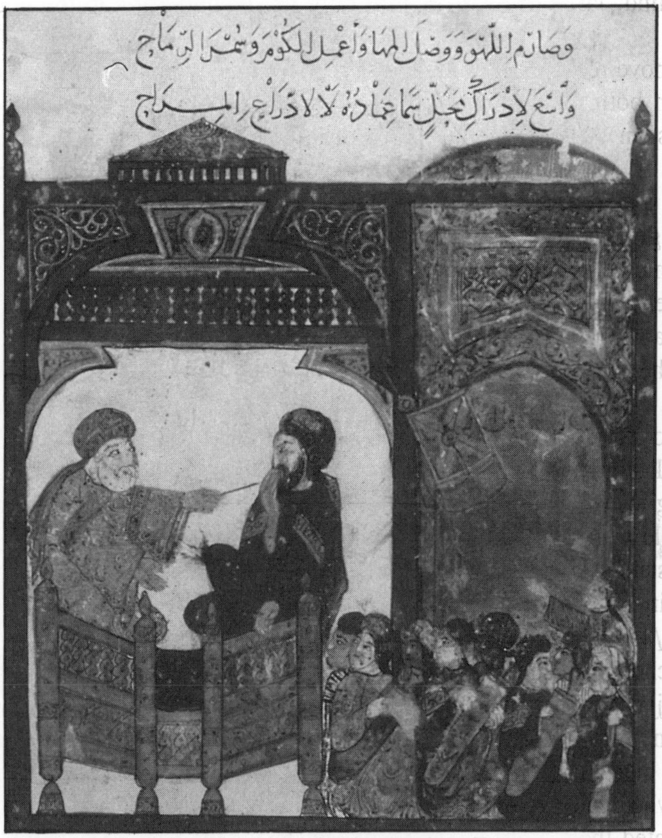

11. A pupil recites for his schoolmaster.

The Schoolroom

Maqāma 46 is set in Ḥoms, in Syria. Homs had the reputation of being 'a foolish and wealthy town' and al-Ḥārith decides to 'sound the [proverbial] stupidity of the people'.[37] He is surprised and delighted to find a schoolmaster setting extremely difficult tasks in composition in rhyming couplets to his pupils. In due course, he realizes that the teacher is none other than his old friend Abū Zayd.

Al-Wāsiṭī has illustrated this schoolroom twice, and it is the earlier, more elaborate classroom scene that we shall discuss. The illustration comes near the beginning of the first composition, which has a pupil reciting:

> Cut off thyself from play, avoid wantonness, but ply the camels and the brown supple spears. Strive to obtain a lofty place, pillared high, not to enrobe thyself in gay dalliance. For lordship means, by Allāh, not quaffing wine, nor gain you glory courting girls full of hip. Hail to one free of hand

and mind, large of heart, whose only joy is giving joy to the good.[38]

The above recitation is a great achievement by a small boy and vindicates the reputation both of the people of Homs and of the oft-maligned schoolmaster. (There is an Arabic saying, 'More foolish than a teacher in an elementary school . . . '.) There seems to have been some ambiguity regarding a teacher's status in society. The prolific Ibn al-Kalbī's *Book of the Claimant [Kitāb al-maṭālib]* gives a long list of people whose ancestors and fathers had practised trades which were despised by the ancient Arabs; these included smith, tailor and teacher. A schoolmaster's testimony, like those of the bath attendant and the pigeon-trainer, was accorded only partial validity by of the jurists. This was despite the Qur'ānic prescription, 'And call two of your men to act as witnesses.'[39] Al-Jāḥiẓ counselled, 'Seek no advice from teachers, shepherds and those who sit much among women.' He also commented on payment in kind: 'Their cakes and bread, that is no good, a plague upon such work and food.' According to Abū Dulaf, however, the holder of a teaching post was considered responsible enough to lead the ritual prayer, and the generally low opinion of schoolmasters does not seem to have deterred al-Tha'ālibī, who taught children early on in his career. We know that the fourteenth-century *Manual of Market Practices [Ma'ālim al-qurba fī ahkām al-ḥisba]* of Ibn Muḥammad al-Ukhuwwa forbade schoolmasters from allowing their charges to read the scandalous *Dīwān* of al-Ḥajjāj.[40] This suggests that teachers were licensed and subject to inspection. In his treatise on pedagogy, al-Zarnūjī enjoined pupils to hold the teacher in high regard by quoting the Prophet's son-in-law, 'Alī: 'I am the slave of him who hath taught me even one letter.' Abū Zayd's boys have clearly demonstrated their diligence and enthusiasm for their lessons.[41]

A Muslim child learns very early on that reading and writing have religious merit, and here the lessons would perhaps embrace religion, the art of versification and polite literature. In this tale, Abū Zayd is apparently only teaching boys, but girls could receive religious instruction at the lower level. Abū Zayd's curriculum appears to be strictly conventional, as he set his pupils elaborate compositions. He seems to be following precedent, for according to Ibn Durayd, who was of Persian extraction:

> My teacher was Abū 'Uthmān Ashnandānī. One day my uncle came in when this person was repeating to me the poem of Ḥārith ibn Ḥillīza which commences, 'Asmā' announces her departure.' My uncle promised me a present if I learned the poem by heart. He then invited the teacher to dine with him, and the teacher went to his room, where the two had their meal and sat for a time afterwards. By the time the teacher left the room, I had committed to memory the whole *dīwān* of this poet, so when he came out I told him this; he was incredulous and began to test me, but found that I had really committed it to memory.[42]

Only 9 of the 10 boys of the text are shown, perhaps due to lack of space. Although they appear to be of a similar age, the text clearly indicates that the first to recite was the oldest. This suggests that in a one-teacher school there was one class for all ages. The pupils are dressed in Arab costume and all wear turbans. Their varied skin tones are evidence of a wide Islamic empire, and they seem to be aged about 9 years upwards.

The whole scene is delightfully balanced and orderly, with the children all holding their writing tablets at the same angle. These boards are extremely functional and of a distinctive, oblong shape, with a haft at the top in the form of a *tabula ansata*, literally a 'clean slate'. In the absence of a desk, children would grip the board with one hand to balance it against the body and write with the other hand. We know from the text that pupils wrote on their boards with a reed pen, and they could wipe the boards clean. An unnamed ninth-century treatise on education states that a *mandīl* (napkin, cloth or handerchief) might be used in school 'for wiping the slate clean'. A scribe holding a similar writing board is found in a fourteenth-century al-Jazarī manuscript; red and yellow writing boards appear in a much later British Museum copy of the *Key of the Eminent Poets [Miftāḥ al-fuḍalā']* by Muḥammad ibn Maḥmūd Shādīyābādī.[43]

The *tabula ansata* motif was also used on tombstones. Herzfeld has catalogued the classical *tabula ansata* form found in Egypt, and there is an early eleventh-century alabaster headstone from Yazd in the British Museum; there, too, a carved *tabula ansata* inset frames the inscriptions. A stone tomb in Damascus, which is contemporary with the manuscript, features a *tabula ansata* window lintel with three rows of epigraphy above. The *tabula ansata* form is also reminiscent of an Egyptian wooden mummy identification label in the Graeco-Roman period.[44] The al-Wāsiṭī tablets seem to be wooden, and white writing boards, with a haft and a band of light wood at the top, also appear in the BN 6094 schoolroom (Plate 13).

In the Wāsiṭī painting, al-Ḥārith and the 'teacher' sit on a fairly high carved wooden chair with bell-shaped feet, pointed finials and small carved balusters. It is made of light wood, not the reddish teak that seems to be shown elsewhere in the illustration. Although chairs were not a typical Muslim feature, Abū Zayd's seat is a recognizable piece of furniture which bears some resemblance to the thrones in later Persian manuscripts. From this vantage point, a teacher could carefully watch his class.

No teaching aids such as blackboard or books are shown. The implication is that Abū Zayd was following a very successful method of rote-learning; this is confirmed by the text. Abū Zayd holds a pointer (*'uṣayya*); this is the diminutive of 'staff', and its root has connotations of disobedience and punishment. Abū Zayd tells al-Ḥārith that his temporary profession as pedagogue is most lucrative, and that a pedagogue can be as despotic in school as any prince in his milieu. This point is well taken in the miniature in the

Istanbul version, where the 'teacher' is administering the bastinado (which, incidentally, is not mentioned in the text).

Schoolroom scenes appear in a variety of media, for example on a candlestick in a private collection which was exhibited in 1976 at the Museum of Mankind, London. An illustration in a fifteenth-century Niẓāmī manuscript in the British Museum shows a more informal scene of teacher and pupils. The teacher is not on a dais, and his girl and boy pupils seem to be left to their own devices, both indoors and outdoors. The theme of the star-crossed lovers, Layla and Majnūn, occurs in a Khurāsānian manuscript in the Victoria and Albert Museum, London, showing them at school.[45] All of these school settings take place in a more relaxed atmosphere than in the necessarily circumscribed architecture of al-Wāsiṭī's schoolroom.

The classroom is in an imposing building, lit and well-ventilated by a wooden roof 'dome'. It has matting of a type that has been noted elsewhere in this manuscript, for example on the narrow house like the 'Ark of Moses' in *Maqāma* 15. It was constructed to encourage air-flow and such features are still seen in the Arabian Gulf. The carved wooden frieze or balustrade may be of teak (*sāj*), and its balusters match those on Abū Zayd's bench. Abū Zayd and al-Ḥārith are highlighted by a cusped archway flanked by two very elaborate, deeply cut inset panels of an unidentifiable material with a vegetal motif. The smaller, lower spandrels appear to be stucco-work. Certain types of carved marble arabesques were specially designed to fit the niches and spandrels of *miḥrābs* and doorways, and perhaps this was also the case with other materials.

Behind the children there is a separate, rather gloomy room, lit by a clerestory window in a large dome. The elaborate pointed entrance to this area is possibly constructed from painted or gilded carved wood. It it reminiscent of a *miḥrāb*, and indeed there are some vestiges of epigraphy on the blue background near the pointed arch which may read part of 'Allāh'. We know that schools were attached to mosques. Niẓām al-Mulk's *Book of Government or Rules for Kings* quotes from a eleventh-century epistle to the Commander of the Faithful where one, Maḥmūd, says, 'One of my servants was walking in the bazaar at Samarqand and he passed by a mosque, where a master was holding a Qur'ānic school and teaching some boys.' It is not clear whether secular works were also taught in a purely Qur'ānic school, but the children were sometimes instructed in grammar, and calligraphy was always included in the curriculum in 'Abbāsid times.

In July and August 1184 Ibn Jubayr visited a school for orphan boys in Damascus which was a religious endowment (*waqf*) and provided instruction and board. He was favourably impressed by the 'virtues of these lands'. His *Travels* reveals that:

> The instruction of boys in the Qur'ān in all these Eastern lands consists only of making them commit to memory; writing they learn through the medium of poetry and other things. The Book of Great and Glorious God is thus kept

undefiled from the markings and rubbings out of the boys' efforts. In most [of these] lands the Qur'ān teacher and writing master are separate persons, and from his lesson in Qur'ān reading the student is dismissed to his calligraphy.[46]

The *Travels* explains that erasure of the word 'Allāh' might discredit it. We know from the text that Abū Zayd schooled his pupils in Arabic literature, and Ibn Jubayr's account confirms that Abū Zayd could not have taught the Qur'ān. Of course it is unthinkable that a character such as Abū Zayd would have been employed in a religious school—this would have been recognized as an elementary school by the Muslim reader.

The following stipulations were among the 'Provisions' of al-Mustanṣiriyya *madrasa*, which was endowed in Baghdad in 1234: 'The House of the Holy Qur'ān shall be provided with a learned man, 30 orphan boys and a reciter'; their food rations and financial remuneration were laid down. In this tale Abū Zayd is teaching boys, although girls could receive religious instruction at the lower level. Elsewhere, we read that in al-Mustanṣiriyya:

Each school [of the four law schools] has an *īwān* in which there is space for lecturing, having a small wooden dome, beneath which the teacher sits upon a bench covered with carpets, a sober figure in his black clothes and turban.[47]

These would be official appointees. It is likely that students in al-Mustanṣiriyya and similar establishments were older than Abū Zayd's pupils, but al-Wāsiṭī may have used a *madrasa* as a model for his junior schoolroom.

An alternative explanation of the setting is that Abū Zayd is teaching at his home. A common expression found in source material is, 'He sat at the door of his house.' This indicates that people frequently sat by the side of the door on mats or carpets, or on a raised platform (*dukkān*). Learned men and teachers used the *dukkān* as a classroom. One hot summer evening in Baghdad, al-Washshā' saw a secretary sitting on a teak platform profusely decorated with verses written in lapis lazuli. If al-Wāsiṭī's schoolroom is set in Abū Zayd's home, then this interpretation is borne out, for the house is commodious and well-constructed and the parents seem to reward him well. However, the architecture is rather monumental in scale and decoration, and the artist's adaptation of a mosque setting is more plausible.

One of Abū Zayd's pupils activates a *punka* by means of cords and pulleys. This runs in fine counterpoint to the angle of the writing boards, as well as tying the class in with the teacher. A *punka* was a fan made from matting called *līf*, produced from the membranous fibres that grow at the base of the palm-tree. Such a utilitarian version would suffice for a schoolroom, and it is repeated in al-Wāsiṭī's second miniature of this scene. The *punka* was the plebeian version of the *mirwa*, a delicately constructed fan with silken cords and fringes dipped in perfumed water. The *mirwa* was also manipulated by 'mechanical devices' (presumably pulley wheels) over an assembly or in private apartments, and the air was suffused with the perfume. Pulley wheels are also visible in the Istanbul manuscript schoolroom.

In *Maqāma* 42 Abū Zayd sets a riddle concerning a *punka* which sums up well the action in this miniature:

> A maiden I know, brisk, full of speed in her ministry, returning the same track that she went by when starting off. A driver she has, kinsman of hers, who is urging her, but while he thus is speeding her on, is her helpmate too. In summer she is seen dew-besprinkled and moist and fresh. When summer is gone, her body shows flabby and loose and dry.

This description indicates that the schoolroom version would also be sprinkled with water. The technical discussion of the ceiling drape in the lawcourt in *Maqāma* 45 of the Istanbul manuscript applies to the *punka*; both were sited in an air current and worked by evaporation.

Al-Ghazālī's *Fitting Conduct in Religion* lays down that:

> The teacher's primary concern should be for the excellence of his own character, since the eyes of his students are upon him and their ears filled with what he says. What the teacher considers good will seem good to the pupils; what he considers base and shameful will seem base and shameful to them.

Abū Zayd, in this instance, gives every appearance of being such a paragon, as he has followed al-Ghazālī's recommendations to the letter:

> The teacher should seat himself silently in the classroom, alertly supervising the students. He should accomplish the major part of instruction and discipline by evoking the awe and respect of his pupils, not by whipping and punishment.[48]

The exemplary behaviour of the class and their mastery of extremely difficult Arabic language, poetry and calligraphy are clear demonstrations of Abū Zayd's success. Once again, al-Wāsiṭī seems to have been as charmed by Abū Zayd as al-Ḥārith was, for he has portrayed Abū Zayd in the best possible light.

Abū Zayd metes out the bastinado in the badly damaged Istanbul manuscript. This is evidently artistic licence, and it may reflect a commonly held opinion of schoolmasters. However, these pupils, like their master, are paragons.

The treatment of the schoolroom scene in BN 6094 appears at the part of the text where Abū Zayd instructs the second pupil (Plate 13):

> '[Display the bridal couplets], even though they be not of the choicest.' Then the child mended his reed pen and nibbed it. He took the tablet in his lap and wrote, 'Fair Tajānī has maddened me and bewitched me with her thousands of wily tricks and beguilements, has enamoured me with the droop of her eyelids, as a doe's, draining mine of tears through her love-charm.'

Al-Ḥārith and Abū Zayd are seated on cushions at the extreme left of the composition. Abū Zayd holds what appears to be a split cane; he would have used this to chastise his pupils. Abū Zayd's pose may be based on royal iconography. He is shown in a frontal position, with one foot raised; his head is slightly inclined to one side. It is almost a mirror image of this artist's governor of Raḥba in *Maqāma* 10. However, a more likely explanation is that Abū Zayd's portrait represents a variation of a medical manuscript illustration, where the doctor is holding up a plant and explaining its properties to a student, as for example the roughly contemporary *De Materia Medica* manuscript in Istanbul.[49] The physician's plant has been transformed here into a split cane which is, after all, a dried plant.

There is an underlying sense of energy in this manuscript which has been commented upon elsewhere in the context of the carriage and manners of the Syrian people. In consequence, these pupils are apparently not well-disciplined, although the movement reflects their eagerness to please their teacher. They are a fairly motley crowd of children; some wear turbans, while others sport a variety of Central Asian hats. The knee-length costume of the boy second from the right is executed in the same curious manner as women's robes by this painter; these accentuate the shape of the hips and stomach.

Abū Zayd is framed by a flat archway which is decorated with a 'meander' and interlace pattern and topped with a dome with finial. The dome is dark and finely decorated with a palmette motif. Al-Ḥārith, in his capacity as observer, is outside the arch. There is no real sense of depth in the composition; perhaps this is why the teacher, although sitting serenely, does not seem to be in full control of his charges. It would be fairly easy to interpret this scene as Abū Zayd sitting at the edge of the reception area of his home, with one foot outside. Perhaps the artist has portrayed a private tutor at court, or the only models he had for youths may have been non-Arab pages from the royal repertoire.

The real importance of this illustration is that it provides us with one of two colophons for the manuscript. The seated boy nearest to Abū Zayd holds up a board proclaiming that the manuscript was executed in the year 1222. Perhaps this information was intended as a visual joke or form of pun. (The second colophon appears on the riverboat in *Maqāma* 22.)

A slightly earlier school scene can be found on a well-known Persian lustre plate from Kashān which is now in the David Collection in Copenhagen.[50] It shows the child lovers, Layla and Majnūn, in the same schoolroom. All the pupils there have similar writing tablets and they sit around the schoolmaster, who is holding a rod. The round plate shape obviously lends itself to a circular composition and achieves an informality which is lacking within the confines of a schematic architectural setting. It also includes a bookstand, which is absent in the manuscript illustrations. This seems yet another indication that an ordinary elementary schoolmaster such as Abū Zayd taught by the rote-learning method. In the schoolroom setting on the candlestick referred to above, the teacher has a pointer, and his pupils also appear to be fairly unruly.

Although each manuscript has its own architectural scheme, no specific school architecture can be gleaned from the illustrations. It is only the inclusion of children with writing boards and a man with a pointer that makes the context clear.

Musicians

Musicians have already been discussed in the context of the military, and of religious festivals. They also appear in scenes of entertainment; they may be vocalists (like Abu Zayd's slave-girl in *Maqāma* 18), professional mourners, instrumentalists in a drinking den, or performers at an outdoor carousing party.

Both of the major musical traditions in the Arab world—those of the eastern lands, including Egypt, and the western area, comprising North Africa—trace their ultimate development from the Umayyad and early 'Abbāsid periods, namely the seventh to the ninth century. By the end of the thirteenth century a complete fusion of Arab and Persian instruments, musical forms and modes had taken place. For example, the Arabs adopted the Persian names and arrangements for the newly tuned outer high and low strings, and for the frets. The prestigious 'art music' which had once been the prerogative of the court at Baghdad was now enriched as a consequence of the fragmentation of centralized power, together with an increase in the artistic activity and patronage evidenced in all art forms.

By the time of these illustrations, literary accounts reveal that the lute (*'ūd*) had become larger, with the resultant variation in pitch. The classical four-stringed lute (*'ūd qadīm*) was smaller than the five-stringed 'perfect lute' (*'ūd kāmil*).[51] The addition of a fifth string, which was coloured red and placed between the second and third strings, is credited to the great Persian court musician, Ziryāb. Ziryāb, who later moved to Spain, is generally recognized as the founder of the highly developed Hispano-Arab school of music. A nine-stringed version of the lute appears in a thirteenth-century religious miniature from the *Canticles to the Virgin Mary [Cantigas de Santa Maria]*, so it was evidently popular among the Christian population.[52]

It should be noted that the music in this section of the *Maqāmāt* is not the highly refined form, but entertainment at the popular level. However, the artists were dependent to some extent on princely iconography for their models, as we shall see.

The emergence of musical entertainment is associated with the slave-girl singer (*qayna*). The *qayna* is portrayed in Arabic poetry as an instrumentalist who might play the lute, the end-blown pipe (*mizmār*) or the frame drum (*daff*). Her specialities were two sub-categories of song, the 'heavy' or ornate *sinād* and the 'light' or gay *hazj*.[53] In the tavern one would surely expect to hear the latter type.

Maqāma 12 finds al-Ḥārith in 'Āna, a town noted for its wine. He is following up a disquieting report that the old man 'in the garb of an ascetic' who successfully led al-Ḥārith and a group of fellow-travellers across the desert has been sighted in a tavern. Since taverns, wine-halls and drinking throughout medieval Muslim society are discussed at great length in Chapter 7 (where, incidentally, there is another lutanist), we shall restrict ourselves here to entertainers and their instruments.

The illustration in BN 3929 (Plate 14) is a confrontation scene between the narrator and the 'holy man'. The text represents al-Ḥārith's description of the sight that met his eyes in the tavern: 'And at one time he bade broach the wine-casks, and at another he called the lutes [to give utterance].' Abū Zayd and a group of attendants and musicians are portrayed in a simple indoor setting. Abū Zayd is correctly seated between a large jar of wine and the square wine-press (*mi'ṣara*). Musicians were generally considered to be of low social status.[54] A handsome mature woman plays her lute at centre stage. The term used in this text for lute is not the usual *'ūd*, but *mizhar*. The lute was suitable for both ensemble and solo performances and known as *amīr al-ṭarab*, 'the prince of entertainment'. It was initially fretless, pear-shaped and short-necked.

Details of its construction have come down to us in an account of the *Poem in Praise of Wine [Ḥalba]* of al-Kumayt. A drunken young man was brought before the Umayyad caliph 'Abd al-Malik ibn Marwān. When 'Abd al-Malik pointed to his instrument and asked what it was, the youth replied:

> O Prince of the Faithful, this is a lute; it is made by taking some wood of the pistachio tree, and cutting it into thin pieces, and gluing these together, and then attaching over them these pleasant chords, which, when a beautiful girl touches them, send forth sounds more pleasant than rain falling upon a desert land.[55]

Less fancifully, the longitudinal shaped strips of the lute body were bent over a mould, and external and internal reinforcement was provided by pieces of the same wood. The straight-sided peg box, set back at an angle of some 80° to the plane of the fingerboard, was attached to the top end of the neck.[56] There was evidently a strong base in the Islamic world for the long-established tradition of construction of musical instruments on mathematical principles.

The lutanist's long hair hangs down loose under her small pointed headdress, her full cheeks are rouged and she has a beauty spot on her lower left cheek. She therefore matches the ideals of female beauty which will be discussed at more length in relation to Abū Zayd's slave-girl in Chapter 6. Lutanists appear in other media. A veiled lute-player occurs on a cartouche of the British Museum 'Blacas' ewer, which was made in Mosul in 1232. Yet another appears on a contemporary tile from Konya, and a group of musicians, including a lutanist, is found on a fourteenth-century Syrian enamelled and gilded flask.[57]

The lutanist is wearing a heavy gold necklace, probably awarded in recognition of her skills. Entertainers were rewarded handsomely, as revealed by a tenth-century anecdote:

> I have been informed by a number of al-Muhallabī's associates that on a certain night al-Muhallabī distributed among them, and a number of singers, entertainers, etc who were present, coin and raiment to the value of 5,000 *dīnārs*.[58]

This was an enormous sum. That other patrons were less generous is obvious from a witticism attributed to one Abū al-Aynā', a master of the sharp riposte. When asked by a singing-girl to give her his ring, in order that she might have something to remind her of him. He replied, 'You can remember that you asked me for it and were refused'.[59]

It is entirely plausible that this lutanist was also a singer, for al-Jāḥiẓ reports that Yazīd ibn 'Abd al-Malik had a singing-girl named Ḥabāba, of whom a poet once said:

> When her lute responds plaintively to her [voice], and beneath its influence the hearing of the noble guests is filled with yearning, and all ears hearken to it in silence, as though they were asleep when they sleep not!

Concerning Yazīd's other slave-girl Sallāma, the poet asked:

> Have you not her heard her [marvellous as she is], when she raises her voice in song, how skilful is her execution; she renders the thread of the lyric in such a way as to render it to a turtle-dove cooing in her throat.[60]

It is reported that she could reduce Yazīd to tears.

Fairly thin lute strings produced a clear, nasal-like sound.[61] In the eastern Arab lands the lutanist plucked the strings with a plectrum; this suggests that the lute was largely a melodic instrument, and the lutanist seems basically to have played one single line of music, insterspersed with strummed chords. Instrumental music was deemed of lesser importance than vocal music, perhaps due to the oral tradition in Arab society.[62] This is reflected in the literary genre of the *Māqamāt* itself and the prizes awarded to Abū Zayd by his appreciative audiences. The vocalist was the 'star' of the musical ensemble; it is thus fitting that the singer in the illustration is somewhat larger than life and wears gold jewellery. According to al-Jāḥiẓ:

11. The robbery in the khān.

12. An altercation in the cupper's booth.

13. The Homs schoolmaster and his enthusiastic charges.

14. The 'holy man' in a drinking-den in 'Āna.

15. Confrontation in the tavern.

> The singing-girl is hardly ever sincere in her passion or wholehearted in her affection. For both by training and by innate instinct, her nature is to set up snares and traps for the victims in order that they may fall into her toils.

He continues by saying that as part of a singing-girl's wiles, she corresponds with a paramour, seals her letter with saffron and 'ties it up with a piece of lute string'.[63] He confirms that they might also be instrumentalists.

There is a further association between playing the lute and singing, for the *Book of Kings* tells how Khusraw's favourite male singer, Barbad, hid in a tree while Khusraw and a group held a picnic below. The illustration for this episode in a manuscript in the Metropolitan Museum of Art, New York, which is attributed to 1522 or slightly later, clearly shows Barbad playing his lute in a tree.[64]

Although the 56th *sūra*, *'Sūrat al-Wāqi'a'*, describes the rewards of Paradise in glowing terms and mentions fruits, goblets, ewers and immortal youths in attendance, there is no mention of the entertainers and musical instruments which are, apparently, so closely associated with scenes of revelry. The Prophet said, 'Singing and hearing songs can cause hypocrisy to grow in the heart, like as water promoteth the growth of corn.' This is indeed true in Abū Zayd's case.

The musician's ample robe features a pale blue vegetal scroll pattern on a darker field. According to Grabar's analysis of this tale, 'no women or young boys are shown' in this particular illustration, but in his later section on women in general in the *Maqāmāt* he mentions a 'female companion of Abū Zayd in a tavern wearing clothes that probably signify the class of singer/prostitute'.[65]

The enemies of Marwān I, the late seventh-century conqueror of Egypt, dishonoured him by calling him 'child of the woman in blue'; this was a reference to his grandmother, who was said to be 'one of the women with blue flags', which were used to indicate houses of ill repute in pre-Islamic times.[66]

Al-Tanūkhī repeats an anecdote which came to him on the authority of the *qāḍī* Abū Bakr, who had been present at a sitting of a lawcourt. The litigant in a debt case told of his son 'who wastes my substance over singing-girls', explaining that the trouble was 'due to a procurer named [he mentioned the name]'. Further, al-Jāḥiẓ was of the opinion that the majority of men who frequented taverns did so for sexual purposes.[67]

There appears to be no way of knowing precisely what the function of al-Jāḥiẓ's 'singing-girls' houses' (*manāzil al-qiyān*) was, but these accounts suggest that singing-girls were sometimes associated with prostitution.

A dark-skinned male musician in Arab robes is playing the *mizmār* of the text. Medieval dictionaries describe the *mizmār* as a 'musical reed, or pipe'. It was about 30–36 cm long and was end-blown, as shown. Since it was apparently easy to play, it is not surprising to find it in a tavern. The old Arabic name was *quṣṣāba* or *qaṣab*. Elsewhere, the *mizmār* appears in a variety of media.[68]

Musical instruments played their part in mystical poetry, particularly that of Rūmī, where they were seen to represent the cadences of eternal harmony;

metaphorically, only the lips of the friend caused the flute to speak.[69] The *mizmār* differed from the flute, which was blown obliquely.

The artist has added a drummer with an unusual, small hand-drum; it seems to be the only example of this type in the whole corpus and is uncalled for by the text, which mentions only 'the pipe and the lute'. Although I have been unable to find this type of drum in medieval Arabic dictionaries, it appears to conform to a modern-day description of the *darabukka*, which is described as a 'conical one-headed hand-drum, open at the small end'. If this is relevant, then Lane's nineteenth-century personal account of the instrument seems to apply: 'It is placed under the left arm, generally suspended by a string that passes over the left shoulder, and is beaten with both hands.'[70] This description fits the drummer's actions in the illustration. Such goblet-shaped drums were made of pottery, metal or wood, with the drumskin secured by wood or nails.

The illustration is at once an adaptation and a parody of the princely cycle, for we know that Abū Zayd has appeared in the guise of a holy man, with eyes glazed over as if in religious abstraction. Here, with his white beard, he recalls later Persian portraits of King Zāl.

Let us now turn to the 'tavern' in the BL 1200 *Maqāmāt* (Plate 15). The association between drinking and music is achieved by the inclusion of a young person of indeterminate sex stirring a large earthenware wine vat. The tambourine (*duff* or *ghirbāl*) and a pear-shaped lute are easily identifiable; a lutanist playing a similar type of instrument occurs on a fragment of a thirteenth-century Syrian bowl with underglaze painted decoration.[71] The tambourine was of Assyrian and Egyptian origin and is a type of small, shallow, single-headed frame drum, with parchment stretched over a wooden ring. The openings in the shell, which are clearly discernible, almost always have small metal bells or discs affixed, singly or in pairs. The tambourine was sometimes used by professional mourners, but without the tinkling plates.[72] Presumably they would be inappropriate in the context of mourning, but the drum effect would help keep time and add sonority to the proceedings. There is no tambourine in al-Wāsiṭī's cemetery scene (Illust. 12).

The small musician in the background at the right-hand side may be playing a dulcimer-type of stringed instrument, although he does not have a hammer or striking implement. Ibn Khallikān's *Biographical Dictionary* mentions the combination of dulcimer and lute in a mid-tenth-century eulogy of al-Mawṣilī, who personified the spirit of classical Arabic music: 'All the apparatus of our pleasant parties is in grief, and the lute sympathizes with the dulcimer.'[73] The courtly themes of drinkers, lutanist and possibly dancers appear on Syrian metalwork of that period, as well as in the Cappella Palatina, Palermo. A tambourine-player in a similar pose is found in a polylobed medallion on a ewer in Cleveland; two tambourine-players occur in a riotous drinking scene in the *Dīwān* of Ḥāfiẓ, dated *c.* 1527; and a tambourine-player accompanies Khusraw's favourite singer and lute-player, Barbad, in the BL 2265 *Five Poems* [*Khamsa*] of al-Niẓāmī dated between 1539 and 1543.[74]

12. Professional mourners in Sāva.

Given the poor overall quality of the BL 1200 manuscript, the painter has surprisingly depicted a very unusual and comprehensive scene in the context of music. In both of the above illustrations, the artists have gone beyond the textual requirements. This is surely further evidence of their automatic association of convivial drinking and musical entertainment, and the appropriation of the necessary iconography.

Professional Mourners

Maqāma 11 is set in Sāva, where the peripatetic al-Ḥārith recounts how he became conscious of 'hardness of heart'. From the tenth century onwards, a new form of piety had sprung up, that of visiting the tombs and cemeteries of saints. Heeding a *ḥadīth* of the Prophet—'Visiting tombs makes one self-denying in this life and mindful of the life to come'—al-Ḥārith set off for a cemetery with devotional intent. Al-Wāsiṭī has once more produced a striking image. Since Rice and James have analysed various aspects of al-Wāsiṭī's cemetery scene,[75] the discussion here is restricted to the professional women mourners.

Three bare-headed, dishevelled women at the top of the illustration stand out from the group around the tomb; their energetic movements set them apart from the wan, sad figures nearest the grave, and each seems to perform a particular role. The principal player in the drama, who stands at the centre, has placed her hands upon her head. Her companion at the right-hand side is beating her breast, an act known as *qayna*, while the other at the left-hand side seems to be pulling her hair into disarray and grasping her robe.

A will from Fusṭāṭ dated 1113 sets aside a sum to cover funeral expenses and specifically mentions 'singers'.[76] *Qayna* also means a female singer. However, the term used for this particular group of professional singers should be *nā'iḥa* or *nawwāḥa*; it is unthinkable that an ordinary singer, who was perhaps morally suspect, could perform obsequies for the dead. The leader delivers a eulogy (*radda*) of the deceased; presumably she will have made discreet inquiries regarding the name of the deceased, family relationships, status in the community, and so on. Her companions enact the part of the *mustafqiha*, that is, one who provides the responses. Al-Wāsiṭī has emphasized this reciprocal role by the eye movements of the principal professional mourner and the *mustafqiha* at centre left. The *Tāj al-'arūs* defines the term as one who 'catches, retains quickly and understands', which implies a talent for deft improvisation of the lament (*nawḥ*) on the part of the wailing women, albeit honed by experience. It is likely that they had a series of standard lamentations, which could be adapted to include the name of the particular deceased. These women formally articulate the grief of the family and strive to introduce the principal players in the drama that will unfold. On this occasion, they are not accompanied by the tambourine.

It is noticeable that the simple garments of all the women are without embroidered *ṭirāz* bands. They are probably 'old clothes'. Abū al-'Atāhiyya mentions al-Mahdī's slave-girls, at his death in the late eighth century, when 'They went in figured silk, then came in sackcloth.'[77] Two of the professionals wear greenish-coloured garments, while their leader is identified by her red robe. We know from al-Bukhārī's authoritative *Traditions [Ṣaḥīḥ]* that in the pre-Islamic period women wore their worst clothes for a funeral. The Prophet proscribed dyed mourning robes for women, except for those made from a Yemeni fabric called *'aṣb*; this had threads which had been dyed before weaving.[78] The red and green robes perhaps indicate that the women were hired for this funeral, for we know that in the tenth century red clothing was 'only worn by Nabatean women and singing-girls of the slave class',[79] and it links them to the two female mourners beside the grave. However, I have found no literary reference elsewhere which suggests that professional mourners were also slaves. It is likely nevertheless that they were perceived as being on the margins of society.

The principal female family mourner also wears red. One wonders if al-Wāsiṭī has deliberately chosen red and green for his composition to emphasize the role of the hired women and their inextricable link with the family, through the deceased. The technical name for a mourning garment, *thawb al-ḥidād*, may be a later development, and seems only to appear in Ibn Ḥanbal's authoritative *Traditions [al-Musnad]*. The word *ḥidād* implies a garment that has been dyed a very dark black. The eulogizing of the dead and the wailing of women were proscribed by the Prophet, on the grounds that they were relics of the pre-Islamic period. Confirmation of the social status of these professional mourners lies in another *ḥadīth*, which says that they are cursed by God. Paradoxically, society depended on them.

It is arguable that there is a need for the professionals' services, because detailed ritual (and public health) prescriptions insist that burial must take place within a very short time-scale, during which the newly bereaved have little or no time to come to terms with the loss of the loved one. The low social status of professional mourners permits scenes of uncontrolled grief at the time of a traumatic rite of passage and, despite their ambivalent social position, they fulfil a valuable role in society.

In the tenth century, Ibn Baṭṭa deprecated what he considered the innovation (*bid'a*) of women following a funeral procession and striking their faces. Al-Dhahabī's *Book of the Dynasties of Islam* tells us that in 1134–5, the death of the long-serving caliph al-Mustarshid bi Allāh provoked great emotion in Baghdad. People wailed and ripped their clothing. Women came out of their houses, their hair undone, striking their faces and weeping, while reciting the merits of the deceased'.[80] Weeping and lamentation by Jews in the provinces of the Persian empire are documented in the Old Testament; Jastrow has pointed out that these customs survived from burial rites in Ancient Babylonia.[81] They continue to this day in the Middle East.

Emotional outbursts of grief were not confined to women, and accounts elsewhere confirm the above practices,[82] together with the rending of clothing and possessions. However, it is noticeable that mourning clothes are usually described as black or dark blue, and it seems that al-Wāsiṭī has diverged from this custom for compositional and aesthetic purposes. He has successfully conveyed a poignant everyday scene in a well-observed vignette.

5

Aspects of Rural Life

Rural life in the *Maqāmāt* appears almost incidentally, in the long and rambling 43rd tale. Contemporary chroniclers saw little relevance in the lives of the peasant class of medieval Muslim civilization, who nevertheless formed the bulk of the population. Their lot was one of service, dependency and exclusion from status, with little control over their own destiny.

Lands and estates were largely in the hands of the state, or its delegates. Land also passed into private hands on an irrevocable and inheritable basis as the gift of rulers. Sometimes land, or the delegation of fiscal rights over it, was granted in lieu of payment for services to the state; these rights were purely personal and limited in period. In other cases, annual sums were set as targets for dues payable to the state; these were exacted through an agent, who ran estates as commercial enterprises. At different periods, rapacious landlords, unjust taxation, climatic changes, civil unrest and destruction by marauding forces would all have been grist to the mill of the exploited peasantry. However, without their toil and the large revenue derived from their produce, the townsfolk could not have survived, and in practice a fragile alliance existed between town and country, based on self-interest. It is likely that the influence of the ruling élite was in direct proportion to the proximity to the seat of power.

It is easy to oversimplify the situation by thinking of the land in terms of a fixed peasantry with their crops on the one hand, and wandering tribes with their animals on the other. In reality, some peasants had firm control over their landholdings and hired people to tend the animals; elsewhere the settled inhabitants shared land use with herders of animals. Populations were partly transhumant and partly settled, according to climatic conditions. However, the symbiosis between tillers of the soil and pastoralists was inevitably somewhat precarious and shifting.

The bedouin were much admired for their resilience and mobility. They, in turn, may have felt superior to their town and country cousins, through their sense of freedom, honour and in some sense noble birth. They appear in the tales as proud, upright people; the hospitality they offer the travellers in the 44th tale exemplifies the extent of their generosity.

As we shall see (Illust. 13), al-Wāsiṭī's portrayal of the village therefore presents a somewhat idealized, even patronizing account of village life. The inhabitants' fine clothes would not have been out of place in al-Ḥārith's metropolitan milieu and the beautiful blue-domed mosque would have graced a decent-sized town. Further, there is an ironic touch in the text, when the village youth expresses his contempt for literature.

The Water-Wheel

The 24th *Maqāma* is set in a quarter just outside Baghdad where al-Wāsiṭī produces an idyllic pastoral setting for al-Ḥārith and his literary friends (Plate 16). (In fact, much of the produce for local consumption came from these areas, and irrigation was a major feature of the landscape.) A lutanist entertains the well-dressed city types, with their wine-flagons, while a young peasant lad and his prodded beast literally tread their weary grind in the background. Much of this passed over the heads of the other illustrators, who, with the exception of the painters of the St Petersburg and Istanbul *Maqāmāt*, generally defined an outdoor setting in rudimentary landscape terms. One further point is that al-Wāsiṭī, here, has clearly made the necessary mental association between drinking and royal iconography and adapted it for his own ends.

The narrative takes place in a meadow on the outskirts of Baghdad, in the populous area known as al-Rābi', so called because al-Manṣūr had granted the land to his chamberlain, Abū al-Faḍl al-Rābi'. Al-Ḥārith and some fine friends were carousing when they were accosted by a ragamuffin, who initially offended them. However, he was able to enlighten them in their arguments over Arabic grammar and he set them 12 apparently intractable riddles. He offered to tell them the solutions if they gave him a gift. The text comprises 2 lines above and 2 lines below the miniature. Addressing the group, Abū Zayd asks:

> What is the epithet which, when it is followed by *nūn*, he to whom it is applied lessens in men's eyes and is set low in reputation and is reckoned among the simpletons and exposes himself to dishonour? Now these are 12 questions to match your number, to balance your disputatiousness.[1]

Al-Wāsiṭī has chosen a wickedly apposite place to insert his illustration, for the answer to the riddle is 'sponger', and it is precisely the opinion that the group held of Abū Zayd. This demonstrates just how tenuous is the dividing line in the Arabic language (and society) between 'guest' and 'sponger'. Abū Zayd then neatly exacted his revenge for the hostility shown him by adopting a high moral tone and declining the group's grudging hospitality.

Abū Zayd is the white-bearded figure in the right foreground, while al-Ḥārith is probably the large man with the dark beard beside the tree. Both wear standard Arab dress, but al-Ḥārith's turban is tied in a more elaborate manner than Abū Zayd's. They are drawn on a much larger scale than the remaining characters, perhaps as a means of identifying them. However, this convention of scale was employed in court iconography and several further points suggest a model from the princely repertoire. Al-Ḥārith could be based on an enthroned prince, and a lutanist was a standard figure from court life in portraits of rulers 'at ease'.[2]

The peasant lad tending the oxen has indefinable facial features and wears a curious pointed hat and a short robe with *ṭirāz* bands. He brings to mind a page at the Saljūq court, his courtly fly-whisk now replaced by a plebeian cane to prod the animals. When these four characters are viewed as an isolated group, it is not difficult to see the transformation of a princely setting by the addition of vegetation, architecture, a dark wine flagon at left foreground and the other eleven revellers as a requirement of the text. The artist may have had several models at his disposal. Further, there is an early textual reference by the narrator to the two boon companions of the son of Malik al-Azdī, a famous Iraqi ruler.

Al-Wāsiṭī correctly shows the 12 men (including al-Ḥārith) mentioned in the caption. Al-Ḥārith's turban is particularly handsome, like that of a ruler, and it serves to identify him. They all wear typical Arab dress. Their robes have *ṭirāz* on the upper arm and are in plain hues of red, blue, brown, saffron, black and violet. Abū Zayd's garment is white, which sets him apart. The folds of the textiles are sinuous and decorative, and highlights are sometimes employed. Two faces have been retouched in a schematic fashion; these characters may be youths, for one of them wears a knee-length red robe with gold edging, a gold-coloured belt or girdle and light white trousers underneath. Handsome youths, wine and song all evoke a paradisaical setting.

One would expect a landscape setting for this tale, and indeed all the manuscripts provide one. The tree at the right-hand side is executed in the 'Mesopotamian' manner. Similar trees have been noted elsewhere in contemporary media. Al-Wāsiṭī's other plants and grass here are typical of his work, but they are now in muted brownish tones. Although they are not particularly intrusive as 'space-fillers', they act as a frame for the composition. The tall papyrus flower on a leafy stem immediately below the pond has already been identified in *Maqāma* 4 in this manuscript.

The parapet of the wall is laid with bricks to form a chevron pattern. These impart a sense of depth to the illustration, suggesting something of the circular course of the path trodden by the beasts as well as directing the eye to the right of the composition where Abū Zayd stands. The water-drawing machine is of solid construction and is evidently a variation of the *zurnūq*, which medieval dictionaries describe as signifying twin pillar-like structures (*manāratāni*). These were constructed by the head of the well, and a wooden beam (*na'āma*) was laid across them. The function of the serrations on the top left-hand side of the beam is unclear. Both draught animals are harnessed to a pole which transfixes the upright, movable pillar. The construction of the black panels of this lifting device shows that it is in the form of a triple Archimedes screw (*ṭunbūr*). When turned, it lifted the water lying not far below the ground surface with its larger end; the water was then discharged down the length of the screw, here through the pointed brick archway. The principles of Archimedes were well known and long applied in the Arab world, and water-wheels are illustrated elsewhere. There are no obvious channels for irrigation, though it is likely that the contraption was functional. The pond is depicted in a very decorative manner, its stylized white outlines recalling the Chinese water convention.

No other illustrator has shown a water-wheel; in this, al-Wāsiṭī has once more gone beyond textual requirements. In his *Chronicles of Egypt*, Ibn Taghrībirdī mentions an oxen slope (*ḥadhar al-baqar*) in the south-east quarter of Cairo, which includes Qusūn's palace and stables, as well as a water-wheel gate (*bāb al-sāqiya*),[3] and in *Maqāma* 42 Abū Zayd composes a riddle concerning the *dūlāb* type of water-wheel. Around 1300, the Anatolian folk poet and mystic Yūnus Emre echoed something of the plaint on the theme of separation even as Rūmī's reed flute did from its reed-bed. Emre's water-wheel laments its separation from the forest in the following terms, yet it evocatively calls up the rhythmic creaking of the wheel as the animals tread their circular path:

> 'O water-wheel, why do you wail?' 'My grief I wail, my pain I wail, I fell in love with God my Lord, and that is why I weep and wail. They found me on a mountain top; they broke my arms, they broke my limbs, they used my wood to build this wheel. My grief I wail, my pain I wail.'[4]

Water-lifting machines were clearly a feature of extensively cultivated regions. To this extent, al-Wāsiṭī's device is a genre element. However, its elaborate superstructure and decorative brickwork are somewhat superfluous if this is an everyday suburban setting, and the explanation may lie elsewhere. This water-wheel scene may demonstrate a further 'royal' connection, in the context of the frontispiece to Volume II of the *Book of Songs* manuscript, dated 1217 and now in Cairo. That painting features an all-female group standing on a brick-built bridge over a water-wheel; genre elements of ducks and fish swim in the water. Women appear shown in the stream. The women may represent a bathing party from a *ḥarīm*, and the requisite musicians in the milieu of courtly relaxation are also shown.[5]

Part of Ibn 'Aqīl's eleventh-century description of the west bank of Baghdad, al-Karkh, reads:

> on the shore . . . are palaces, in orderly disposition, all with water-wheels, gardens and balconies facing [those across the Tigris]. And the ducks playfully swim together on the wharf of the riverside palace. Many a time would the singing voices of this quarter mix with the sound of the water-wheels.[6]

Al-Wāsiṭī's variation on a contemporary scene may have been inspired by the *Book of Songs* frontispiece or by a similar illustration, by literary accounts or merely by personal observation of an everyday phenomenon. He has, however, gone further, by creating the landscape setting and then using a quite separate model of people to exploit his pictorial space, by determining his main characters and then building up the group around them. In this he has been more successful than the artist of the contemporary Pseudo-Galen *Book of Antidotes* frontispiece,[7] where the separate registers retain a certain frieze-like quality. Overall, this apparently decorative landscape scene yields a surprising amount of information concerning the state of scientific knowledge in the Middle East in the early thirteenth century.

The Village

Maqāma 43 is set in the Ḥaḍramawt, in Yemen. The tale, which is extremely long and complicated, affords Abū Zayd the opportunity of displaying his mastery of Arabic. The full-page illustration in BN 5847 depicts the penultimate incident in the story and there is no text as caption. Al-Ḥārith related how he and Abū Zayd travelled on 'until the journey brought us to a village . . . and forthwith we entered it to forage for provender, for we were both of us short of provisions'.

The painting represents two distinct scenes, the meeting in the foreground with a local lad, and a panorama of the village (*qarya*). There was evidently some sort of official halt before or shortly after a traveller entered a village: the text tells us that the two men had 'not reached the halting-place and the spot assigned for the kneeling down of the camels'. Landmarks such as roads and highways, waterways and hills were used to fix the boundary and the pond for the animals may be such a feature.[8] A *ḥadīth* invokes God's curse on anyone who changes boundary signs. The illustration makes it clear the pair have not yet gone into the village, for the peasant with the mattock over his shoulder is entering it through the gate in the surrounding wall.

Al-Wāsiṭī has 'framed' the encounter within landscape elements of grass, bushes and flowers. The date-palm is very realistic; this feature is shared with the relevant BL 1200 illustration. Its positioning beside the mosque vividly

13. Abū Zayd and al-Ḥārith approach a village.

recalls verse 14 of *sūra* 76, 'The shade thereof is close upon them and the clustered fruits thereof bow down.' This allusion to Paradise would not be lost on the audience. In general, *Maqāmāt* landscape merely indicates an exterior setting. Here, landscape elements have been carried up and around to create a quite separate register at ground-level and to capitalize on the increase in the spatial planes. We have already seen al-Wāsiṭī employ this device in the pilgrimage procession (Plate 1).

The grass is suggested by a solid wall of green, interspersed with pale brown plants with reddish blossoms. Three large plants to the left foreground appear to be papyrus. The dark plants serve to define the framework and they also act as foreground space-fillers. This same compositional device occurs in the *Book of Farriery*.[9] The linking of different planes of action, using features of landscape, is implemented to good effect, too, by the artists of the Istanbul and St Petersburg manuscripts.

Abū Zayd and al-Ḥārith in their city finery are mounted on handsome camels. It should be noted that the villagers wear similar garments, although, in reality, this is unlikely to be the case. Both men have dark beards and look much younger than their usual portrayals; indeed, they are not particularly recognizable in this instance. This is surprising, as we are now reading the 43rd *Maqāma*, and the period of the tales stretches over many years. One elaborate camel-saddle with carved wooden mounts can be seen and both camels are covered with expensive fringed cloths.

The young man of the text is not depicted as a youth, but as a mature man with a full beard, nor does he carry the bundle of grass described. Moreover, he is dressed in metropolitan-type clothing, whereas a peasant returning from the fields with fodder would surely have worn short, practical clothes of the type found in the genre agricultural scenes in manuscript painting and on metalwork of the period.

The boldly coloured, full-length garment was clearly chosen for its impact on the composition—much of the force of the encounter with al-Ḥārith and Abū Zayd would have been lost if the man had been scantily dressed and superimposed upon a plain light background, as in some agricultural scenes.

A panoramic effect is achieved in the upper register by depicting a series of five vaulted niches as houses and one as a cattle byre. The individual semicircular vaulted structures are shown to good effect in cross-section; they are solidly built of roughly hewn stone bound with mortar. There were two methods of stone-working. It could be smoothly cut or, as appears to be the case in this illustration, it was left undressed on most of the outer face, but with smooth edges, in a technique known by masons in Mosul as *qubbadar*. Popular before the advent of Islam, this technique was used in the seventh century BC in the walls of Nineveh. Stone was plentiful in northern Iraq, and it was also available in south-western Iraq at Shithatha, near al-Ukhayḍir. Substantial reserves of gypsum, for use in mortar, were also found in the south-west. These archways, whatever they represent, skilfully encapsulate glimpses of village routine and occupations and suggest a closed community. Any tendency to flatness in the composition has been somewhat mitigated by setting the archways on a slope. The wall around the settlement is constructed of small regular-shaped units, which may be kiln-burnt bricks (*ajūrr*). By combining these bricks with quicklime (*sarūj*), their strength was considerably increased. They would be ideal for a defensive wall, in which case a lime mortar was used.

The matronly woman who seems to be arguing with her husband bears a strong resemblance to al-Wāsiṭī's singer with the herd of camels in *Maqāma* 32.[10] She therefore represents a 'type' of middle-aged Arab woman in this manuscript. Two young girls are in an adjoining 'house', while an adolescent girl to the right weeps; they all have plump, round faces and are again dressed in surprisingly fine garments for a rural scene. The men are typical examples here. The man at the extreme left and the person with the distaff at the right-hand side are enigmatic figures. The man seems to be concerned with something happening outside the composition, although he is not part of it. A finely drawn character in his own right, he has perhaps been appropriated from elsewhere.

The person at the right holding a distaff must be a woman, although she seems to be wearing a man's turban. The bare leg to the knee would certainly have been considered indecorous for a female outside her home. However, covering up would be more strictly adhered to in the towns, among strangers. It might be a plump youth, but women are traditionally associated with the art of spinning. The centre of the woman's domain was the spindle. From her endeavours, spinning became an extensive home industry; for example, there was a thread market (*sūq al-ghazl*) in Baghdad. There seems to be no reason why she should be sitting outside the village wall. A spinning woman is also found at the right-hand side of the Istanbul manuscript village and a common source for both artists is possible.

At the extreme right of the composition, a peasant carrying a mattock returns from the fields; he enters the village through an elaborate vaulted gateway in the defensive wall of the settlement. He too wears the fine clothes more typical of an urban environment. These garments may have been chosen for their colourful, decorative qualities, as a foil to the dark interiors and rough-hewn masonry; alternatively, they may have been taken over wholesale from other genre sources. Each of these characters is a well-drawn individual, giving a strong genre flavour and indicating a keen sense of observation on the artist's part.

A white ox or water buffalo looks out of one of the dark recesses, just above the pond. This device lends depth and interest to the composition, and the association of beast and water calls to mind the *al fresco* carousing scene in *Maqāma* 24 (Plate 16). A similar stylization of water can be seen in his ocean in *Maqāma* 39 in the St Petersburg *Maqāmāt*. Goats graze by the water-side; their depiction is less satisfactory and more clumsy than that of the camels. Although they and the farmyard fowls perched on a vaulted roof-top are a minor theme, they are nevertheless an integral part of the natural setting of the countryside.

While it is not inconceivable that poultry might fly up on to roofs, one is reminded here of the birds on the domes of the King's Pavilion in the late twelfth-century *Book of Antidotes* in Paris, as well as an early fourteenth-century illustration of al-Jazarī's *Treatise on Automata* in New York. A single bird sits prominently on a dome in the 13th *Maqāma* in the later Oxford manuscript and the conjunction of birds and the mosque in Basra occurs in the Istanbul *Maqāmāt*.[11]

A handsome mosque of stone construction dominates the left-hand side of the upper plane. The surface of the large outer wall blocks is highlighted. The tall corner buttress, which has a pointed finial, is constructed of smaller building units. An epigraphic frieze in foliated Kūfic script runs the length of the outer wall. The first word is not legible, but the inscription continues, *huwa Allāh*, 'He is God'; this is a common Qur'ānic reference which stresses the Oneness of God, and it is a reminder to all that Allāh has no peers. In this type of popular Saljūq Kūfic, foliated motifs grow out of the letters or from the upper edge of the epigraphic band, relieving the otherwise strict angularity of a carved script.

Al-Wāsiṭī's epigraphic minaret frieze is enclosed within a narrow band; no decoration is discernible from the painting. If al-Wāsiṭī had enclosed his inscription within bands of cable moulding, they would have emphasized the cylindrical nature of the minaret. Alternatively, he could have followed the example of the artist of the Istanbul work in *Maqāmāt* 28 and 50, where the shaft bricks are laid on a diagonal course. Al-Wāsiṭī's minaret is incomplete: there is no small pointed dome with finial which should have crowned it.

Epigraphic friezes were a prominent architectural feature at that time.[12] Al-Wāsiṭī has depicted an epigraphic wall frieze in the last tale, a feature that also appears in the Istanbul *Maqāmāt* on the wall of the mosque in the 48th tale; however, both these inscriptions are in Naskhī script. Above our mosque frieze are two rows of crenellations with a heart-shaped motif.

The relatively smooth-textured cylindrical minaret shaft (*bādan*) suggests the brick construction which was the preferred medium for the Iraqi minaret. Brick sizes varied considerably, and their colours also fluctuated according to the degree of firing.[13] This latter feature is noticeable in the illustration. Cut stone minarets are found elsewhere, particularly in Syria. Two epigraphic bands of floriated Kūfic script on a plain background encircle the shaft below the gallery (*ḥawḍ* or *shurfa*). It is not possible to decipher them. These two bands of Kūfic are separated by a 'meander' border of a type also found on the frieze of double engaged pilasters on the *miḥrāb* in the tomb of Imām 'Abd al-Raḥmān in Mosul. The same simple pattern occurs frequently in manuscript illumination elsewhere.

The base (*qā'ida*) of the minaret is not visible. Bases usually took one of three forms, the square, the octagonal or the dodecagonal. If this minaret is Iraqi in inspiration, its model may have been built on the most common, octagonal form of the later 'Abbāsid period, although there was a transition in plan from the square, through the octagonal to the dodecagonal. Cylindrical minarets with octagonal bases are found in the Khaffāfīn mosque in Baghdad, as well as at 'Āna, Sinjār, Arbīl and Daqūq.[14]

The minaret gallery, which provides a walkway for the caller to prayer (*mu'adhdhin*), rests on two rows of honeycomb (*muqarnas*) vaulting. Carved terracotta pieces were used extensively; these were affixed to panels by plaster (*juṣṣ*) which was applied only on the back of the pieces. It is likely that some form of template was applied to the surface of the cut brick shapes before the carving was executed. Examples of terracotta relief are found on the

Mustanṣiriyya and Sharābiyya colleges (*madāris*) in Wāsiṭ, and the Mirjāniyya *madrasa*.[15]

The form of the gallery probably resembled the base of the minaret, if only for symmetry. Given the small scale, it is difficult to determine the shape of the balustrade. It seems to be hexagonal, but the artist may have distorted it to introduce an element of compositional depth—we have seen how he previously misrepresented architectural features to this end.

The main mosque structure is topped by a beautiful large turquoise ribbed dome (*qubba*) with a gilded bulbous finial. The dome represents a major space form and creates an impression of monumentality. Perhaps this mosque was built on the domical plan which had spread from Iran in the twelfth century. It is a beautiful building, of elaborate construction and at first sight surprising in a village context.

In his *Geographical Dictionary [Mu'jam al-buldān],* the great twelfth- to thirteenth-century geographer Yāqūt mentions several villages in Iraq covering large areas and housing a considerable population. He describes one as a 'big village' (*qarya kabīra*) and another as a 'small town' (*bulayda*); sometimes he simply says a 'town' (*balda*) and/or a 'village like a city' (*qarya ka al-madīna*). Some 'villages' apparently even had a Friday mosque;[16] if so, they should theoretically have had at least 10,000 adults who were obliged to perform the Friday prayer. Since these would have been male adults, a sizeable population can be assumed. It is therefore not impossible for al-Wāsiṭī's village to possess a very fine Friday mosque.

The niches in the miniature recall the artist's two domed tombs in the Sāva cemetery (Illust. 12), but they have now been stripped of buttresses and crenellations and are set on different levels. Village stone has also replaced the bricks of the tombs as the building medium, and both illustrations have a tree at the left-hand side. A plausible alternative explanation of the miniature is that al-Wāsiṭī's inspiration and model lay in an actual mosque complex with adjoining mausoleums, which he adapted to provide both a framework and a backdrop for the human elements. Iraqi mausoleums might be free-standing or attached to a mosque. They were (and still are) a very common architectural feature; those which have survived represent the bulk of buildings from the period of the *Maqāmāt* illustrations. They were associated with famous people and were accorded great importance.

We have here a remarkably self-contained community of men, women and children, together with their animals and fowls. One must ask whether it is likely that everyday working folk in a prosperous village would be wearing such fine garments. Their prosperity depended on their industry, and more plebeian clothes would have been in order, as outlined above. One can imagine the complete self-sufficiency of village routine and occupations. All the staples of life are here: water, the heavily laden date-palm which holds out the prospect of paradise (*janna*) for the faithful, the labourer, the woman with her distaff who is central to the home and, most importantly, God.

One should not be too surprised to find that such a pious and hardworking community should have little time for literature. This delightful scene is perhaps intended to show the bucolic aspect of life to a literate urban audience—the youth in the foreground advises al-Ḥārith and Abū Zayd in metaphorical language that in his milieu, literature is 'utterly valueless' and poetry fetches 'not a barley-corn, nor prose a breadcrumb'. On the other hand, the peasant may be displaying a hostility towards city-dwellers that was reciprocal and never far from the surface, because al-Ḥārith says of the village, 'May the good keep aloof from it.'

There are two relevant illustrations in the Istanbul manuscript, but, unfortunately, they have been too badly defaced to reproduce. It is clear that they share common features of iconography and composition with the Wāsiṭī work. It is tempting to suggest that the former copied directly from al-Wāsiṭī (especially in the light of the highly unusual setting of al-Wāsiṭī's village) and then experimented in exploiting the pictorial space to the fullest extent. In view of al-Wāsiṭī's originality, his unique position as scribe and illustrator, and his going beyond textual requirements on several occasions, it would be necessary to compare the most original al-Wāsiṭī compositions with the Istanbul miniatures in the same tale. One would also have to take account of their place in the text, and this is an area which merits further study.

The Bedouin

The 27th, 32nd and 43rd tales are set within a specifically bedouin environment, which, since they are concerned with admiration of the bedouin and the purity of their Arabic, is entirely appropriate. Al-Ḥarīrī stresses the philological importance of *Maqāma* 27 in particular by appending his own brief commentary, and *Maqāma* 44 deals with the hospitality in a tent afforded to travellers on a winter's night, where al-Wāsiṭī provides a very comprehensive family scene on two adjoining pages (Plates 19 and 20).

Maqāma 27 refers to the 'people of the hair tents' (*ahl al-wabar*), and this is one of several expressions used for the bedouin. Ibn al-Athīr explains it as follows: '[The name] is derived from "camel's hair" because they make their dwellings out of this material.'[17] Each tent represents a family and forms part of an encampment (*ḥayy*). Members of the *ḥayy* form a clan (*qawm*) and a number of kindred clans then constitute a tribe (*qabīla*). Encampment scenes almost invariably include camels, thus underscoring their owners' dependency on them. 'Umar, the orthodox (*rāshidūn*) caliph, reportedly said, 'The Arab prospers only where the camel prospers.' This point is exemplified by the fact that Arabic is said to include some 1,000 names for the camel, encompassing all stages of growth of the numerous breeds.

Maqāma 32 finds al-Ḥārith travelling from the pilgrimage to Ṭayba (one of the names for Medina) to visit the tomb of the Prophet. He is yet again mindful

14. *The 'legist of the Arabians' and Abū Zayd.*

of the Prophet and his example, for there is an allusion here to a reported *ḥadīth* which runs, 'He who performs the pilgrimage, and visits me not, wrongs me.'

In the homestead of the Banū Ḥarb, al-Ḥārith encounters Abū Zayd in the guise of a juriconsult (*faqīh*), gravely pronouncing on the 'decisions on ambiguous legal questions' posed by the spokesman for the tribe. Al-Ḥarīrī has alluded to these in his Preface. Each of the 100 questions posed to the 'expert' on laws of religious ritual contains at least one *double entendre*. The questions are pertinent, bearing in mind that al-Ḥārith has just completed the pilgrimage, for he and the assembly are still fired with religious zeal. The real literary purpose of this very long tale is to illustrate proverbs and rare words in the bedouin vocabulary.

The illustration in BN 3929 appears early on in the tale. It is correctly placed in relation to the text, which reads:

> Verily, I am the legist of the Arabs of the Arabians, and the most learned of those that live under the star-pocked sky.' Then there stalked up to him a man glib of tongue, stout of heart, saying, 'Know that I have had converse with the legists of the world to the effect that I have selected from them 100 decisions, and if thou be one of those who loathe the daughters of others [meaning lies, untruth, falsehood], and desire from us sound food, then listen and answer, so that thou mayest get thee thy due.

The caption in large script advises the reader that this is 'The picture of Abū Zayd and the Arab who questions him.' The small, sprightly Abū Zayd is seated on a cushion at the right-hand side of the composition. He is the man, 'glib of tongue, stout of heart', who has 'donned the turban in the orthodox fashion and gathered his garment in proper style, and was sitting crosswise, while the great ones of the clan surrounded him, and their medley enwrapped him from all sides'.

There is of course no crowd, although the two grave bedouin are larger than Abū Zayd, which could be a compositional device to suggest a greater company. Alternatively, this may be an adaption of an enthronement scene, where the ruler is 'larger than life'. Abū Zayd readily and fearlessly takes up the challenge, and he sits confidently expounding. His hand gestures indicate that he is carrying on a spirited conversation with one of the bedouin, with some element of give and take. Abū Zayd carries a staff, which confirms his peripatetic role, for we know that it was one of the 'appurtenances' of the itinerant pilgrim, as defined by al-Sharīshī. Four of the tales mention the prescribed way of sitting for men when there is nothing to lean against. Steingass describes the bedouin method of sitting at ease as follows: 'They drew their knees to their bodies, and kept them in that position, either by knitting their hands before them, or holding a sword in front, or tying them with some improvised sash to the back.'[18] It is evidently a comfortable way of sitting, for it is forbidden during the Friday sermon (*khuṭba*), as it is conducive to sleep.

The two tribesmen sit on similar cushions; they are distinguishable by their turbans worn in bedouin fashion, tied under the chin. The chief nomad wears a dark, heavy robe with a trefoil pattern; his companion's garment, like that of Abū Zayd, is plain. All the robes bear *ṭirāz* bands, although no epigraphy is discernible—garments bearing this embellishment are unlikely to be found outside a metropolitan environment. The patterned robe serves to draw attention to the questioner and suggests that the colours and textile designs were regarded as important compositional 'markers'.

Bedouin costume differed considerably from that of the urban-dweller (except the poorest). Due to the rigours of the desert, the bedouin's clothing tended to be extremely simple and—unlike high metropolitan fashion—it has remained fairly constant over a long period of time. A more realistic mode of dress for males in a desert setting would have been the *kisā'*, a type of wrapper that was generally made of wool and could be used as a wrapper in the cooler seasons. It was much in use among men and women in the general populace, although the *Book of Songs* mentions it particularly in relation to the bedouin. Also common to both sexes was the *'abā'*, defined by the *Tāj al-'arūs* as 'a well-known sort of woollen garment of the kind called *kisā'*, in which are [generally] stripes; and said to be a *jubba* [woollen cloak-like garment] of wool'. Dozy's *Detailed Dictionary of Clothing in Arab Lands [Dictionnaire détaillé des noms des vêtements chez les Arabes]* confirms that this was a characteristic garment of the bedouin, made from coarse cloth or wool of different colours.[19] Such garb would be fairly basic, practical and well-suited to the climate and natural surroundings.

The bedouin is brown-skinned, as befits a senior tribesman who has long been exposed to the desert sun. Alternatively, he may have been appropriated from an 'author portrait', where wise philosophers were sometimes depicted with dark skins. He is distinguished-looking and entirely credible as an urbane man who has conversed with 'the legists [*fuqahā'*] of the world'. His companion is fair, like Abū Zayd. Perhaps the fair man is meant to be al-Ḥārith, in bedouin garb; his paleness sets off the dark skin tones of the nomad posing the legal questions.

The small, bearded, middle-aged man with a 'topknot' seems to be based on an Indian model. Although he wears Arab clothing, he does not have a turban and so presumably is not a Muslim. He recalls the foreign ruler in al-Wāsiṭī's illustration of the childbirth scene (Illust. 16), and he represents a transformation of this painter's usual youthful, pig-tailed attendant of court settings. This would confirm the theory of an adaptation from the princely cycle, and also ties in with the relatively large size of the two bedouin.

Both tribesmen carry swords, another example of this artist's extremely literal interpretation of the text. As their name indicates (*ḥarb* means war), the Banū Ḥarb were a fierce tribe, and in the tale they have 'just returned from the war'. According to *al-Qāmūs*, *ḥarb* in its root meaning has connotations of plunder and despoliation of wealth and property. The raid (*ghazw*) was the economic basis of pastoral society. An early Umayyad poet outlined the guiding principle of such a life thus: 'Our business is to make raids on the enemy, on our neighbour and on our own brother, in case we find none to raid but a brother!'[20] Plunder was considered the prerogative of bedouin raids and it is arguable that the harsh social and economic conditions of life in the desert elevated the raid to something of a national institution in bedouin eyes.

A reference is made in the 49th tale to *ghārāt* (bedouin excursions for the purpose of plunder), which were considered to be chivalrous exploits and not flagrant attacks. Along with the virtues of manliness (*murū'a*) and fortitude and enthusiasm (*ḥamāsa*), raiding was considered by the bedouin as one of the three supreme virtues. It seems to have assumed the status almost of a sacred duty in the face of a hostile environment. Even a nineteenth-century writer, discussing a *shaykhs'* market (*sūq al-shuyūkh*), states that, 'No inconsiderable portion of their gains is derived from the purchases of plundered goods brought in from the desert by the bedū.'[21]

It has been suggested that during the contemporary Saljūq period in Iraq, the bedouin played a somewhat anarchic role. Then, as today, there were stages of quasi-urbanity and semi-nomadism, seemingly with no great line of demarcation. Tribesmen frequently raided the western side of Baghdad, and sometimes even north-eastern Baghdad. Districts and towns were often illegally annexed through warfare; this would have contributed to Baghdad's shifting medieval population and explains the variety of ethnic features of the characters in the *Maqāmāt* miniatures. Yāqūt's *Geographical Dictionary* confirms the desolate state of some parts of the city in the early thirteenth century.[22] Therefore, however much al-

Ḥārith's personal high regard and motives would be well understood by the reader, it should not be assumed that admiration for the bedouin was universal in the period. According to al-Dūrī, 'the urban population usually espoused the cause of the rural population' and, in some cases, 'they both stood together against the bedouin'.[23]

Unusually for this painter, he has provided a groundline in the form of bolsters, although they are consistent with the bedouin context; they underscore his practice of placing the characters in rows. The presence of a figure of some importance is implied through the association with enthronement scenes. However, as usual, the artist has portrayed Abū Zayd as himself, thus missing an opportunity to inject some humour into the situation by having him seated incongruously on a throne. The flat foreground in the bedouin setting is counter-balanced, and a sense of depth indicated, by the feet and robes protruding over the edge of cushions, and also by the smaller attendant, who dovetails in to the side and behind a foreground figure. The swords also reinforce this impression of depth and, literally, the thrust of Abū Zayd's arguments.

A proud bedouin boast is that they have turbans instead of diadems, tents instead of walls, swords instead of bulwarks and poems instead of written laws.[24] These are demonstrated in both texts and illustrations. The emphasis on rhetoric and philology explains the bedouin munificence at the end of this tale, when Abū Zayd is rewarded for his erudition with the gift of a female singer and a fine herd of camels. Here we see the reverse side of the coin of the principle of raiding, namely great hospitality (*ḍiyāfa*), which mitigates the harshness of life in a nomadic environment. *Ḍiyāfa* is dealt with extensively in a bedouin context in *Maqāma* 44 (Chapter 7).

These accounts of the bedouin afford the reader some insight into the nomads' values and traditions, many of which persist up to the present day. A modern reader might well identify with the world-weary al-Ḥārith, who, when seeking respite from his constant travels and business dealings, relates in *Maqāma* 27 how he was inclined 'in the prime of my past life to make my residence among the people of the desert, in order to acquire their high-minded temperament and their pure dialect of the Arabian language'.

6

Women

In the early days of Islam, women enjoyed a greater degree of freedom in society than their *Maqāmāt* counterparts. The Prophet's first wife, Khadīja, for example, was a highly successful and widely travelled merchant in her own right and was by no means an exception, although it would be naive to imagine that this was generally the case. Al-Khaṭīb al-Baghdādī's eleventh-century writings on 'Abbāsid society demonstrate the societal changes since the early days of Islam, the most notable of which was the veiling of women. Veiling seems to have been more readily adopted with the increasingly cosmopolitan ethnic groups, urbanization of society, greater mobility and the relaxing of family ties, complicated by the issue of family honour. Covering up was probably less common in the desert and small villages, where there were large extended families and much traditional intermarriage, and people tended to know each other. Al-Wāsiṭī shows unveiled bedouin women with trays of food mixing freely in a tent with strangers (Plate 19).

The subject-matter of the *Maqāmāt* is far removed from that of the court circles of Persian literature, which embraced the themes of undying love and—the ultimate renunciation—death for love. Where women appear in the *Maqāmāt*, their presence is required by the text. Abū Zayd's wife has a relatively minor role and is not even given a name, although she has a necessary part to play in several tales as accomplice and foil to Abū Zayd. There is no love or tenderness in this marriage; indeed, in the seventh tale, Abū Zayd describes his wife in a metaphor for 'disastrous' or 'inconvenient'. The couple's relationship is a purely business affair based on deceit. As such, it incidentally embraces the element of intrigue generally imputed to women.

Abū Zayd's wife is quick-witted and resourceful in her skirmishes with *qāḍīs*, highly articulate and fearless. She is well aware of her prerogatives enshrined in the Sharī'a, which grants her inheritance and other rights and affords a measure of protection against the alleged cruelty of her husband. There is no textual guidance for the painters beyond the mention of Abū Zayd's wife or companion, the deserted wife in Kūfa, or the singing-girl, and *Maqāmāt* women usually appear unveiled. All these portrayals of women are the creation of individual artists who did not necessarily heed the text. In the bustling, public, urban settings, the characters are all male. When Abū Zayd's wife's face is uncovered before *qāḍīs*, it is likely that this was interpreted by the painter as a device to elicit sympathy and upset the *qāḍī*'s equilibrium for financial gain and a quick exit.

It is perhaps significant that when the two most finely drawn, impeccable female characters appear in a 'plot within a plot' scenario in the 5th and 18th tales (Illust. 15, Plate 18), they are highly idealized figments of Abū Zayd's imagination. First, we meet the virtuous deserted wife with a famous Arab name, coping admirably on her own with a young son and an example for all. She conforms to two further Islamic attitudes to women, that of women's spiritual superiority and the Arab poets' concept of womankind. Second, we have the theme of woman as costly commodity and sound investment, in the portrait of the highly educated young slave-girl musician of whom Abū Zayd is enamoured. It could be argued that the rigid seclusion of high-born and bourgeois women in the 'Abbāsid period gave slave-girls an enhanced social cachet as possessions which could be proudly paraded before one's peers.

Women are illustrated in several manuscripts in 14 of the tales. They are mentioned in 9 stories, including 4 where they act as Abū Zayd's accomplices, and they form part of a larger genre scene in 5 tales, although they are not specifically referred to. Further, they are crucial to the plots of 2 other tales, as flights of fancy on Abū Zayd's part.

The Virtuous Wife

Maqāma 5, which is set in Kūfa, provides yet another excuse for Abū Zayd to exercise all his powers of imagination. One evening, 'when the gloom of night had thus drawn its curtain', al-Ḥārith and a group of companions, 'who had been nourished on the milk of eloquence', heard a knock at the door. A stranger who sought hospitality so intrigued the party 'by the sweetness of his language and delivery' that they invited him in; a candle was lit and revealed Abū Zayd. In a 'tale within a tale' format, Abū Zayd recounted an earlier occasion when he unsuccessfully sought hospitality. The child who answered the door told him that his father, 'one of the nobles of Sarūj and Ghassān', had deserted his mother when she was pregnant and they were now very poor.

Al-Wāsiṭī's second illustration correctly illustrates Abū Zayd's arrival at the house, while the young boy recites the following verses, which appear in four lines above the illustration. The lad mentions Abraham, who is credited with

15. The deserted wife and child.

ordaining the rites of hospitality, but explains apologetically that all he can offer is good conversation and a bed:

> 'For how should we to guests impart a meal, while thus the pangs of want our slumber steal, or bounty toward the indigent display, while hunger thus consumes our bones away? How seems to thee my offer? Speak and say!'

Abū Zayd's reply, and the child's response, which comprise the two lines below the miniature, read:

> [And I replied] 'What can I do with an empty house, and a host who is himself thus utterly destitute? But what is thy name, boy, for thy intelligence charms me?' [He replied] 'My name is Zayd, and I was reared at Fayd, and I came to this town yesterday with my kindred of the Banū 'Abs.' And I said, 'Give me [yet further explanation].'[1]

Abū Zayd realizes immediately that he has arrived at the house of his erstwhile wife. He is delighted that this child, his son, has inherited all his powers of eloquence. The little boy is well dressed in outdoor clothing which is identical in style to that of an adult male. In an indoors genre scene, he is overdressed.

Abū Zayd's wife sits spinning beneath an elaborate, pale blue cusped archway. This arch is decorated with a type of loose floral arrangement. At the centre of each spandrel there is a large golden rosette or sun motif of the sort found in Qur'āns to mark the pause (*juz'*) when reading. A decorative pair of heavy brocade curtains is draped above the spinner; they feature a gold vegetal design on a dark field. They may have been manufactured at Wāsiṭ, which produced the best type of wall and window curtains, as well as tapestry-woven carpets.[2]

The woman sits on a shallow brick dais, covered by a dark rug with a pearl roundel design at the edge of the border. A lighter gold-coloured drape has been thrown over the rug, and its folds are sharply delineated. However, it does not look like a tapestry-woven carpet or a conventional woven rug, as it has the look and texture of clothing fabric and suggests a degree of opulence.

The commodious house has a pyramid-shaped roof 'dome'; this may be made from woven matting which could be rolled back. If the material is matting, it is likely that the house is in an area of low rainfall. There is a similar domestic roof on al-Wāsiṭī's merchant's house in Sinjār in *Maqāma* 18. Above the entrance portal is a three-tiered crenellation of geometric form which may be cut brick or terracotta. The three-tiered dome (*mīl*) with clerestory windows is identical to that depicted by the painter in *Maqāma* 50, where the 'dome' slides back on wheels and there is, in addition, a pair of roof wind-vents. Al-Wāsiṭī has also included a pair of handsome honeycomb (*muqarnas*) domes on the palace on the exotic island where the childbirth scene is enacted. A similar smaller dome, without lights, occurs on the house in BN 6094 in this tale of the wife and child.

Honeycomb elements of varying shapes and purposes are found throughout the Islamic world. The late 'Abbāsid mausoleum of Sitt Zubayda in Baghdad is famous for its conical brick *muqarnas* dome, while the tomb of Imām Yaḥya in Mosul, built in 1229, features an interior *muqarnas* dome.[3] Iraqi *muqarnas* domes of the period were executed in brick or stone and of geometric form. In Syria and Egypt the motif was generally carved in stone or wood. An early thirteenth-century example of *muqarnas* work embellished the portal to the Damascus citadel, and the porch of the Ẓāhiriyya *madrasa* in Damascus was similarly decorated.

Such domes were highly visible elements of the architectural landscape of the period. In this instance, the dome suggests a vault over a long corridor. The portrayal of the house is surprising, considering the circumstances of the poor deserted wife and child, and it is unlikely that a lone woman with a young son acting as 'man of the house' would really have considered offering shelter to a male stranger.

A similar red wooden roof balustrade occured in this manuscript, in the school. On the spinner's right there is a storage niche containing two tapered stemmed vessels, which are apparently of decorated glass; this niche also includes a large metal candle stand on a pedestal foot, similar in type to those in the Dioscorides *De Materia Medica*.[4] Although the text requires a lighted candle, and indeed the other manuscripts stress the light, al-Wāsiṭī has deliberately omitted it. The explanation is that flames, particularly a lighted fire, are Arabic metaphors for hospitality. In *Maqāma* 48, for example, Abū Zayd tells his audience of a time when 'my flint refused to give sparks', that is, when he was 'indigent and unable to be bountiful'. Later in the same speech, he makes a well-known allusion to hospitality and fire. The empty candlestick here is thus a metaphor for the lack of hospitality on offer.

Open niches or built-in storage cupboards for household utensils were fairly common in the Islamic world. These might be decorated, as in our example, where it is not clear whether they are of terracotta or carved wood. Above this niche and the entrance at which Abū Zayd stands are large panels, presumably made of wood. They are deeply cut and bevelled with an ogee design and a repetition of the heart-shaped leaf motifs which commonly occurred elsewhere. Decorative terracotta plaques are inset; these were affixed with plaster, applied only to the back, and there are no visible joints. The use of such terracotta ornamentation was centred in Baghdad in Saljūq times.

This structure seems to be the reception hall of the house and adjoining vestibules. Similar tripartite structures for houses appear elsewhere in the *Maqāmāt*, and they may be an accurate rendition of the houses of the bourgeoisie in the medieval Arab world. A document in the Cairo *Geniza* describes a reception hall in a well-to-do family home in Fusṭāṭ in the following terms:

> One reception hall is long; its walls are of marble and it has two passages panelled with carved wood, each of which has a door leading to an adjacent 'cabinet' [in Arabic *kumm*, literally a sleeve], thus the reception hall has two cabinets attached to it, very much like the Roman house.[5]

Such a wealth of architectural detail in no way overshadows Abū Zayd's wife in her central role as a spinner. This is emphasized by her large size in comparison with the slight figures of Abū Zayd and the child, and also by her very dark robe which one would reasonably expect to have been light, flowing and comfortable in the privacy of her home. Spinners held the distaff in the left hand, or under the left arm, or fastened in a girdle. The fibres were twisted or drawn out with the right hand and then attached to the spindle. The spindle was then revolved rapidly, its speed controlled by a small wheel. Abū Zayd's wife also spins in the St Petersburg manuscript, where the position of the wheel and the distaff bear out the standard use of the implements.

The Prophet said:

> Sitting for an hour employed with the distaff is better for women than a year's worship; and for every piece of cloth woven of the thread spun by them, they shall receive the reward of a martyr.

The Prophet's wife 'Ā'isha said:

> Tell the women what I say: There is no woman who spins until she hath clothed herself but all the angels in the Seven Heavens pray for forgiveness of her sins; and she will go forth from her grave on the day of judgment wearing a robe of Paradise and with a veil upon her head.

Abū Zayd's wife is aptly called Barra, which is a celebrated and honoured woman's name among the Arabs. Another Barra was an ancestress of the Quraysh, to whom the Prophet's clan was affiliated. Abū Zayd seeks to imply that his wife is of noble birth, and thus a commodious house is in keeping with her status. Young Fayd has mentioned his kinsmen, the famous Banū 'Abs. The implication must be that Abū Zayd, too, is of very good lineage. However, one is immediately struck by the incongruity between the tenor of the child's speech and al-Wāsiṭī's elaborate miniature. There is certainly an emphasis on the successful struggle of a deserted woman to bring up and educate a son, but there is surely an element of humour and irony on the part of the artist.

This idea of women being at the centre of the home finds parallels elsewhere in the Near East. In the Jewish tradition, for example, spinning is among the virtues of the celebrated Old Testament 'woman of worth', whose price is 'far above rubies', in the 31st chapter of the *Book of Proverbs*. One wonders why Abū Zayd's intelligent audience do not ask why he deserted such an obvious treasure. They are clearly mesmerized by his eloquence.

The twin themes of spinning and virtue also appear in the Annunciation scene in al-Bīrūnī's later *Chronology of Ancient Peoples* manuscript in Edinburgh, where Mary is shown with a distaff. Both Mary and al-Wāsiṭī's Barra have extremely broad, oriental, non-Semitic faces; despite the illustrious Arab name, Abū Zayd's wife is patently not an Arab and she may have been appropriated from elsewhere. Annunciation scenes depict Mary spinning, and spinning women also appear in genre scenes in Persian manuscripts. Throughout the ages, women and spinning have been closely associated through myth with the fate of mankind, and the great goddesses became mistresses of the destinies they created according to their will. Both the Hittite goddess Ishtar and the Syrian goddess Atargatis carried distaffs.[6] Abū Zayd's wife is portrayed as a woman who is firmly in control of the destiny of herself and her child, and who has no need of the husband who has deserted her. It should come as no surprise to the reader that she is a figment of Abū Zayd's imagination.

Childbirth

The 39th tale finds al-Ḥārith and Abū Zayd taking refuge during a storm on an island in the Arabian Gulf, while they are *en route* from Ṣuḥār in Oman to an unspecified destination. In spite of the dangers of a sea voyage, al-Ḥārith finds

16. A complicated delivery in the palace.

it preferable on this occasion to an overland route, as he is encumbered by a large quantity of merchandise. The pair decide to leave the ship and seek provisions on land. In due course they arrive at a large palace, whose owner is described by one of his slaves as 'the lord [*shāh*] of this castle . . . the pole-star of this place, and the *shāh* of this territory'. Al-Ḥarīrī may have used the Persian term *shāh* in order to conjure up an image of the mysterious East, for towards the end of the tale the ruler is merely referred to in Arabic as the *wālī*. The *shāh* and his household are distraught at the possible outcome of his pregnant wife's complicated delivery.

Al-Wāsiṭī shows a bold interior view of the palace; strictly speaking, the illustration should have come before this juncture, for the text clearly indicates that the birth has already taken place. The Arabic above and below the miniature reads:

and our voyage to Oman became easy. Abū Zayd was contented with the largesse received and prepared for departure; the *wālī*, however, would not allow him to move after he had experienced his blessing, but bade him enrol in his household so that his hand might make free with his treasures.

The ruler's wife is 'labouring in the throes of a difficult childbirth'. Help is at hand, however, for Abū Zayd advises a sorrowing retainer, 'Be still, O such a one, and of good cheer, and receive news of joy and proclaim them, for I possess a spell for childbirth, the fame of which is spread abroad amongst mankind.' We find Abū Zayd writing his spell in a small ante-room at the top of the picture. There are two anomalies here in relation to the text: he is not in 'tattered garments', nor is he writing on a piece of ambergris (*zabad baḥrī*). Al-Wāsiṭī has evidently modelled Abū Zayd on a scribal figure. This might restore his credibility in the eyes of the reader, who will remember that his earlier eloquent 'spell for travellers' for their safe voyage had proved totally ineffective.

Scribes and secretaries appear elsewhere in thirteenth-century Iraqi manuscripts; in the St Petersburg *Maqāmāt*, for example, there is a scribe in the court at Ṣa'da. Munkar and Nakīr, the two 'recording angels', can be seen busily engaged in writing down someone's deeds or misdeeds in the Munich version of al-Qazwīnī's *Wonders of Creation ['Ajā'ib al-makhlūqāt]*, from Wāsiṭ. Scribes are also found in the Istanbul *Epistles of the Sincere Brethren.*[7] Abū Zayd ostentatiously writes out this second spell in a saffron solution; this should be tied to the woman's thigh with a shred of silk after perfuming it with ambergris, in accordance with the text and Arab practice. Some of the earliest Islamic medical manuscripts established the connection between medicine and the occult. For example, according to al-Ṭabarī's mid-ninth-century *Paradise of Wisdom*, 'If you put a magnetic stone into the hand of a woman in labour, it will help her in a difficult birth.' This seems to be a reiteration of a recommendation by Hippocrates, who mentioned a lodestone, and sympathetic remedies were especially associated with midwifery. Several further palliatives are found in the extensive tenth-century work, the *Book on Pregnancy and the Care of Infants [Kitāb al-ḥabālā wa al-aṭfāl]*, by al-Baladī. For example, al-Baladī recommends the following: 'A snake-skin wound around the hips of the woman accelerates the birth.'[8] This appears to have a connection with ophiomancy, or divination by means of snakes, which is mentioned in Parsi-Persian omen calendars dating from the late sixteenth and early seventeenth centuries. Abū Zayd's instruction, therefore, seems to be entirely appropriate in the context.

A painting in the Turcoman style in BL 3299, the *Key of the Eminent Poets [Miftaḥ al-fuḍalā']*, probably dating from the early sixteenth century, shows a talisman being prepared with saffron.[9] Abū Zayd cautions that no menstruating woman (*ḥā'id*) should touch the amulet. He seeks to emphasize his power by bestowing religious sanction on his spell in his allusion to the proscription on menstruating women touching the Holy Qur'ān, since they are in a ritually impure state.

Al-Ḥārith sits at the top right-hand side of the composition, consulting his astrolabe on three matters: questions (*masā'il*) concerning the soon-to-be-born child; the selection of a propitious moment for the midwife to deliver the baby; and the foretelling of the baby's future. Astrolabes were in use before the advent of Islam. They were of three kinds, of which the flat type in the illustration (known as *saṭḥī* or *musaṭṭaḥ*) was the most common. Al-Ḥārith's model appears to be correct in size, material (brass) and components, if one compares a twelfth-century Saljūq example, a thirteenth-century Andalusian model and a thirteenth-century Egyptian type.[10] All somewhat wider than a handspan, they were obviously suspended from a long cord (*'ilāqa*) fixed to the heavy ring (*'urw* or *ḥabb*) at the top. Suspension would protect the intricate moving parts, namely the revolving dials and plates on the front and two clock-type hands on the reverse. Each ring was engraved with symbols and Arabic letters. The outer rim (*ḥajra* or *ṭawq*), which could be rotated, had gradations from 0° to 360°; this allowed calculations involving the earth and the planets. Presumably all these components moved in conjunction with each other, after a fixed point had been chosen as the basis of the calculation.

Hippocrates was of the opinion that, 'Astronomy does not contribute the smallest part to medicine, but the greatest one, indeed.' He imposed three tasks upon the physician: 'Declaring the past, diagnosing the present, foretelling the future.'[11] However, the first and second points brought the doctor (and the third point brought the astrologer) into conflict with the Sharī'a: the Hellenistic concept of cause and effect seemed to pose a danger to the concept of Divine Providence.

The 'intellectual' view of medicine that is enacted here on the upper storey of the palace is reinforced by the term used for a physician (*ḥakīm*), with its connotations of wisdom. Visual confirmation of this is found as an annotation in a Paris *Kalīla wa Dimna* tale, where *al-ḥakīm* is written above the figure of the doctor who has been summoned by the king to heal the sick princess. Further evidence of the perception of the intellectual quality of medicine occurs in the Paris *Book of Antidotes* dated 1199, where the physician is invariably shown seated with a book and a pupil, or in the pensive pose of a philosopher, almost as if to confirm that the messy business of touching the patient is beneath his dignity.[12]

The inclusion of Abū Zayd and al-Ḥārith thus occupied in the context of a palace reflects an account by Yūsuf ibn Ibrāhīm. According to this astronomical calculator, in the early Islamic period 'Umm Ja'far had a special conference room in her palace reserved for astronomical calculators and physicians—there is a clear inference of the interdependence of medicine and astrology, via astronomy. The seventh Īl-Khān Ghāzān Maḥmūd, under whom Islam was finally recognized as the state religion of the Īl-Khānate was advised by the *amīrs*:

> If the king wishes events to take place according to his desires, he must become Muslim, for in the stars and in the ordinances and biographies of the *shaykhs* it is said that in the year 694 [21 November 1294–9 November 1295] a Muslim king will ascend the throne.

A further royal connection with astrology is demonstrated in the early fifteenth-century Fārsī illustrated horoscope of Iskandar Sultan.[13]

The tenth-century physician al-Qurṭubī lists three potential threats to a safe delivery: from the mother, from the foetus or from external factors. In this tale, the obesity of the mother would surely count as an 'external factor'. Part II of al-Ṭabarī's *Paradise of Wisdom* covers pregnancy, while al-Rāzī's ninth-century encyclopedic *Comprehensive Book [al-Ḥāwī]* cites the clinical case of a pregnant woman who was 'extremely fat' and suffered paralysis on delivery (and subsequently epilepsy).[14] It is not clear to the lay person whether the woman's being overweight had caused these problems.

No obstetrical instruments appear in the miniature, although they were available in the East, but possibly not the West, at that time; their use was perhaps outside the expertise of a midwife. The midwife's head is covered in a white wrap—al-Qurṭubī's medical treatise, in the section on midwifery, does not specifically recommend this. This scarf is quite different from the head-coverings worn by the two attendants in saffron robes; it sets the midwife apart and might represent her 'badge of office'.

The female figure beside the Prophet's mother in the miniature of the birth of Muḥammad in the Edinburgh *Universal History* also wears a distinctive white headdress. Here it is worth quoting from al-Tha'ālibī's *Book of Curious and Entertaining Information*, where al-Ṣūlī cites some elders' comments on midwives in Aḥwāz. The midwives reported that they had frequently delivered infants suffering from a fever at birth. This fact was apparently well-known to midwives and discussed by them.[15] It suggests that they did not work in isolation and there may have been some form of regulation and a midwives' 'guild'. They may well have adopted some type of 'uniform' which identified them, although they were probably viewed as marginal in a society which had proscriptions regarding blood and menstruation. Hence the taboos and mystique surrounding childbirth.

The young girl at the left is bringing in a brass brazier. This has a specific function: it indicates that the woman is about to be delivered, since it was the practice to fumigate the genital area with the powerful medicaments of yellow sulphur, henna and bitumen after the extraction of the placenta. This attendant has a long piece of thread or string in her right hand, to tie the ambergris to the woman's thigh in fulfilment of both textual requirements and current practice. The foot of the kneeling attendant and the hands of the girl standing at the right-hand side are monumental in scale and and may have been modelled on statues. The mother wears a heavy gold necklace, gold bracelets and gold anklets and her immediate attendant also wears gold anklets, whereas the two girls in

16. The uninvited guest at an al fresco gathering.

17. *Abū Zayd's wife before a miserly judge.*

18. Abū Zayd's slave-girl 'unrivalled in perfection'.

19. Famished travellers enjoy bedouin hospitality.

20. A camel is slaughtered for the honoured guests.

saffron robes do not. This might imply a mother and daughter relationship, with the midwife and her attendants being relegated to a subservient role.

The miniature confirms the recommendation by early physicians that the midwife should be assisted by three women: one at the right-hand side; one at the left-hand side; and one behind, to support her back and to allow the pregnant woman to lean back, if necessary.[16] Three women stand behind the Prophet's mother in the Edinburgh *Universal History*, but there is also another woman there, beside the angel holding the child. The midwife was obliged to be seated, and the term 'seat of the midwife' appears in the text of the preceding *Maqāma* to indicate close proximity. This would allow her to use her hand after the breaking of the waters to facilitate the baby's exit 'by the grace of God'. Al-Qurṭubī prescribes that the midwife should have short nails;[17] such a recommendation would be to prevent uterine damage and the introduction of infection.

The midwife's outstretched right leg, as illustrated, would both assist the mother in pushing the baby out of the womb and cushion the newborn infant; the woman has pushed her clothing up her thigh and out of the way for obvious reasons. Al-Qurṭubī also instructs the midwife to strap up the mother well, and then make her sit down in the place prepared for the birth. This practice has been adopted, for one can clearly see a low red stool and two bands, outlined in light grey or white, around the mother's upper abdomen. These acted to control the mother's breathing and thus help her to push the child out.

Al-Wāsiṭī's illustration is, therefore, technically correct on a number of key points, all of which imply a detailed knowledge of current obstetrical practices on his part. It is difficult to say whether this sprang from contemporary documentary or illustrated evidence, or common knowledge of these practices in society in general, but the possibility of current illustrated medical manuscripts being available to the artist cannot be precluded. In addition to the Greek sciences, Indian works were also known to Muslim scholars in the Islamic sciences, and Mesopotamian material occurred in Sanskrit works and in South Indian traditions.[18] The women in the birth scene seem to be Indian and the ruler is not Semitic.

Mother and infant scenes appear elsewhere, but in less explicit form, and certainly not in a fully frontal pose, for example the representation of a Caesarian section in the early fourteenth-century al-Bīrūnī's *Chronology of Ancient Peoples* in Edinburgh. The nativity scene in the *Universal History* manuscript shows the Prophet and Amīna his mother, though in such a context it is necessarily a restrained image and the fully clothed mother is covered in bedclothes. The late fourteenth-century copy of the Paris *Wonders of Creation* shows Tibetans adoring a newborn child being cradled by a very large clothed woman. Finally, a miniature of the birth of Rustam, executed in *c.* 1450, shows a fully dressed woman on a type of day-bed.[19] Four women in white shoulder-length headdresses attend her; there is a man, presumably a doctor, in attendance and another female attendant, both of whom have the cloth or napkin known as *mandīl*.

One curious point which has been noted in medical manuscript illustrations is the lack of distress suffered by the patients, and their compliance with the medical attendants; in the days before general anaesthesia, this is well-nigh incredible. However, the availability and use of opiates in other contexts has been discussed, and it is likely that drugs of some kind were administered. Perhaps it is indicative of the mystique created by medical practitioners and the hedging-in of practices associated with taboos. The magical properties of Abū Zayd's ambergris in the text appear to be efficacious and his reputation is vindicated—al-Baladī said of the onyx to be wrapped in the woman's hair, 'Even if it is placed near her, it will drive away all pains.' Nevertheless, no talismans appear in the fifteenth-century illustrations of a man having his haemorrhoids cauterized or of another man having a dislocated hip set with some sort of implement over the top of his hips, which was presumably tightened from underneath.[20] This is surely one more confirmation of the prevalence of secrecy, superstition and occult practices with particular regard to women, blood and ritual impurity.

Illustrations in these other manuscripts are purely didactic in function, yet the artists are careful not to overstep the bounds of propriety: the man with the dislocated hip is naked, but his genitalia are not shown, while the man with haemorrhoids is shown clothed and in profile, with his robe pushed up over his buttocks. These examples serve to emphasize how shocking al-Wāsiṭī's birth scene would be in a book intended for the non-medical Muslim reader. Thus it is quite possible that the scene represents an iconographic borrowing from foreign sources and its adaptation to an Arab milieu. The full frontal pose itself, although technically correct, is reminiscent of figures in anatomical treatises. Al-Wāsiṭī has, however, mitigated the potentially shocking aspect of such a pose for his readers by depicting an unnaturally gross and obviously non-Arab woman. There is nothing titillating about her.

The man of the house, albeit a ruler, has necessarily been relegated to a secondary, if central, position in the illustration but even he is excluded from the women's quarters at this time. Like his wife, he is shown frontally; this pose, as well as the stillness of the other characters, is characteristic of Persian royal iconography. The man's face is gaunt and long, an impression reinforced by the halo. His dark skin, long black beard and long hair with a topknot all suggest an Indian origin.

An almost identical face, but inclined slightly to the right, occurs in the portrait of an enthroned figure on a pointed cushion in the Dioscorides *De Materia Medica*.[21] Significantly, perhaps, he is a doctor, which seems to confirm an Indian school of medical material that drew on and adapted Persian iconography. However, the *shāh* in our illustration sits on a pointed pink bolster in the pose of an Eastern holy man, not a Persian ruler. His ankles, crossed right over left, are much lighter in skin tone than the rest of his body. He is sitting in the natural posture of ease from Turkish iconography which had been adopted in several lands, including India.[22]

The throne has the pointed ends found elsewhere in *Maqāmāt* manuscripts, with elaborate corners that look like book-ends. However, its cut-away sides are unusual in that the other thrones have straight, swept-up sides, whereas in this painting the throne resembles that of a fifth-century Buddhist statue from a temple of Tun-Huang. The pale blue background in the illustration has an unusual fleur-de-lis motif with a darker, feathered edging. Behind the throne is a cut-off circular drapery resembling the curtains below; and the large pearl roundel motif of its border, which is also found on the bolster, suggests a Sāsānian influence. Like the halo, it acts as a frame, reflects the outline of the domes and ties the composition together. The circular backcloth recalls the circular motif of a bronze plaque representing a Buddha from the seventh/eighth century at Aq-bešim in Yeti-su. It is also echoed in a ruler portrait on an early twelfth-century enamelled dish from Mesopotamia, now in Innsbruck.[23] The *shāh* is wearing non-Arab clothing, although his body-wrap bears a *ṭirāz* band. Two youthful attendants replace the flying genies or angels who usually appear in Islamic iconography, and they have long, uncovered hair like their master.

The whole architectural setting is very detailed, its format resembling the artist's tavern in 'Āna that is discussed in Chapter 7 (Illust. 18). The two-storey building consists of a central reception room on each floor and a side chamber on either side. This must be seen as the interior of the two-storeyed palace with an iron door depicted by al-Wāsiṭī earlier in the tale. It is obviously a commodious structure, as the domes have clerestory windows like those in the public bath-house (*ḥammām*). The splendid pair of drapes are in a heavy brocade with a golden floral scroll pattern; similar vegetal whorls have been noted elsewhere in a variety of different media. We have already seen lavish curtains in the house of Barra, the 'poor' deserted wife, and we know that splendid drapes were manufactured locally at Wāsiṭ.

A yellow brick floor occurs elsewhere in this manuscript and a similar type was noted in the St Petersburg work. The red carved wooden rail below the ruler, which may be a platform, could be of teak (*sāj*). According to al-Jāḥiẓ, al-Hamadhānī and others, teak was the best wood for doors, windows and roofs, and lumber from East Africa was imported into the Arabian Gulf.[24] The doorway is decorated with stucco or marble spandrels, and a small plaque in the same material appears above the narrow ante-rooms. These plaques are carved or moulded in relief and set in wood, and they could be decorative ventilation grilles. Stucco decoration featured widely in house and palace decoration in Sāmarrā at an earlier period, where it was used for dado, window and door ornamentation, frame decoration, window lattices and *miḥrābs*, among other things. Heart-shapes recur in al-Wāsiṭī's birth scene on the two small plaques above the ground-floor ante-rooms, and on the carved red wooden frieze above Abū Zayd and al-Ḥārith. They also appear on stucco-work in a similar position in the saintly Barra's house (Illust. 15). The central part of the upper storey of the palace carries a carved or moulded crenellated frieze, variations of which occur elsewhere in al-Wāsiṭī's work.

The architecture of the palace therefore appears to be an accurate reflection of contemporary style and construction, and the birth scene, which is unique in *Maqāmāt* illustrations, reveals a detailed knowledge of current midwifery practices. References to the recourse to the occult on the part of both author and artist are substantiated by source material. Diverse iconographic and stylistic influences have also played their part in this remarkable scene.

Women and the Law

Maqāma 9 is set in Alexandria, where the prudent al-Ḥārith saw fit to introduce himself and pay his respects to the local *qāḍī* in order to strengthen his case in the event of litigation in his business affairs. While he was attending court one evening and the *qāḍī* was about to distribute alms to the needy, a woman, who was dragging along an 'ill-conditioned old man', entered and addressed the *qāḍī*.

In al-Wāsiṭī's painting, there is a commentary on the text written in red in zigzag fashion down the left-hand side of the folio. The three lines of prose text above the miniature and the two lines of verse below it indicate that the illustration is out of place in the text. Strictly speaking, it should appear earlier as the text reads: 'Whereupon the *qāḍī* sent after him one of his trusty servants, and commanded him to observe his proceedings: but it was not long before he came back in haste, and returned laughing immoderately.' (The servant explained that he had seen the old man gleefully singing and dancing because of the success of his deception. The *qāḍī* took it in good part and laughed so much that his hat fell off.) It should be noted here that the text gives *dānniyya* for 'hat', because it resembles the long, tapering wine-jar (*dānn*). The thirteenth- and fourteenth-century *Maqāmāt* manuscripts, as has been pointed out, invariably show the *qāḍī* wearing a head-shawl over a turban, unless he is portrayed as a governor, where he does not, in any case, wear a *dānniyya*. Fashions appear to have changed between the time that the manuscript was written in the twelfth century and illustrated in the thirteenth.

Abū Zayd's wife has unsuccessfully petitioned the *qāḍī* for restitution for herself and her child, who is 'feeble as a lath'. She maintains that her husband is a malingerer who has dissipated the proceeds of the dowry (*mahr*) he made over to her for her exclusive use and benefit, in accordance with the Sharī'a. The Muslim dowry thus differs from practices elsewhere, where it is regarded as a 'bride price' payable to the bride's parents. The actual amount of the *mahr* is not prescribed by law, but depends on an agreement between the two parties. In Islam, the wife forfeits her right to her dowry if four independent witnesses testify that she has been guilty of immorality;[25] in practice, such a charge is exceedingly difficult to prove. Abū Zayd's eloquent counter-claim and impassioned plea to 'decide with justice, or to wrong incline' results in the pair receiving money from the *qāḍī*, who has urged conciliation in conformity with

17. A woman and an 'ill-conditioned old man'.

the Qur'ānic prescription in *sūra* 4.

Abū Zayd's wife is unveiled; it was, apparently, acceptable for women's faces to be uncovered in public in times of distress, and she doubtless dresses in this way so as to appear more vulnerable and to elicit sympathy. She wears a fine, long outer robe with gold edging; this is of a smokey-grey hue, and it conforms in description to what al-Washshā' had outlined in the tenth century as being the fashionable, smokey-grey coloured wrap (*ghilāla dukhāniyya*). Underneath she wears a red patterned shift with gold braid around the hem. It should be remembered that, although the same names may appear for clothing in different parts of the Islamic world, the garments themselves might vary according to the material used, and so on. Ashtor, in the Egyptian context, describes the *izār* as a 'figure-enveloping wrap' and a 'ubiquitous garment' which is seldom mentioned in Hebrew documents. A Jewish marriage contract written in 1083 prices an *izār* at 1¼ *dīnārs*.

The *thawb*, which is still common today, was an ample, enveloping robe with wide sleeves, worn by both men and women. In the first third of the twelfth century a half-silk (*mulḥam*) *thawb* cost ¾ *dīnār*, while a fine linen *thawb* of Dabīqī fabric cost 10 *dīnārs* in 1134. Ashtor describes the *ridā'* as 'an ample cloak with which women covered themselves when going out of the house'. He says that in 1134 a half-*ridā'* could be purchased for 3 *dīnārs*, while a muslin one, which was presumably full-size, cost 2½ *dīnārs* in 1115.[26]

Abū Zayd's wife's soft leather ankle-boots (*khifāf*) have an inset of a different colour at the side, and pointed toes; thus it is possible that they are the *khifāf zaniyya*, which description emphasizes their narrowness. One might have expected her to appear in her oldest clothes, but she tells the *qāḍī*, 'Now when I went away with him, I had rich apparel and household effects, aye, and superfluities [plumage] with me.' She seeks to impress upon the *qāḍī* that she was a woman of some style and substance who has fallen on hard times through no fault of her own.

The text describes Abū Zayd's wife as 'the mother of children', 'a woman of enticing beauty', and al-Wāsiṭī has portrayed her as a handsome, mature woman, typical of the amply built females who appear throughout his miniatures. The women he painted may have worn the undergarment called *ghilāla*, described by the thirteenth-century lexicographer Ṣāghānī as 'a piece of cloth with which a woman makes her posterior [to appear] large, binding it upon her hinderpart, beneath her waist-wrapper'. It should be noted that this definition varies from the tenth-century description which was given earlier.

The *qāḍī*'s two outstretched fingers are a placatory gesture, but Abū Zayd's wife's eloquent hand gestures show that she is far from happy with his legal opinion (*fatwa*) that Abū Zayd 'ought to be acquitted from all blame'. Nor is she pleased at the *qāḍī*'s admonishing her to 'return to the retirement of thy home, and pardon the husband of thy youth; and cease from thy sad complaining'. She has no intention of submitting to the will of her lord, as she has been exhorted to do. The seclusion of women in Baghdad appears to have been an 'Abbāsid innovation. According to Raḥmatallāh, it was 'a Persian or Turkish import into Arabic society'[27] and the *ḥarīm* therefore represented a new social order. The freedom which women had enjoyed in the early days of Islam was largely lost, the major change being the veiling of women. Al-Khaṭīb, writing in the eleventh century, cannot have rated women very highly, for he includes the biographies of only 29 women in a period spanning 300 years.

Ibn Munqidh tells how his mother acted during an emergency when no male family members were present. She distributed weapons to those capable of fighting and she sat her daughter beside the balcony of the castle of Shayzar. She was even prepared to throw her daughter over the edge, rather than have her fall into the hands of the Ismā'īlī, 'peasants and ravishers'.[28]

Miskawayh's *The Experiences of the Nations* describes Ḥusn, the mother-in-law of Abū Aḥmad al-Faḍl ibn 'Abd al-Raḥmān of Shīrāz, as 'strong-minded, astute and intellectual'. She spoke both Persian and Arabic and was all-powerful as stewardess at the court of al-Mustakfī, having been instrumental in his appointment on the deposing of al-Muttaqī. The theme of a woman boldly seeking justice from a ruler recurs in a Persian illustrated manuscript in the British Museum which was copied at Baghdad in 1396: here an old woman seeking redress for her wrongs fearlessly confronts the Saljūq Sultan Mālikshāh, who ruled from 1072 to 1092. This, in turn, is derived from an illustration in Niẓāmī's *Treasury of Secrets [Makhzan al-asrār]* where the king is the Saljūq ruler Sanjar, who reigned from 1117 to 1157.[29] There is a recurrent theme of strong women confronting males in authority running through Islamic literature.

A somewhat discomfited al-Ḥārith sits at the right-hand side with his hand to his mouth, pondering the moral dilemma of whether or not he should reveal his friend's duplicity to the *qāḍī* with whom he has just ingratiated himself. Al-Ḥārith knows that his friend has fallen well short of al-Ghazālī's guidelines for the witness who appears before a *qāḍī*:

> [A witness should] feel his responsibility for telling the truth, bear himself with modesty and keep in mind his religious duty [that is, conduct himself as a man of piety and faith]. He should not commit perjury, but should only bear testimony to that of which he is sure, guarding himself against error through forgetfulness, and arguing as little as possible with the *qāḍī*.[30]

Although the witness's hand-to-mouth gesture seems to express this well, it is in fact a motif well-known in classical antiquity and adopted in Byzantine art, for example in biblical painting, and appropriated by Muslim painters. One should note the marked similarities (the Semitic features, for example, and the turbans worn to the back of the head) between this and other contemporary Arab miniatures and certain Syrian gospel illustrations. In terms of iconography and human types, these similarities evolved within Islamic painting. Vestiges of the influence of the earlier Baghdad school of painting persisted until the end of the thirteenth century.[31]

Abū Zayd bows obsequiously and kisses the *qāḍī*'s hand in thanks for the alms he has received and for the considered judgment of his marital plight. In the fourteenth-century Vienna *Maqāmāt*, Abū Zayd is shown in mirror image, bowing deeply from the waist before a *qāḍī* in *Maqāma* 8; he, too, may be about to kiss the *qāḍī*'s hand. A contemporary example of Mosul metalwork, the 'Blacas ewer', captures exactly al-Wāsiṭī's genre flavour, and its lowly subject bears a close resemblance to Abū Zayd; this suggests the influence of 'types'. The ewer scene is also a mirror image of that in the manuscript version but its figure of authority is a prince. A rather more formal version of the theme of kissing the hand of a prince is seen on another ewer from Mosul, in the Walters Art Gallery, Baltimore, and it is possible that such signs of obeisance are unique to Mesopotamian metalwork. These metalwork scenes seem also to be related to the frontispiece of Vol. XI of the Cairo *Book of Songs* dated 1217.[32] There is undoubtedly an element of satire in the Abū Zayd portrait, for he has successfully duped the *qāḍī*, and then he kisses his left hand. It is unthinkable that Abū Zayd would do such a thing because the left hand is considered ritually impure—both scenes on the above-mentioned ewers involve the kissing of the right hand. The full implication of al-Wāsiṭī's painting would be well understood by, and cause great merriment among, his literate bourgeois audience. In describing how his poverty has enfeebled him in body and mind, Abū Zayd has also used the metaphor, 'My power of stretching out my arm became straitened.' The painter has taken up this reference to Abū Zayd's act of soliciting for money.

There are literary precedents for Abū Zayd's impudence. Ibn Ṭiqṭāqā records how, early in the ninth century, a poet addressed a vizier as follows: 'Money and intelligence enable a man to stand in the courts of the princes; as you see, I possess neither.' The vizier 'Alī ibn 'Īsā recounts how he was petitioned by one Muḥammad ibn Ḥasan, who seized his hand and said:

> 'May I be no descendant of 'Abbās if I let the vizier go before he has signed this paper, or else kiss my hand as I kissed his.' Standing up, I signed the paper, but marvelled at his unmannerliness and impudence.[33]

Perhaps the secret of Abū Zayd's freedom to act in a similarly impertinent manner lies in his ability to make people 'marvel' at him. Having capitalized on this element of surprise, he then makes a hasty retreat. Poets and other entertainers could inspire fear in those in power because of their ability to expose them to public ridicule and undermine their jurisdiction. It was a double-edged sword, however, as a ruler's retribution could be swift and cruel.

This composition is yet another adaptation of the courtly repertoire. On at least three further occasions al-Wāsiṭī seems to elevate Abū Zayd's status in an adaptation of royal iconography. In *Maqāma* 30, for instance, an old man—probably Abū Zayd—is seated on a throne with pointed ends in the beggars' mansion. In the childbirth scene, to give another example, we saw him cast in the role of wise man to the foreign ruler (Illust. 16). However, the number of possible models is limited. Al-Wāsiṭī had another tilt at authority in *Maqāma* 10, where we saw him portray the governor of Raḥba in the worst possible light (Illust. 4). These portraits are gentle forms of satire and never approach a lampoon. This element of adaption from the royal repertoire is also present in other *Maqāmāt* manuscripts.

Servile ceremonies from the old Sāsānian court were adopted by the 'Abbāsid caliphs, whose subjects had to kiss the ground before them. What may be the earliest instance of kissing the ground in the Islamic world involved a drunken jeweller, Ibn al-Jaṣṣāṣ, and Abū al-Ḥusayn ibn Ṭūlūn (Khumarawayh). *The Experiences of the Nations* reports that when Ḥamīd ibn 'Abbās was invested as vizier by al-Muqtadir in the early tenth century, 'He kissed the ground before the caliph.' According to Ibn Khaldūn, 'In the case of higher personages, permission was given either to kiss the caliph's hand or foot or the edge of his robe or *ṭirāz*.' Miskawayh describes how, when Sulaymān ibn Ḥasan was summoned around the year 932 to be appointed as vizier, 'He presented himself in his barge, and was met by the commanders and the people, who kissed his hand.' Ibn Munqidh's *Memoirs* tell how in fourteenth-century Azerbaijan, when the Ashrafīs from all around the districts assembled, he 'bestowed on every one, according to his rank, a favour and special honours. Some had come to kiss the foot of his highness—may his government be perpetuated.' Finally, the memoirs of Abū al-Fidā' recall how, in 1390, 'All the army was mounted and they kissed the ground before him [Sultan al-Mālik al-Nāṣir].' These accounts bear out well Hogarth's assertion that, 'Never has captor more swiftly been captured by his captive than Arabia by Persia.'[34]

The *qāḍī* in al-Wāsiṭī's miniature under discussion is seated on a type of throne draped with a circular rug. He wears a very fine shawl of office over his turban, and his tunic, which is of a heavy, rich material, has extremely wide, red-lined sleeves with brocade at the edge and upper arm. The shawl may well be of a Nīshāpūrī half-silk fabric or it could have come from Kirmān. The *qāḍī's* pointed beard is somewhat longer than the accepted norm of measuring a hand's breadth below the chin, following the example of the Prophet. Such concern with personal appearance is perhaps intended to indicate a foible on the *qāḍī*'s part. Source material confirms that the judiciary tended to be vain. For example, the renowned juriconsult Abū Ḥanīfa, who was both a silk manufacturer and a merchant, paid 400 *dīnārs* for a robe in the eighth century, while the tenth-century vizier 'Alī ibn 'Īsā, himself a model of probity, castigated a *qāḍī* for his extravagant clothing.[35] These points underscore for the reader the extent of Abū Zayd's duplicity and his skill in exploiting the weaknesses of those who, in theory (because of their supposedly superior station in society), should have known better than to be deceived.

The miniature from the BN 6094 version offers a different treatment of the same scene, but Abū Zayd's wife again wears a padded head-dress, which covers the shoulders. Similar head-dresses have been noted in BN 3465 *Kalīla wa Dimna*, a mid- to late-fourteenth-century *Book of Animals [Kitāb al-ḥayawān]* and a mid-fourteenth-century Hebrew *Haggadah* from Barcelona.[36]

Turning now to the 40th tale, al-Ḥārith relates how he has witnessed an altercation between a man and his wife before a miserly *qāḍī*. The relevant caption for the illustration in BN 3929 reads:

> I intended leaving Tabrīz at a time when it was unwholesome [irksome] for high and low, and empty of patrons and men of largesse; and while I was making ready my travelling-gear and foraging for some company on the journey, I encountered there Abū Zayd, the Sarūjī, wrapped up in a cloak and surrounded by females.

There is a parenthetical addition in bold gold Thulūth script down the side of the illustration announcing, 'The picture of Abū Zayd with the women around him' (Plate 17).

Abū Zayd kneels at centre stage before the *qāḍī* to plead his case. This is one instance where the '*qāḍī*' of the text is not shown wearing the head-shawl, and he is probably adapted from a governor; for example, he is very similar in type to the governor of Merv in the BL 1200 *Maqāmāt*. This may indicate that the artist has not read beyond the beginning of the text to establish the scenario, although governors did preside in a judicial function in the higher court for the redress of grievances (*dīwān al-maẓālim*).

The usual youthful attendant stands to the *qāḍī*'s right, wearing a pointed hat. This slightly exotic element is reinforced by the long ends of the *qāḍī*'s costume, which are reminiscent of the Persian ribbon denoting royalty (*patev*). (A similarly attired youth appears later in this manuscript in the 37th tale.) The position of his hands suggests that the lad has been appropriated from the courtly repertoire and that he should be holding up a fly-whisk or fan. Two women stand to the left, and a new item of female clothing appears now, the *naṭāq*, which is mentioned in the text of *Maqāma* 14. It is described by Steingass as 'a kind of body veil, tied by a woman round her waist in such a manner that the upper part hangs down over the lower as far as the knees, the lower reaching down to the feet'.

The woman nearest Abū Zayd must be his wife, for she is gesticulating with her left hand in refutation of his accusations, and she has secured her white *naṭāq* over her left shoulder. This reveals her all-in-one head and shoulder covering (*khimār*), her unveiled face and her calf-length shift. The *khimār* appears to be a modified form of turban and confirms reports of women wearing a headdress wound like a turban which are found elsewhere. A similar heavy headdress is worn by the old woman who is sent out by the king of Syria to find Gulshāh's mother in the Istanbul *Romance of Warqa and Gulshāh* manuscript. Such headgear might account for the very large, round appearance of women's heads in some other *Maqāmāt* illustrations, for example in al-Wāsiṭī's village scene in the 43rd tale (Illust. 13).[37]

Abū Zayd's wife's companion wears a wrap over her shift and she partially covers her face with it. This may indicate her embarrassment or consternation at hearing (especially in male company) the intimate personal details of her friend's marital plight. Her shift has a large, single leaf motif on a striking dark red field. Although neither woman wears trousers, no bare legs can be seen since they both wear dark leather boots. The garment folds suggest a diaphanous material. Similar lightweight garments and boots occur in the same *Romance of Warqa and Gulshāh* manuscript.

The caption and text mention 'women', and it should be borne in mind that, in accordance with the Sharī'a, two female witnesses are regarded as equivalent to one male witness for testifying in court. This would pose no problem for the Muslim reader. Even if this were not so, the nature of Abū Zayd's allegations against his wife deal with conjugal rights; they are extremely personal and scurrilous, and she would doubtless feel in need of encouragement and moral support from a woman companion. Once again, the 'entertainment' value of these tales should be remembered, and the fact that their audience was exclusively male.

Divorce (*ṭalāq*), which Abū Zayd is threatening, is seen as a last resort in Islam. It is likely therefore that Abū Zayd's wife is accompanied by a family member who seeks reconciliation at any cost, in accordance with the prescriptions laid down in *sūra* 2. This would accord with the advice of the *qāḍī* in *Maqāma* 9, who urged her to 'return therefore to the retirement of thy home, and pardon the husband of thy youth'.

Although the miniature lacks the architectural props of the shadow theatre, Grabar's point about the topical and 'scabrous plots' of shadow plays in general, and the important part played in them by women, is relevant in this context. Once more, the lively depictions by this particular artist highlight a possible connection between the subject-matter of al-Ḥarīrī's text, the element of the 'playing out' of his scene, and the immediacy of the shadow play.[38]

Both the *Maqāmāt* discussed here show that women in the thirteenth-century Muslim world were quite capable of successfully pursuing their rights. They are far removed from the stereotyped Western view of veiled, submissive creatures.

The Slave-Girl (Jāriyya)

The most entrancing female *Maqāmāt* portrait appears in BN 3929, in *Maqāma* 18, where we find the young slave-girl described by Abū Zayd as a *jāriyya* (Plate 18). The word *jāriyya* has connotations of 'running about' and, by extension, 'being at someone's beck and call'. Al-Ḥārith related how, on his return journey from Damascus to Baghdad, when he stopped over at Sinjār, he and his travelling companions were invited to a banquet by a merchant. This gave Abū Zayd the opportunity to display his eloquence before an assembly and launch into one of his convoluted tales:

> Now I had a maiden, who was unrivalled in perfection; if she unveiled, the two lamps of heaven were put to shame, and all hearts were inflamed with the fires of desire. If she smiled, she [displayed teeth that] made pearls despicable and [in comparison whereof] choice pearls would be sold for pulse; when she gazed earnestly, she excited deep emotions and made the fascination of Babylon to be realized.

He goes on to tell how he was tricked out of this treasure. There is a Qur'ānic allusion in the last line to the witchcraft of Babylon mentioned in *sūra* 2, which is doubtless intended to convey how beguiling the girl was. Abū Zayd's composition echoes that of the contemporary Ṣūfī poet 'Umar ibn al-Farīd, who said of his mistress: 'You rave about the full moon in the vault of heaven; leave off thy delusions, for she is my beloved not that [moon]. Her charms survive the revival of the dawn.'[39] Five lines of text in Naskhī script above the miniature extol the girl's singing. It was deemed superior to that of Ma'bad, an early Umayyad precentor at the Medina mosque, and her minstrelsy outshone even that of Zunām, a celebrated musician at the court of Hārūn al-Rashīd. The caption in large gold letters simply reads, 'And this is her picture'.

Although Abū Zayd's maiden is described as a *jāriyya*, she is obviously extremely cultivated and no ordinary maidservant. She may have undergone a long and expensive training and she would therefore represent a considerable investment on the part of her master. The unveiled girl is dressed in a heavily brocaded deep blue and gold robe reaching to mid-calf, with an open front; this would be worn over other clothing and fulfils the category of a cut and sewn outer garment. The robe's unusual sleeves are extremely deep and measure from the girl's breast to below the knee. It sounds similar to the fashionable, fourteenth-century Mamlūk *bahtala* (shift) with a long train and sleeves 3 ells wide which was to incur official wrath and led to the punishment of women who wore it (although this had little effect on popular fashion). Very wide sleeves also seem to have been popular among men at that time—they appear on clothing on metalwork, as well as elsewhere in contemporary manuscript painting. They were practical both because they were cool and because they could be used as pockets.[40]

Since this type of brocaded robe was a costly garment, the generous cut implies that no expense was spared for the girl wearing it. It must be what Stillman calls the *ṭirāz farajiyya*; a somewhat unsatisfactory description, since it seems merely to denote a garment with decorative bands of embroidery and that is split or open down the front. Al-Dhahabī's *Book of the Dynasties of Islam* reports that Nūr al-Dīn received a set of robes of honour around the year 1171; these included 'a long, flowing open robe with large sleeves [*farajiyya*]'. The girl in the illustration seems to be wearing a variation of the male garment, the *jubba*; *farajiyya* literally denotes that it is split and without closures. The caliph Amīn offered a *jubba* of gold-figured silk to a singer who pleased him; subsequently regretting his rashness (since it was presumably extremely costly), he spoilt it. Although it was usually a woollen garment, a more luxurious *jubba* could be manufactured in silk, or embroidered with gold and silk. Cairo *Geniza* documents mention only two colours of *jubba*, blue and green, which may provide further confirmation of my use of the term. Because it is rarely mentioned in (Jewish) marriage contracts relating to Egypt and Tunisia, the *jubba* was clearly more popular in Syria than in Egypt in the medieval period.[41]

That male clothing could be varied to suit the female form is confirmed by al-Ṭabarī, who describes a type of Rashīdī cloak, the *ghilāla*, of 'women's cut'. This is yet another variation of the term *ghilāla*. It is unlikely that the girl would appear outdoors in this exquisite robe: not only is it expensive, but it would be considered immodest to expose so much of her arm. The fabric is extremely richly patterned, with a heavy, pale blue, vegetal design on the dark blue field. Realistic, single birds (not enclosed in a 'frame') are also shown in gold. There is little of the earlier, static heraldic quality of decoration on this textile. It is entirely plausible that the fabric was manufactured in Baghdad, as Marco Polo reports that, 'In Bandas they weave many kinds of silk stuffs and gold brocades . . . and other tissues richly wrought with figures of beasts and birds.'

On the upper half of each sleeve there is a gold *ṭirāz* band with elements of incomplete Arabic epigraphy within a border of white roundels. Writing in the late ninth and early tenth centuries, Ibn 'Abd Rabbihi of Cordoba reveals that, as well as featuring the more common religious invocations or political inscriptions, the *ṭirāz* sometimes bore verses of an amatory or sentimental nature.[42]

Al-Wāsiṭī shows the famous herd of camels in *Maqāma* 32 being tended by a singer (*qayna*) wearing a robe with equally wide sleeves, which she may have received as a gift for her musical prowess. Her robe is of a blue-green diaphanous material and it has heavy gold edging, *ṭirāz* and a red lining. Underneath the *jubba*, Abū Zayd's maiden here wears a light shift which opens at the front. It has an ornamental neck-band and falls below the knee. This *qamīṣ* was basically a type of shirt for men and women, with a round hole for the neck. It seems to have come with or without a front opening, and the length could vary; the women's *qamīṣ* might also have a band of embroidery. Other versions for women were the *itb*, the *sidār*, the *shawdar*, the *qarqūr* and the *qarqal*. According to Dozy, these terms designated chemises of a similar shape, but with subtle variations on the basic shirt and its fabric, and according to the place of origin.[43] They came under the classification of clothes worn next to the body.

Below the shift one can clearly see the light, patterned trousers (*sarāwīl*), which are very similar in cut to the male version. These are of the smokey-grey colour adopted for the elegant woman's lingerie in 'Abbāsid times. A trouser cord (*tikka*) was used with the trousers, and as the maiden surely fits al-Washshā''s definition of 'the elegant woman', one could expect her *tikka* to be made of *ibrīsm* (a type of silk).

Indigo was extensively cultivated in Syria during the medieval period. In Alexandria in 1396, indigo from Baghdad cost 35 *dīnārs* per *qinṭār* (a dry measurement). Women were well-practised in the art of cosmetics and used various aromatic shampoos to keep their hair lustrous. There was a range of hairstyles: waved or curled, plaited or falling into ringlets. A band of black silk was frequently tied to the head, and ribbons, lace and other head ornaments were common.

In the earlier *Maqāma* of Ḥulwān, Abū Zayd was inspired to eulogize a weeping maiden who bit her hand in anguish on parting from her loved one. The lover spoke of her as follows: 'When last I met the idol of my love, her crimson veil I prayed her to remove, whose glowing tint obscured her aspect bright, as eve's red lustre dims the queen of night.'[44] Around her head the maiden wears a long, fine red scarf with gold circlets—this garment may be the silk embroidered with a circular motif (*al-ḥarīr al-mu'ayyan*) that was favoured by ladies of refinement. A twelfth-century document reveals that red dye was obtained from baqam, an Indian wood; its price at that time in Egypt fluctuated between 30 and 40 *dīnārs* per *qinṭār*.[45]

Pearls frame the maiden's face and neck. This type of headdress is the *'iṣāba mā'ila*; the adjective *mā'ila* has connotations of wealth, in particular of silver and gold. Head-coverings with gold coins sewn on as decoration are worn up to the present day. Ibn 'Abd Rabbih recounts, on the testimony of an eye-witness, that the girls at al-Rashīd's court wore the type of turban (*'iṣāba*) that was encrusted with pearls and jacinth (*yāqūt*) and featured love poems. Jacinth was brought from Ceylon. Strictly speaking, it was a a blue gemstone, possibly sapphire, but the term could include a variety of stones such as garnet, quartz, topaz and even pearls (*lu'lu'*), which came from Oman and the Gulf around Bahrain. The *'iṣāba* appears to have been an innovation of al-Rashīd's half-sister, 'Ulayya.

A Persian variation of the *'iṣāba* may be seen on the base of a Persian polychrome pottery bowl dated *c.* 1200, which shows a noble lady being bled.[46] Her headdress, however, is heavier and of rather more elaborate design, with a fringe of pearls at the forehead and what may be small gold or silver ornaments sewn on the sides.

Around the *'iṣāba* the maiden wears a head-band (*wikāya*), which might also be embellished with a poem. Ibn 'Abd Rabbih's *The Unique Necklace* has a typical example of such a verse, where a lover writes of his mistress, 'Across her brow with musk three lines I traced, as stray soft moon-entangled clouds; "God curse those who betray."'[47] The girl's *wikāya* is tied behind her left ear in a manner reminiscent of the Sāsānian ribbon denoting royalty. From its lightness and delicacy, the fabric appears to be silk. Although the hair-band was also known as *zunnār wikāya*, the *zunnār* more properly refers to a belt which was at one time worn by the 'People of the Book', the Jews and Christians.

The girl stands near a small stylized tree, depicted in the Mesopotamian style; she may be outdoors. It would be surprising if this were so, unless she is in the immediate precincts of the house, since one would expect her face to be covered with the outdoor veil (*niqāb*). Medieval dictionaries describe this as a veil 'that is upon [or covers] the pliable part of the nose' or which 'extends as high as the circuit of the eye'. The girl's serene pose is in marked contrast to the lively postures generally found in the BN 3929 manuscript. This may indicate that the manuscript was the work of more than one artist.

Plants and trees had long been popular metaphors for female physical attributes, and the small bush in the illustration may well be a pomegranate tree; this would provide a visual metaphor for the embodiment of womanly beauty. Al-Firdawsi's *Book of Kings* describes Miḥrāb's daughter, Rūdāba, in the following terms: 'Her cheeks are like pomegranate blossoms, she hath cherry lips. Her silver breasts bear two pomegranate seeds; her eyes are twin narcissi in a garden.'[48] Zāl, predictably, found her irresistible. Perhaps the use of rouge to achieve the 'pomegranate blossom' effect was considered seemly only in the very young—the traditionalist al-Baghandī is reported to have castigated a slave-girl, saying, 'The time is passed wherein you used to paint with rouge.' This is a Qur'ānic allusion to *sūra* 80, which refers to God's bounty. The lips and cheeks were stained red with a concoction called (in Persian) *chehra barafurukhtan*.[49]

It was the fashion to stain the fingers and toes up to the first joint, as the girl in the illustration has done on both hands. She seems to be gesticulating in a precise manner, perhaps indicating that she was modelled on a singer or dancer. Red henna was applied to the nails to give 'a more bright, clear and permanent colour than to the skin', while the dark grey variety was applied to the rest of the fingers and hand. Henna from the banks of the Nile continued to be widely exported into the nineteenth century,[50] and it is still the custom in the Middle East to trace delicate henna patterns on the palms of the hands and the soles of the feet.

Kohl (antimony), used to make the eyes seem more luminous, was kept in small bronze flasks and applied with a bronze 'stick'. We know that kohl sticks and toilet flasks were manufactured at Nīshāpūr, and two examples from the early Islamic period measure 7.6 cm and 7.4 cm respectively. A small flask from Nīshāpūr has a conical body with a rounded profile and vertical ribbing. Its neck is cylindrical, it has a sloping shoulder and it is undecorated.[51] The shape was evidently dictated by the need to exclude as much air as possible, to prevent the product drying out.

The girl wears a heavy gold bracelet (*siwār*) in a cable pattern on each wrist. Such bracelets were either handmade or cast. Silver was also used for jewellery, and an Egyptian pair of fourteenth-century silver bracelets with dragons' head finials can be seen in the British Museum.[52] Hebrew trousseau lists from the twelfth century throw valuable light on the customs of the time and the prices of goods. In Egypt, bracelets came in a variety of materials; those decorated with pearls could cost anything from 2 to 5 *dīnārs*. A marriage contract for a member of the bourgeoisie records a pair of bracelets valued at 28 *dīnārs*. Under her voluminous sleeves, Abū Zayd's *jāriyya* might also be wearing the type of large gold armlet (*dumluj*) designed for the elbow. Because of its relatively large size, it was more expensive than the *siwār* and, depending on the materials and the quality of the workmanship, could cost between 5 and 15 *dīnārs*.[53]

Although the maiden's feet cannot be seen, she is possibly wearing the type of fine narrow boot, made of black leather, that we have seen on other occasions. A light *rahāwī* shoe from Edessa and a split type (*maqṣūr*) were worn in summer, while fur-lined shoes (*musha'ara*) were used in winter. The girl would probably wear an anklet (*khalkhāl*) of gold or silver. The word *khalkhāl* is onomatopoeic, suggesting the clinking of the anklets when the wearer was walking. An Arab song runs, 'The ringing of thine anklets has deprived me of my reason,' while the Old Testament mentions 'the daughters of Zion . . . making a tinkling with their feet'.[54]

Since the head-band covers the girl's ears, it is impossible to see if she is wearing earrings. We know that the gold *ḥalqa* could be purchased in Egypt for between 1 1/2 and 2 *dīnārs* (although Ashtor considers this price rather low). More affluent ladies of leisure could expect to pay around 5 *dīnārs* for a pair. Medieval dictionaries describe the *ṭūma* as having a large bead, possibly a pearl, at its centre. A trousseau inventory in Cambridge University gives the value of a pair of earrings worked in gold as 2 *dīnārs*.[55]

In her right hand the girl is holding a small bronze mirror by its handle. Its size is the same as a roughly contemporary Persian cast bronze mirror measuring 14.7 cm, and it is slightly smaller than a similar Persian mirror in the Fogg Art Museum. The mirror appears to be undecorated, but it might have figurative designs in relief and an inscription of blessings for its owner on the obverse. Relief casting did not appear on mirrors from Persia much before the beginning of the twelfth century. Its sudden appearance then was probably due to Chinese influence, following the uniting of the Tartars of Mongolia and northern China.[56]

In addition to plain disc mirrors, bronze mirrors with central bosses were used in Persia in the twelfth and thirteenth centuries. Two mirrors of this type are found in the Louvre. One mirror of the period with a handle is decorated with a mainly geometric design, while on another five kings' heads appear in roundels. Hebrew documents reveal that in Egypt a simple iron mirror cost from 1 to 2 *dīnārs*, while mirrors made from porcelain, steel or glass cost from 4 to 5 *dīnārs*. The latter were more elaborate and might be covered with silver and encrusted with precious stones, or embellished with filigree and gold ornamentation.[57]

A lady and a maid with a mirror are found in a cartouche on the 'Blacas ewer' in the British Museum. There is a similar scene in the early fourteenth-century *Universal History* manuscript (formerly in the possession of the Royal Asiatic Society), which portrays Abraham and the Three Strangers. Sarah is seated on one side, with a silver mirror in her hand, before a small tree which may be a space-filling device. Gray considers that there is almost certainly a Christian, or 'more probably, a Jewish', original behind the Rashīd al-Dīn miniature.[58] One cannot preclude this possibility for the portrait of Abū Zayd's maiden. Behind her head there is what appears to be a combination of halo and classical wreath; this represents an extension of the 'halo as frame' usually employed by this artist. Alternatively, the *jāriyya* could have been modelled on the female attendant of a noble lady. This would explain the hand gestures, which may be proferring the mirror, while her fine clothing would mirror that of her mistress. In an Islamic context, however, the girl's eloquent hand gestures might also suggest that she is singing or reciting, and her portrait may have been based on a performer at court. In support of this thesis, it should be remembered that Abū Zayd paid testimony to her musical prowess in the earlier allusions to the court musicians of Mu'āwiyya and Hārūn al-Rashīd. Further, her garments and accoutrements are costly, and historical accounts confirm that entertainers were well rewarded for their skills.

In his *Encyclopedia of Arab Manners [Nihāyat al-'arab fī funūn al-adab]*, al-Nuwayrī (d. 1332) describes the ideal of feminine beauty. Her stature should resemble bamboo (*khayzarān*), with wide hips and a pomegranate-like bosom. A round full moon face, framed by hair black as night, should preferably sport a mole to suggest the effect of a drop of ambergris upon an alabaster plate. The eyes should naturally be large like those of a deer and intensely dark, without kohl, and with languid (*saqīm*) eyelids. A small mouth, with teeth resembling pearls set in coral, was considered most attractive, as were tapering fingers dyed with red henna at the tips.[59]

Ibn Khallikān's *Biographical Dictionary* records yet another example of the ubiquitous ideal of female beauty in the Arab world of the time. He quotes a mid-twelfth-century poem by al-Ṭarābulusī, which runs:

> Such a one's daughter, she has vanquished me by the variety of her perfections [charms], which consist in the sound of her voice and the aspect of her form, the haughty pose of the Persian, the voluptuousness of Syria, glances like those of the maids of Iraq, and language [sweet as that] spoken in the Ḥijāz.[60]

These images complete the idealized view of the Muslim woman, an image far removed from that of the classical age. Such notions of female beauty have undergone little change over the centuries, and the painter of BN 3929 has captured well the essence of ideal female beauty in the medieval Near East. Illustrations in the manuscript are invariably literal, and this portrait bears testimony to Abū Ẓayd's eloquence and the spell he could cast—'his' *jāriyya* is yet another figment of his fertile imagination.

While some terms differ according to region, the picture of women's costume which has emerged is one of a fairly universal type throughout the Islamic world, in that female modesty is stressed. A great variety of luxury items was purchased from all corners of the medieval Islamic world, with women putting their individual stamp on their style of clothing according to their means and sense of fashion.

Women in the Mosque

We now return to al-Wasiti's Rayy mosque illustration in *Maqāma* 21 (Plate 5). (The remainder of the scene was fully analysed in 'The Arab Governor'). Six adult women sit together in what is presumably a separate galleried area of the mosque. Although we—and apparently the congregation—see the women, this is unlikely to have been so in real life. The upper gallery in the Istanbul manuscript illustration contains (presumably female) figures behind a wooden baluster, but no latticework is shown.

While there is no prohibition on women entering the mosque, a *ḥadīth* declared that women could attend a mosque if their husbands permitted. According to the *ḥadīth*, however, women were not actively encouraged to do so. If a woman did choose to attend, she would not be perfumed, nor be in a state of ritual impurity, in other words, menstruating. Other sources recommended that women should leave the building before the men, and we know that some mosques had a 'ladies' section'.[61] Women have variously been required to stand at the back of the mosque, had a special enclosure cordoned off for their exclusive use, or been concealed behind a wooden grille, as in present-day Medina. Following the introduction of the ruler's enclosure, chambers enclosed with wooden latticework were constructed in mosque hallways for the use of religious students. The female members of the congregation shown in the illustration may have gathered in such an area.

Ibn Jubayr's report of 1184 throws further light on the segregation of women for worship. He describes the Bāb al-Badr in the palace square of Baghdad as 'part of the *ḥarīm* of the caliph, whose belvedere overlooks it, and [it] is set apart for the reception of those who come to preach here, so that the caliph, his mother and the ladies of his *ḥarīm* might listen from the belvederes'.

A Jewish legal document describes a house in Fatimid Egypt as having a 'secret door', which gives on to a different street from the main entrance. It reveals that, 'The entrance to the women's gallery of a synagogue, and certainly also of a church, was also called a "secret door".'[62] This would confirm the existence of a separate mosque entrance for Muslim women.

The main character seems to be the ample matriarchal figure at the right-hand side. Over her shift she wears a striking, decorative outer wrap with floral scroll patterns of white and red on a darker red field. The proscription on the wearing of red garments in the tenth century has the proviso 'except that which is by nature . . . red, such as the red silk stuff called *ladh*, silk [*ḥarīr*], brocade, figured stuff [*washī*] and *khazz* [a type of silk]'.[63] This must mean that the woman belongs to the upper class. She appears to be wearing a type of small gold brocaded turban (*'imāma*) with a peak underneath her all-enveloping robe, and this item could account for the large round heads of all the women.

The unusual black silken veil—resting on her forehead above the eyebrows and extending to the bridge of her nose—appears to hang from the headdress. Strictly speaking, she would not have needed to wear this veil when in the company of other women. Perhaps it is an indispensable fashion accessory on this occasion. Al-Washshā''s *Section on Fashionable Ladies* mentions the *mi'jar* (black veil) perfumed with hyacinth. An important component of the headdress, the *mi'jar* was a piece of cloth, usually muslin, bound around the head. Commanding a high price (from 2 to 15 *dīnārs*), it was an important item in the trousseau. Medieval documents mention the *mi'jar* in silk and linen from Dabīq and elsewhere, and gilded versions were extremely popular. They might have a border (*mu'lam*) or be doubled. Black was also fashionable in fourteenth-century Egypt;[64] neither Mayer nor Serjeant, however, describe or show veils of this type. The women in the illustration will have left their footwear outside. The principal female character's wardrobe, and her demeanour, suggest that she sees this outing to hear the great preacher as an important social occasion; it gives her an opportunity to vie with other women within her social circle.

Despite a rousing sermon on the themes of the transitory nature of life, and sin and repentance, by a highly regarded preacher (said to be even greater than the tenth-century Ibn Sam'ūn), the preacher's words seem to have been lost on the female worshippers. The woman second from the left is being reproved by two of her companions. Her chin resting on her left arm, she seems to be asleep. However, an examination of the manuscript reveals that this is not the case; perhaps she is bored. One authority denounced conversations in the mosque, on the grounds of disturbance to the pious. This woman's outer robe is predominantly gold and green and almost covers her red shirt. She wears a pair of gold bracelets on her left wrist. Al-Wāsiṭī's woman in labour wears gold bracelets, as does Abū Zayd's maiden, and so they were evidently popular items of jewellery. They are tight-fitting and must have fastened with a clasp.

To the right, a woman is conversing with the matriarchal figure. Her pointing finger confirms this conversation and provides a link between the two characters. A further decorative link is provided by the similar patterns of the two women's robes. The wrap of the pointing woman has a similar, if denser, floral scroll pattern of white on red; it is reminiscent of that found on a man's robe in the fourteenth-century *Maqāmāt* in London. Al-Wāsiṭī did not allow pattern for pattern's sake to detract from the very human element of his compositions and their relationship to the text, as happens in Mamlūk manuscripts, and in particular the *Maqāmāt* in Vienna. However, we do not know if these are authentic textile patterns, or whether the artist employed them for their aesthetic qualities.

Well-dressed women are found in the frontispiece to Volume II of the *Book of Songs* in Cairo. Patterned and coloured garments also appear on ceramics and Persian polychrome ware. Very similar decoration occurs on metalwork and in book illumination[65] as well as architectural ornament in various *Maqāmāt*. The robes of the other four women are of a fine material in plain colours (pink, dark green and silvery-blue) with heavy gold edgings. Their diaphanous qualities, and the contours of the female form, are achieved by white highlighting in a manner reminiscent of Byzantine painting. These figures provide a foil to the central character, and their robes are obviously expensive. Plain colours with highlighting also occur on robes and female trousers in the Istanbul *Romance of Warqa and Gulshāh* manuscript. The woman in the pink wrap at the centre of the group wears a gold-coloured veil; it rests on her forehead above the eyebrows and is of a similar type to that worn by Abū Zayd's slave-girl. A pattern of circlets can be made out, but it is impossible to say if these are gemstones, gold ornaments or a design printed on the material. All of al-Wāsiṭī's women are portrayed as amply built and perhaps conform to an 'ideal' of mature womanhood.

A young serving-girl, standing in attendance on her mistress, holds a flag-shaped fan with a handle which may be of palm matting (although a more realistic means of ventilation would have been the *punka* on pulleys and cords as described previously). Alternatively, since this is a central congregational mosque, a large wet felt carpet (*khaysh*) suspended from the ceiling—clearly depicted in the St Petersburg manuscript mosque in the final tale—would have been in order.

A similar hand-held fan appears in the BN 3929 *Maqāmāt* in the context of a figure of authority. The model for the girl may therefore lie in the royal repertory of illustrations, where an androgynous-looking attendant carried a fly-whisk, for example in BN 6094. In our illustration, her gesture resembles that of the prince's youthful attendant on the companion page. (Somewhat incongruously, the Oxford *Maqāmāt* shows a youth holding a similar fan over the assembled company at the beggars' wedding in the 30th tale.) The girl shown here may be the only example in the *Maqāmāt* illustrations of a female Arab attendant; all al-Wāsiṭī's other youthful servants seem to be non-Arab.

The servant-girl wears a dark green wrap with a gold embroidered edge (*mu'lam muthaqqaq*), the weight of which exaggerates the folds of the robe and suggests that it, too, was made from a fine material. Underneath her wrap, she has a pale shift. Servants' costumes would have reflected their mistresses' own financial circumstances and position in society. One should not discount the possibility that these ladies represent the ruler's *ḥarīm*.

A striking feature of all these female outer costumes is their colour and gaiety, in striking contrast to the dark *'abā'* worn in public in the Middle East today. From what little can be seen of the women's shifts in the illustration, they were also brightly patterned. Contemporary Egyptian documents confirm the popularity of the colours used by al-Wāsiṭī for female clothing. The following shades are mentioned as being in vogue: pomegranate, blue, green, yellow and red, as well as pearl or grey/white.

According to Yāqūt, the Tuesday market (*sūq al-thulathā'*) in Baghdad, which was adjacent to the cloth-makers' *sūq*, was the busiest market in the city. Baghdad and Tabrīz, like Nīshāpūr, manufactured silk and velvet garments.

The miniature confirms Samadī's description of the ladies' section of the mosque as a brilliant scene 'which could well be compared to springtide in a garden'.[66] An amusing vignette of well-to-do contemporary women, it probably shows the types of females whose husbands were the readers of this and similar literature.

7

Hospitality

As in so many other worldly spheres, Islam impinges on precepts regarding etiquette and hospitality. Tradition has it that Abraham entertained the angels and poor men, and in Muslim eyes he is the paradigm for the liberal host. At the end of the 4th tale Abū Zayd left a note for his generous hosts. He justified his apparently impolite hasty departure by alluding to *sūra* 33, reminding them of the Prophet's command to his followers to finish their meal and depart. The hospitality offered travellers, its duration, and the conduct incumbent on both host and guest, are all covered by elaborate canons of behaviour. There are prescribed ways of sitting, eating and drinking. Very little background information about the guest was either sought or volunteered. Many of the rules governing hospitality derive from the bedouin. In an exceedingly harsh environment even one's enemy would be offered the basics, for who knew when the roles might be reversed?

All acts of generosity are greatly appreciated, even al-Ḥārith's 'hasty meal of my capability' (*Maqāma* 7) and the simple meal of dates and fresh milk offered Abū Zayd by the poor old man who lived in a house 'narrower than the ark of Moses, more fragile than a spider's web' (*Maqāma* 15). Even when he behaved very badly and provoked personal hostility, Abū Zayd was invariably invited to eat and drink. He compounded his misdeeds by haughtily refusing, to prove whatever point he was intent on making.

Drinking

The 12th tale is set in a tavern in 'Āna, on the Euphrates, an appropriate setting as the city was famous for its wine. The dissolute court poet Abū Nuwās said,

18. The dénouement in the tavern.

'I vow that I shall drink the cool wine of Fallūj and 'Āna—a wine that is unlike any other wine.'[1] Al-Ḥārith and his party had just been escorted across the desert from Damascus by a man 'with the features of mature age, and the garb of an ascetic', who had composed a talisman for their safe journey. However, they were bemused by the old man's abrupt departure after they had generously rewarded him with jewellery and gold coins. Deciding to follow up a rumour concerning the whereabouts of this paragon, al-Ḥārith visited a wine-hall, described in the text as *daskara*.

Al-Wāsiṭī has provided a comprehensive miniature for the tavern scene. The dénouement is revealed in the two lines of text above. The first line, which is the end of Abū Zayd's poem in mitigation of his conduct, reads, 'Now the brother of want, who has a household, is not blamed if he be wily.' Immediately above the illustration, the beginning of al-Ḥārith's prose runs, 'Then I knew that it was Abū Zayd, the man of ill fame and disgrace, he that blackens the face of his hoariness.' This may be a reference to unbecoming conduct in an older person, who should know better. Three lines of text below the miniature complete the confrontational dialogue and include al-Ḥārith's castigation of his friend. The commentary is written in al-Wāsiṭī's usual manner down the side of the folio. Since part of it is in dark ink, this may have been over-written at a later stage. Reference is made to 'poverty' (*'ayla*), possibly an ironical comment on the first three words of the first line of text in the illustration, 'the brother of want'.

The two-storeyed building is commodious and handsome. The simplified, theatrical architecture suggests a 'staging' of the various activities. An even greater feeling of theatricality is evident in the wine-hall in the St Petersburg *Maqāmāt*. (In some ways, it is more successful than al-Wāsiṭī's: the creation of rooms on different levels and the bustling, lively figures are reminiscent of shadow-play characters. The long, dangling sleeves are similar to those in illustrations of dancing Ṣūfīs, and the essential elements for the making, pressing, straining and storage of wine are shown.)

In the Wāsiṭī tavern, the three rooms on the upper landing have domes with insets for light and ventilation. The large central dome indicates that the building extends backwards for some way. Al-Ḥārith finds Abū Zayd in what Preston familiarly renders as the 'tap-room'. This was the principal chamber in the centre of a tavern; used for the entertainment of guests, it was surrounded by different areas of wine-making activity. The illustration conforms to this description. We see various stages of wine-making in the surrounding chambers. These activities confirm that the tripartite architectural setting on two storeys represents six different rooms.

Abū Zayd, who has just 'bade broach the wine-casks', appears set for a long sojourn. He sits on a type of throne, his head graciously inclined towards al-Ḥārith, patiently listening to (and by now perhaps oblivious of) his friend's harangue. There is more than a hint of irony in this portrait: Abū Zayd has introduced himself as a holy man and his eyes are glazed, apparently in religious contemplation. His drinking cup is daintily held in his left hand and with his right hand he grasps a white napkin (*mandīl*). Abū Zayd holds his *mandīl* in the correct manner; it was usually folded double and held in the hand closer to the looped end. Its fine *ṭirāz* band sets it off as a more elegant item than the *mandīl* held by the less refined fellow quaffing greedily in the upstairs room and who is also prepared for a long drinking bout. Both napkins are white, the most popular colour. They could be made of silk, fine Egyptian Dabīqī linen, cotton, wool or other fabrics. Napkins appear in *Maqāmāt* manuscripts and elsewhere, and in other contexts.[2] The great, late, modern Egyptian singer, Umm Kulthūm, invariably held a napkin which she used to theatrical effect.

In the tenth century, al-Washshā' quoted part of a lover's quatrain written on a *mandīl* by an artistically trained slave-girl. The napkin 'speaks' in the following terms: 'I am the *mandīl* of a lover who never stopped drying with me his eyes of their tears. Then he gave me as a present to the girl he loves, who wipes with me the wine from his lips.' This phrasing of inscriptions as if 'put into the mouth of the object' also occurs on metalwork from an early period. An earlier example of a napkin in the royal context occurs in the Istanbul al-Jazarī *Treatise on Automata*. Here the female servant holds the cup which is mechanically filled with wine; in her left hand she has 'a *mandīl* which the king can use to wipe his mouth after drinking'.[3]

The drinking ruler on the frontispiece of the fourteenth-century *Maqāmāt* in Vienna has an elaborately decorated *mandīl* in his left hand. Still in the context of the Mamlūk court, the napkin known as *fūṭa* was associated with the office of the *jandar*, who was a court official, possibly a scribe. Evidence of this is found on Mamlūk shadow figures, dated to between 1290 and 1370, which show a square in a blazon—the square is taken to represent a kind of *fūṭa*.[4] There are many examples of the napkin's role in court etiquette.

Because we know of the stern disapproval of wine-drinking by Islamic society in general, and by al-Ḥārith in particular, al-Wāsiṭī's *mandīl* here serves both to highlight Abū Zayd's newly found refinement, and in some way to mitigate, even justify, his conduct in the eyes of the reader. The composition is evidently a parody of royal iconography and matches exactly Abū Zayd's duplicity.

In all these particular situations there was an implicit notion of refinement—accounts of the *mandīl* in the *Arabian Nights* apparently correspond with its use in contemporary urban society. In time, it replaced the flower held by drinkers of an older tradition. By now, the flower had outgrown its capacity to symbolize drinking as a socially acceptable pastime. Earlier examples of drinkers with flowers are found in a variety of media,[5] flowers (along with youthful attendants) suggesting a vision of Paradise. In the tavern in the fourteenth-century London *Maqāmāt*, the flowers have been retained in place of the *mandīl*. If a Syrian provenance for the work is correct, it confirms a notion that older traditions in manuscript painting survived there, especially when one considers the BN 6094 *Maqāmāt* manuscript dated 1222.

According to the *Biographical Dictionary*, the apparatus of social occasions also included cushions, perfumes, flowers, musical instruments and wine. Several of these elements are present in the illustration, and the miniature therefore represents a contemporary convivial scene. The myrtle (*ās*) and violet were particularly popular; myrtle and jasmine perfume Abū Zayd's tavern and are mentioned in the text immediately before the musical instruments. According to al-Suyūṭī, the Prophet said that myrtle was one of the three things which Adam brought from Paradise and that it was 'the chief of sweet-scented flowers in this world'. Plants were also elements in the language of love of the Ṣūfī mystics, and each had its own metaphorical significance. For example, the narcissus represented eyes to look at the Friend, the hyacinth reminded the poet of the beloved's curly hair, and the lily was silent and had ten tongues.[6]

It is not possible to say whether the dark-coloured drinking cup in Abū

Zayd's left hand is made from glass or metal; since metal would adversely affect the taste of the wine, it is probably a heavy moulded glass. A fresco in a bath-house in eleventh-century Fatimid Egypt portrays a drinking man, holding a long glass beaker in his right hand; he is not in a full frontal formal pose, and he faces slightly to the left. As previously mentioned, the rules of ritual purity dictate that the left hand should not be used when eating or drinking. However, there is a seated ruler with a fluted glass in his left hand on two cartouches on a candlestick from Mosul, and another Arab with a drink in his left hand is found in an al-Jazarī manuscript dated 1354.[7]

Al-Wāsiṭī's portrait of Abū Zayd is not necessarily a parody of the courtly repertoire because his glass is in his left hand, although it could be interpreted as an amusing adaptation of royal iconography, and a lampooning of royalty. It correctly implies that his critical faculties are impaired by alcohol. According to Grabar:

> Since the act of drinking was a central mode for the representation of the prince, Abū Zayd has been transformed into a prince in pose and composition. Drinking and power have been so fully associated visually with royal images that it is only in such terms that Abū Zayd could properly be represented in these activities.[8]

While this may be true, it is also possible that the artist adapted royal iconography as a convenient short cut. It is also significant that we saw Abū Zayd in lordly pose being serenaded by the female lutanist in BN 3929 (Plate 14).

Drinking bouts throughout the *Maqāmāt* illustrations are by no means restricted to the royal scenario, and there is little doubt that such scenes were a true portrayal of some milieux in contemporary Muslim society. Objects relating to wine-drinking were sufficiently well-known to be depicted and reproduced; and the use and adaptation of the princely cycle for entertainment did not preclude the existence of drinking among the lower orders. The illustration may therefore be based on the common wine-hall of the text or on some other drinking establishment.

The Umayyad ruler Yazīd I paid an incognito visit to a well-known vintner (*khammār*).[9] Each time the *khammār* opened a jar, he washed his hands, strained the drink and supplied his customers with a fresh napkin so that they might wipe their mouths after each mouthful. Presumably wine was consumed on the wine-maker's premises, as in the illustration. Ibn Munqidh, on his visits to Nāblus, used to lodge with a man called Mu'izz who ran a guest-house for Muslim travellers; this was situated on the opposite side of the road from a house belonging to a Frank, or European, who sold wine for merchants. This Christian used to appear with a bottle and cry out, 'So-and-so the merchant has just opened a caskful of this wine. He who wants to buy some of it will find it in such-and-such a place.'

Many *aḥadīth* reiterate the evils of alcohol, for example, 'Prayer of him who drinks wine is not accepted by God,' and 'Cursed is he who drinks, buys, sells wine or causes others to drink it.'[10] Sentiments such as these may underscore another possible motive for the hardening of the official Muslim attitude to wine: the decreasing esteem in which Jews and Christians were held. Over a period of time, as attitudes changed, it appears that the wine-trade devolved largely to these two communities. (Similarly, Christianity's earlier disapproval of usury had led to the Jewish community's involvement in money-lending.) In both instances, activities disapproved of by the majority religious community were tolerated when engaged in by a minority group.

Some of the finest wines could be sampled in taverns attached to monasteries. When al-Wāthiq built his wine-hall at Sāmarrā in the middle of the ninth century, he commanded that an expert vintner should be engaged—a Christian from Quṭrabul fulfilled his requirements. Quṭrabul, a town near Baghdad, was a well-known drinking haunt named frequently in Arabic poetry. Its reputation lasted at least until al-Wāsiṭī's era, for it is also mentioned in Yāqūt's *Geographical Dictionary*. Magians, too, were associated with the wine-trade, and a poem by Zuhayr refers to Christian friars laying up wine.[11] Even given the fact that the guide was in 'the garb of an ascetic' and carried a rosary, it is surely significant, in this tale about a tavern, that in the BL 1200 version (Plate 15), Abū Zayd looks remarkably like a Christian priest—perhaps the artist made an automatic association between wine and Christians.

There are numerous accounts of wine-drinking in Arabic literature: the *Book of Songs* and the poetry of Abū Nuwās, 'Umar ibn al-Farīḍ and al-Fīrūzābādī are but a few examples.[12] *Nabīdh* (lightly fermented wine) was permitted, however. It was made by soaking grapes or dried dates in water, to extract the sweetness, then allowing just enough fermentation for the mixture to taste sharp. *Nabīdh* was permitted for even the most devout Muslim, as the Prophet himself partook of date wine which had fermented for no more than two days. Ibn Khaldūn says that Hārūn al-Rashīd and al-Ma'mūn, both of whom were accused of debauchery because they drank fermented wine, had in fact only drunk *nabīdh*.[13]

Some explanation is required regarding the 'foulness of the report' which came to al-Ḥārith's notice. It is not clear whether al-Ḥārith refrained from taverns on account of the disreputable company to be found there or because he had religious objections to alcohol. He was certainly a scrupulous and upright person. On another occasion, in *Maqāma* 41, Abū Zayd masqueraded as a preacher in the Tannīs mosque and, after being caught out by al-Ḥārith, further outraged him by suggesting that they 'pass [wine] between us from hand to hand'. Al-Sharīshī says the word for tavern (*ḥāna*) is derived from the noun 'destruction' because 'wine-shops are destructive to property and reputation'.[14] That would explain al-Ḥārith's reluctance to enter the inn.

There is no unambigious proscription on wine (*khamr*) in the Sharī'a, although most Muslims abstain from alcohol. The relevant passages in the Qur'ān vary both in import and in guidance to the pious. Initially, the value of wine as an excellent source of nutrition was recognized. However, its association with gambling and divination, and its deleterious effect on the correct performance of the ritual prayers, provoked general disapproval, and this in turn led to its proscription in *sūra* 5.[15] This might be explained by the revelation of *sūras* at different periods and their taking into account the exigencies of the times. Despite some disagreement between the four schools of Islamic law, the prohibition on wine was adopted by the jurists.

Al-'Umarī's geographic, historical and biographical work, *Paths of Perception among the Kingdoms and Cities [Masālik al-abṣār fī mamālik al-amṣār]*, has an eyewitness account from the mid-ninth century on the presentation and service of alcoholic beverages. He describes how the servants in al-Wāthiq's wine-hall on the river (*ḥānat al-shatt*) at Sāmarrā brought trays, measures (*makāyīl*), ewers (*kizān*), and tools (*mabāzil*) to broach the fragrant plaster plug of the wine-jar. Al-Wāsiṭī may be showing an adaptation of a princely scene with a ruler 'at ease' and holding court at a drinking bout (*majlis al-sharāb*). A similarly relaxed setting is found in the contemporary *Book of Antidotes*.[16]

Al-Wāsiṭī's miniature captures something of the flavour of revelry and almost fulfils a poet's description of al-Wāthiq's wine-halls, where:

> The choicest wines were procured and the taverns were furnished with the caliph's own furnishings. Curtains were put up, gilt vessels and painted jars were supplied; altogether, the wine-halls presented a splendid and joyful sight.

Abū Zayd is being entertained by a musician with a fine eight-stringed lute. Eight strings seem to be unusual. Al-Tanūkhī tells how an *amīr* in Baghdad had a lute made for a singing-girl called Futuwwa with whom he was in love; it was costly and made of 'Indian wood'.[17] It is not possible to say where al-Wāsiṭī's type of lute originated, but the Persian lute (*barbat*) was an improvement on the skin-bellied lute of the *rubāb* type (*rubāb* refers to the skin of a ewe or she-goat). An extremely elaborate lute (it is not possible to determine the number of strings) appears in the Vienna *Maqāmat* tavern.[18] It is very decorative and has carved hexagonal insets in geometric star patterns which are similar to those found on doors and other panels.

Al-Wāsiṭī's tavern obviously boasts a good wine-cellar. The room at the upper right of the composition is used as a store for the jars (*dinān*) of fermenting wine; these do not have the thin, elongated points found on jars at Sāmarrā and in al-Wāsiṭī's miniature of the cave in the first tale. There were two types of alcoholic wine, the naturally fermented *mushammas* and the artificially fermented *maṭbūkh*. Fermented wine was stored in the pottery vessels shown in the illustration. They accord with Rice's description in his re-examination of an account of jars excavated at Sāmarrā and measuring some 20 cm wide at their widest point and standing 80–85 cm tall.[19] There was a large opening at the top, while the bottom tapered sharply to form a thin stalk; the stalk presumably allowed the sediment to gather. The *dann* must have been stored in sand or earth, if the method of stacking in the illustration is correct. *Dinān* were coated internally with bitumen and hermetically sealed with plaster. This practice of making cheap, porous vessels watertight had been in use since the ancient Mesopotamian period.

A fitting metaphorical description of a *dann* has been handed down by Abū Nuwās, who said, 'Hasten the first wine from the bottom of the *dann* which has two coats of armour, one clay, one bitumen.' The amphora used to store alcoholic beverages was usually corked with putty and cloth.[20] This is confirmed by the text, when Abū Zayd calls for a wine-jar to be broached. We read of a *dann* in a wine poem by Ibn al-Fāriḍ: 'And were the revellers to gaze at its seal, this sight alone would intoxicate them.' As in the St Petersburg *Maqāmāt*, the wine-jars here are stacked in the top right-hand corner, but al-Wāsiṭī has expanded his composition by having another set leaning to the left in the bottom left-hand corner. These jars in close formation recall a verse by the poet Ibn al-Mu'tazz: 'The wine-jars are like a row of men drawn up to dance a *dastaband*.'[21]

The action of passing down a fresh jar from the upper storey provides a visual link between the two floors and also lends an air of bustle to the scene. The boy in the gallery is Arab and wears the turban. It is not clear if the small lower figure receiving the *dann* is turbanless; this would indicate that he (if it is a male) is not an Arab or, alternatively, that it is an unveiled female attendant. If this centre of wine-making is run by non-Muslims, it is not surprising to find an unveiled woman. The sex of the person stirring the wine mash in the London *Maqāmāt* tavern—where there are strong Christian connotations—is also ambiguous (see 'Musicians' in Chapter 4).

Two people are engaged in wine-processing at al-Ḥārith's left-hand side, and the slight, dark-skinned figure in a waist-cloth is trampling grapes in a wine-press (*mi'ṣara*). To enable as much weight to be exerted as possible, and to lend support, straps were fixed to the ceiling. These are illustrated both here and in the St Petersburg miniature. It is a very unusual image, and it is likely that the person trampling the fruit would be spattered with grape juice. A poem attributed to al-Nuwayrī likens the wine-press to 'a sea of red flames' in which the labourer stands, as his lower body becomes spattered with the juice. Some liquid is running out into a small red terracotta pot. Another similar small figure, but clad in short, knee-length trousers, is shown by al-Wāsiṭī on the island in *Maqāma* 39. Both these men are small and dark-skinned, which may indicate that they are foreigners. It also points to the involvement of non-Muslims in wine-making.

A verse by al-Quṭāmī sheds further light on the involvement of non-Arabs in the wine trade: 'He put [the wine] in pitch-coated jars, dark in appearance and clad in clay, upright, defying the heat of the sun like Aramaeans in short trousers.'[22] Similar short, practical trousers are worn by peasants at work elsewhere in Islamic miniatures and on metalwork. The cloth strainer in al-Wāsiṭī's miniature was known as *rāwūq* or *najūd*. The corners of this straining-bag, which was probably muslin, are knotted to each side of the tripod. The process is confirmed by al-Kumayt, who quotes al-Ṣadr ibn al-Waqīl, 'While tears of blood trickle from the strainer the ewer beneath it giggles'.[23] The quotation is apposite, as the wine being served here is red.

An earlier wine-strainer, possibly made of basketry-work, is shown at the foot of a Persian silver plate dating from the eighth to ninth centuries; its rope handle is attached over the three points of a tripod and it is suspended over a pot. In the medical context, a strainer for aromatic wine occurs in an illustration for the *De Materia Medica*. A similar strainer appears in a medallion on a late thirteenth- to early fourteenth-century candlestick, possibly from north-west Persia. This filtering-cloth is suspended on strings, held by a suspension ring,[24] a variation on the method used in the St Petersburg manuscript, where the top of the cloth is attached to a suspended crosspiece.

The attendant in white, who has just pierced the jar's perfumed plaster seal, is straining the contents into a large yellowish footed bowl which rests on the floor. It seems to be of metal with a band of epigraphy on the exterior. It is not clear if the wine filtering through was presented directly to the drinkers from a bowl of this size or was decanted into a smaller, intermediary vessel.

A very similar metal container being borne by an attendant in the regal context occurs on a Mamlūk bowl with gold and silver inlay now in the Louvre. Once more, there is no sign of an intermediate stage between the large bowl and the drinking vessel. However, several wine-pourers—in silver from Persia, and in beaten brass inlaid with gold and silver and a black compound from Egypt—have survived. These take the form of a flattish bowl with a long spout. One appears in a feasting scene on the lid of a contemporary metal wallet, and they are also illustrated in two fifteenth-century manuscripts. Such vessels may well have contained a filtering device. A sixteenth-century Turkish manuscript in the British Museum depicts an attendant pouring wine from a similar flat pourer with long spout, but the liquid passes through a metal funnel and then into a glass flask.[25] In al-Wāsiṭī's tavern, the wine may have been decanted into something smaller or, alternatively, it might have been ladled, 'as is the wont in public taverns', according to al-'Umarī. A verse from another poem in praise of wine runs, 'Not wine of the white grape, fragrant as musk (when the jar is broached) and set on the strainer to clear, and ladled from cup to cup'.[26] In this refined milieu, ladling from cup to cup was perhaps considered unseemly.

Upstairs, two companions also appear set for a long drinking session, and the flared tops of two large glass flasks can be made out above the balustrade. These carafes represent the last stage in the path of the beverage from the storage jars to the table in this miniature. Similar vessels occur on metalwork, and there is a thirteenth-century lustreware flagon from Kashān with a tulip-shaped top in the Victoria and Albert Museum.[27] A drinker with a glass and a flask appears on an eleventh-century ivory casket from Cordoba, and there is an Ayyūbid example of a long-necked Syrian glass flask in the Museum of Islamic Art in Cairo; it bears a dedication to Sultan Ṣalāḥ al-Dīn Yūsuf.[28] Both the body and the neck have enamel and gilt decoration. Although this is a luxury item, its shape and function would probably remain constant in any environment, on grounds of practicality. Another possibility for pouring directly into the glass is the spouted type of glass flask that appears in BN 6094 in *Maqāma* 18. Four similar Mamlūk examples occur on the trays on which two shadow-play figures, street vendors, are hawking drinks around the market; similar 'carafes' rest on the trays that they carry on their heads.[29]

In the Wāsiṭī painting, the man on the right in the tavern gallery is quaffing from a stemmed drinking-cup and holding a napkin, so this may be no common drinking den, an impression reinforced by the fine Arab costumes with *ṭirāz* bands and gold edging of those present. At official drinking bouts, it was the custom for both guests and host to wear bright robes in shades of red, yellow and green.[30] The salon was perfumed by a censer containing ambergris, aloe-wood or some other fragrant substance (this is alluded to in the Arabic text, where Abū Zayd is mentioned inhaling the 'fragrant odours', or *rayḥān*), and the men perfumed their moustaches and beards with rose-water or civet. No censer is shown in the miniature. A wide selection of fruit, including apples, quinces, grapes and pears, was offered as dessert at these drinking sessions—a large dish of fruit stands prominently in the foreground of the miniature.

Al-Wāsiṭī's illustration is an adaptation of royal iconography, and his architectural representation is intended as a refined setting for an evening's entertainment. This may have been based on literary accounts or on personal knowledge. His portrayal of Abū Zayd's enjoyment of wine brings to mind a verse by Ibn al-Fāriḍ: 'Were you to be for one hour only, drunk with it, you would fancy the world your slave, to rule and command.'[31]

There are some interesting similarities between al-Wāsiṭī's composition and the pharmacy in the *De Materia Medica*. Bearing in mind that there are parallels with some of the techniques in the preparation of pharmacological compounds, it is interesting to see a good selection of medical jars with incised and painted decoration, as well as what seems to be either trails of bitumen coating or tails of cloth which were inserted with the seal and which will be used to remove it. People in the pharmacy are also busily engaged in different areas. We have already seen a large, incised jar in BL 1200 (Plate 15).[32]

Another miniature from the same *De Materia Medica* manuscript shows a physician supervising the preparation of an aromatic wine for colds and coughs, and there is a strainer on a tripod.[33] This does not suggest that the pharmacy and the wine-hall were identical buildings. Rather, the architecture as depicted is an artistic convention to convey the impression of a series of rooms where various activities take place simultaneously, in these cases preparation, storage and a reception area.

An accessory from a Mamlūk shadow play, a stand with eight pitchers with tapered bases and decorated bodies on two shelves, suggests a further possible connection with the architectural framework in the manuscripts. In addition, two huge *dinān* for the storage of the oil for the lamp occur in the Mamlūk shadow figure for the Lighthouse of Alexandria[34] (as one of the Seven Wonders of the World, this subject-matter underlines the topicality and genre elements of the shadow theatre which are shared with the *Maqāmāt* literary genre).

We have seen that the theme of drinking was found throughout medieval Arab society, both in court circles and in humbler milieux. The posthumous papers of an otherwise pious Cairo jurist (which reveal him as an author of somewhat erotic verse) should therefore occasion no great surprise. One example of his work reads, 'O God, I ask not for Rest. Give me not Peace—only a waist to embrace and a wine-cup that never shall cease.'[35]

Food and Etiquette

Food is mentioned in eight of the *Maqāmāt*,[36] and several meals are illustrated in the manuscripts. BN 5847 provides an encampment scene on adjoining pages in *Maqāma* 44, which exemplifies Arab hospitality. The tale opens on a bitterly cold winter's night, when a famished al-Ḥārith and his friends are welcomed by a generous bedouin host. At first glance, one might ask whether the slaughter scene should not have come first, but an examination of the Arabic text confirms that the tent setting is in the correct place, and that the slaughter of the camel follows it. Therefore the proper interpretation of the illustrations is that the travellers arrive at the camp fire, are brought *hors d'œuvres* (*nuql*) and then warm themselves at the fire while waiting for the main courses (Plate 19).

Al-Ḥārith and his benighted fellow-travellers seem momentarily to have lost their sense of propriety, for the caption above them reads, 'We spurned what is said about gluttony and saw sense in plunging into it with the measure of the greedy.' Even if the guests were famished and cold, they risked being rebuked by their hosts, as the following tale illustrates. Abū al-Ḥasan, who had devoured several types of kid at the table of Abū 'Abdallāh al-Barīdī, tells how:

> I was about to take the shoulder, but was anticipated by the hand of Abū 'Abdallāh, in consequence of which I withdrew mine. He said to me, 'Abū al-Ḥasan, you are the modern Sābūr of the Shoulders!' I was very much ashamed, knowing that he said this out of annoyance.[37]

Abū Zayd had an illustrious paradigm in the sage Luqmān, who inspired the saying, 'More voracious than Luqmān'.[38]

The Sharī'a prescribes the correct methods of eating, such as eating less than one's fill and eating slowly. This was perhaps out of concern with the direct medical effects, as well as the niceties of social behaviour.

Arabic humanistic literature had encompassed culinary works since the first half of the ninth century. They not only dealt with the preparation and cooking of food, but covered dietary concerns and etiquette, all of which were deemed indispensable for refined members of society. The earliest scientific work on diet, the *Book of Nutrition [Kitāb al-aghdhiya]*, made its appearance in the twelfth century; its author was the illustrious Andalusian physician Abū Marwān ibn Zuhr.[39]

In the illustration, two women are bustling around, bringing in another tray of *nuql*, an important constituent of any meal. An anecdote concerning the caliph al-Wāthiq tells how he asked some courtiers for their opinion on the best *nuql*. Some preferred savouries such as salt and biscuits, or vegetables (*nabāt*). Others chose fruit such as pomegranates, or sugar soaked in rose-water.[40] The women are unveiled, although their heads are covered with very long dark scarves; this might be surprising in the presence of strange men, but one should remember that this is not a metropolitan scene. In the context of entertainers, al-Jāḥiẓ says in his *The Epistle of Singing-Girls*:

> An indication that looking at women in general is not prohibited is that a middle-aged spinster will appear before men without any bashfulness. Were this prohibited when she is young, it would not be permissible when she is middle-aged.[41]

A commentary on a *ḥadīth* concerning guests says that a stranger approaching a camp without a friend or acquaintance there will go to the first tent, whether or not the man is at home. The wife or daughter will immediately set about spreading a carpet and preparing a meal. Al-Wāsiṭī's mature women certainly act decisively in the entertainment of their guests and seem eager to please them. A late twelfth-century account confirms the welcome which even the unexpected guest received. When 'Imād al-Dīn al-Iṣfahānī rejoined Sultan Ṣalāḥ al-Dīn in Damascus, he described how:

> the tablecloth was spread out; the carpet rolled out, tables were made ready; deep dishes were lined up. The cooks presented sheep, fowls, very sweet, fiery, acidic, with no particular flavour, stinging, boiled, roasted, already-made, fried foods.[42]

The ladies wear fine, dark-green robes with *ṭirāz* bands on wide sleeves. Here the robes seem to be the variation of the *jubba* called *ṭirāz farajiyya*. The woman in the centre of the composition has a marked resemblance in features, build and clothing to al-Wāsiṭī's celebrated singer; this again might indicate that the painter regarded her as a 'type' who represented a capable, spirited, mature Arab woman. Here she is very much mistress of her own domain.

Two of the guests sit on woven matting carpets and, in view of the weather, sensibly wear their turbans in the bedouin manner, tied under the chin. The standard small table (*khīwān*) has been placed on a patterned rug, with two bowls and food laid out on it; one wonders whether the platters might not, in fact, have been spread on rugs, in the context of an encampment. The guests are holding some unidentifiable white food in their right hands. Although we cannot see what the bowls contain, the two round objects may be fruit. Two other men are warming themselves beside a flaming fire at the right-hand side. It is unlikely that the fire was inside the tent itself, especially as shown in the painting, although a charcoal brazier might have been used in a tent. However, this would be extremely dangerous if used in an enclosed atmosphere, unless proper ventilation in the form of a smoke-hole were provided.

The two men by the fire would be seen as sitting indecorously, with their legs exposed, especially as they were guests and, more particularly, in the presence of the women of the family. However, BN 6094 and the fourteenth-century BL 22.114 also show men round a fire, with their robes far pulled up, and it is evidently a genre feature. Here, it serves to emphasize the extent of the hosts' hospitality, as the guests are clearly 'making themselves at home'. The scene is enacted inside a large tent open to the elements, which allows it to appear as a backdrop. As explained in the general discussion of tents, the orange-red interior is a separate hanging—here the colour indicates the welcome of a fire-lit scene.

A thirteenth-century account by Abū al-Fidā' describes the tent of al-Malik al-Muẓaffar while on a military expedition to Aleppo. The tent 'had a red exterior, and was made of western cloth. Its interior was decorated with fine dyed linen-work.'[43] In a nomadic setting, woollen wall hangings would have been more appropriate and more likely. While decorative, they would of necessity have been more of a craft than an art, their shadings and weaving tensions reflecting the gathering of diverse materials and the hurried packing and unpacking of a rudimentary loom at the dictates of the environment.

Although the exterior of al-Wāsiṭī's tent has reinforced places for poles to be affixed, none are included because they would inhibit the composition. A single spear behind the tent points upwards and outwards to the edge of the folio to suggest an element of depth; the encroachment into the text is an early innovation. This tent is of the same basic, wide type which also appears in the miniatures for this tale in the St Petersburg manuscript; one tent had to serve many functions and a large and perhaps extended family. There is very little difference as regards shape between al-Wāsiṭī's tent and his cave setting in *Maqāma* 1 (for both are semicircular) but the cave is naturally in gloomier hues. In both illustrations, the artist has used the semicircular shapes as a decorative framework and compositional backdrop.

Al-Ḥārith and his companions would have agreed with a contemporary poem by Ibn Mammātī, quoted in the *Biographical Dictionary*, which runs:

> How brightly his fires burn at night to attract the tardy guest! He who draweth to the light of his fire will not have reason to complain, provided

he never received hospitality from the family of Muhallab.[44]

Again, we see the metaphor of light and fire for hospitality.

The text at the second painting describes how the company have wiped their hands with napkins (surely an irrelevance here) and settled down to civilized conversation. A rather aloof old man, later revealed as Abū Zayd, turns aside 'as the lofty turns aside from the lowly' and quotes a passage from the Qur'ān: 'Verily this is nought but idle tales of the ancients.' (Plate 20)

The miniature shows the cooks outdoors, who are evidently about to provide a sumptuous repast, for the scene is dominated by the ritual killing (*dhabḥ*) of a camel. Although the eating of camel flesh is not proscribed by the Qur'ān, it was not consumed universally among the Arabs. The name of Allāh must be invoked over an animal about to be slaughtered, but this is not the full *basmallāh*, merely 'In the name of Allāh'. It seems that the use of the epithets, 'The All-Compassionate, the All-Merciful' is considered inappropriate, in the light of what the beast is about to undergo, although every effort is made to avoid unnecessary suffering.[45] Al-Ghazālī's *Counsel for Kings* quotes the Prophet as saying: 'God loves kindness in all [human] actions. Let the man who is to a slaughter a sheep therefore sharpen his knife, so that he may deliver that living creature from pain sooner.'[46] In nineteenth-century Egypt, Lane reports that some women would intone over the animal about to be killed for food, 'In the name of God! God is most great! God give thee patience to endure the affliction which He hath allotted thee!'[47]

Camels are stabbed in the throat, at the part nearest to the breast. Other animals have the throat cut at the part next to the head (as in the miniature) and the windpipe, carotid arteries and gullet are then removed. The camel in the illustration has had its limbs tied, and the man is forcefully holding its head down. Al-Wāsiṭī has cleverly accommodated the contours of the hillock to the camel's humped outline. It is not difficult to imagine the beast's distress and its fearful bellowing. Elsewhere in the *Maqāmāt* there is mention of the facial bags of the throats (*shaqāshiq*) of camels which emit a roaring sound. An extract from *Maqāma* 25 captures something of the slaughter: 'My humped camels mourned the morning I made the feast.' A literary account masterfully sums up the occasion: 'There bounty ever kindles high the flame of hospitality; and camel choice and stately steed full oft are doomed for guests to bleed.'[48]

Another man stirs a large cooking pot or cauldron (*qidr*), the most important culinary utensil. Interestingly, the cook is male. According to al-Baghdādī, the most superior pots were stone (*baram* or *ḥijāra*) followed by those of clay baked (*fakhkhār*); others were made of copper (*nuḥās*) or lead (*anuk*). Syrian pots were of good quality and larger vessels from Merv, Ṭūs and Sughd were also highly thought of. The text indicates the size of pot used, for it refers to *a'shar*, which was originally the plural of *'ushr* or a tenth part. *A'shar* is applied to a cooking pot so large that its capacity is ten times that of an ordinary pot. These huge utensils were also used in cooking dishes of grain, among other things. We know that they were exactly the same as the 'pots of fire' containing naphtha that were thrown during the siege of Acre in the Crusades.[49]

An enormous vessel such as the *a'shar* would be needed to cook this camel, so perhaps the pot on the fire contains a first-course dish. It is clear that the actual feast is some time off. Abū al-Aynā', who was famed for his quick wit, was being entertained by Ibn Mukram, who set a pot before him. It was full of bones, so Abū al-Aynā' said to his host, 'This is evidently a gravy-pot.'[50] Arab hosts may have feared criticism by their guests if they did not live up to the expected standard of hospitality; this might explain the tolerance of the behaviour and deportment of these guests.

The cook ladles the contents of the pot directly into a serving bowl; his ladle has a long, straight handle with a knop. If the ladle were metal, he would surely have used a cloth to hold it. In the bedouin context, the ladle is probably wooden, as the trunks of palm-trees are used to make utensils. Everything in that environment would be put to good use, and no part of this camel would go to waste: meat not used for the meal might be pickled in vinegar with salt, herbs and vegetables, or dried (*qādīd*); and the bones could be used to make combs and needles.

In the scene of the Prophet's night journey (*mi'rāj*) in the Edinburgh *Universal History* manuscript, an angel offers the Prophet celestial fare from a bowl which is carried on a shallow dish with a foot. There the ladle has a swan-necked, short handle. A fourteenth-century feast scene has also been noted in the *Universal History* manuscript in the Asiatic Society of Bengal, which is not much earlier than 1430. It is on a rather grander scale, however, for it depicts the Feast of Hulagu Khān in an *al fresco* setting. Nevertheless all the basic ingredients are there: a slaughtered animal on the ground; a man with a sharp knife who is carving a bird; a large uncovered pot with two handles, storage jars and flasks; and wine cups.[51]

A boy is tending a fire with sticks in al-Wāsiṭī's miniature, and he seems to be blowing on the fuel. This genre element of watching a pot on a fire occurs in the *Five Poems [Khamsa]* of Niẓāmī, and was to become a cliché in Persian miniature painting. Blowing on a fire to keep it alight was nonetheless a vital task, to provide sustenance, to keep away wild animals, and so on. It is obvious that for cooking in such quantities as in this tale an abundant supply of good wood would be necessary, and the date-palm at the left of the illustration would provide some fuel in the way of dried branches; also, to encourage growth, the trunk would be regularly lopped and the fibrous growth could be burnt. A proverb concerning firewood is mentioned in *Maqāma* 37. Fuel from the palm, ilex and olive trees were particularly popular because they gave off little smoke. *Markh* and *'ufar* excel as firewood as they are easily set alight when rubbed. These trees can also be set alight merely by the wind.[52] These are perhaps in general vegetation of the settled lands (*al-ḥāḍira*); otherwise nomads could gather spikes and thorns (*shawq*).

Fuel, whether in the form of wood or charcoal, was a basic commodity in settled areas. A *raṭl* of charcoal of inferior quality cost 6 *dirhams* in Damascus in 1246, and according to a text concerning the founding of the Mustanṣiriyya *madrasa* in 1234, a lecturer received part payment in kind, including 'firewood'.[53] As well as being a reminder of its importance as a staple of the bedouin diet and its indication of a water source, the palm here acts as a 'space-filler' and as a balance in the composition.

When the camel has been cooked, generous portions will be carried to the guests on large serving dishes; this is confirmed in a commentary to *Maqāma* 48. A woman bears a large tray, possibly a *ṭabaq*, carrying two dishes. During the 'Abbāsid period, the term *ṭabaq* was also synonymous with a feast or banquet in the caliph's palace, or more frequently, in the vizier's official residence.[54] *Ṭabaq* is still used today for any type of tray, of whatever material.

The serving-woman is dressed like the other females in the family, but her pale blue robe is very beautiful and elaborate. It is lightly figured in red, with its folds highlighted in a darker tone. One is reminded of the design of the extremely elaborate spandrels of the house of the virtuous wife Barra (Illust. 15), even if the floral motifs there were quite definite and there were golden sun motifs. So far as this bedouin robe, at least, is concerned, while luxurious garments existed, their price put them beyond the purse of the average citizen, and one assumes that al-Wāsiṭī depicts them for their aesthetic qualities. Papadopolou plausibly suggests that the space in this miniature has been organized around a spiral which runs from the hand of the man ladling food from the pot down and round the fire, up through his eyes, along to the woman's eyes and then up round the figure of the man, ending through his hand with the knife.[55]

These scenes of a flickering fire must have proved as enticing to the weary traveller as they did to the romantic poets, who often composed verses to the departed lover, of whom only the traces of the beloved's camp fire were left. Even in modern times, a song by Umm Kulthūm tells of the ruins of the home of the lover. A poignant metaphor was conjured up by Miskawayh, in his obituary of a man who died in 970:

> In this year perished Abū Ṭāhir Ḥusayn ibn Ḥasan, governor of Basra, with all his connections; their traces were obliterated, their fortunes dissipated; there remained not on the face of the earth a blower upon tinder from among them.[56]

Al-Wāsiṭī has captured well the narrator's description of arriving at a 'house' (*bayt*) 'whose camels roared, whose cauldrons boiled'. His scene recalls a report in the *Biographical Dictionary*, where Ibn Khallikān quotes one Abū al-Manṣūr Sadar:

How often, during the shades of night, have we arrived, without previous notice, at the encampment of an Arab tribe; but found not, by their fire, a person who could direct us to our way. And yet their scouts were not remiss; but we fell in among them, gently as falls the dew.[57]

Conclusion

Each manuscript represents an individual response by artists to a previously unillustrated abstruse work which called for the creation of new imagery or the adaptation of existing sources. Illustrations were clearly highly dependent on the text, and a definite *Maqāmāt* visual idiom evolved, with specific settings which had no apparent parallels elsewhere. Both the book and the illustrations demonstrate a preoccupation with a sophisticated metropolitan audience and the anecdotage in the guise of the exploits of Abu Zayd which was so much a part and a reflection of Arab social life.

These fascinating paintings help to compensate for the somewhat repetitive nature of the author's plot and setting and the inevitability of the outcome of the tales. This is particularly true of al-Wāsiṭī's work, where his unique knowledge of the text in his dual role of scribe and artist enabled him to make leaps of the imagination far in excess of the other painters. My decision to analyse the text and commentaries and other literary material was fully justified since it has yielded a wealth of information on Arab society.

Although the influence of Arab painters is seen in later Persian painting, there is an apparent failure of the *Maqāmāt* idiom to perpetuate itself; it was evidently exclusively to the taste of an Arab audience and irrelevant to Persian literature and artistic expression. Despite the present lack of evidence concerning patronage and the existence of workshops, the proliferation of figurative representation generally, and the presence of a highly literate bourgeoisie suggest that the readership of the *Maqāmāt* was influential in the appearance of illustrated literary works. Illustrations were added for their aesthetic appeal and were perceived as a necessary dimension to the most Islamic of all the arts, the creation of a book.

Notes

Initial entries are given in full; thereafter book titles are abbreviated, and the following abbreviations are used for journals:

AR *Arabica*
AI *Ars Islamica*
AO *Ars Orientalis*
AAsiae *Artibus Asiae*
AA *Arts Asiatiques*
BANIPAA *Bulletin of the American Institute for Persian Art and Archaeology*
BM *Burlington Magazine*
BSOAS *Bulletin of the School of Oriental and African Studies*
CAJ *Central Asiatic Journal*
DI *Der Islam*
EI *Encyclopaedia of Islam*
IJMES *International Journal of Middle East Studies*
IC *Islamic Culture*
IS *Islamic Studies*
IOS *Israel Oriental Studies*
JSAI *Jerusalem Studies in Art and Islam*
JAL *Journal of Arabic Literature*
JIH *Journal of Indian History*
JPHS *Journal of the Pakistan Historical Society*
JRAS *Journal of the Royal Asiatic Society*
JWH *Journal of World History*
KdesO *Kunst des Orients*
NGDMM *New Grove Dictionary of Music and Musicians*
NGDMI *New Grove Dictionary of Musical Instruments*
SIr *Studia Iranica*
SIsl *Studia Islamica*
SUM *Sumer*

Introduction

1. T. Preston, *Makamat or Rhetorical Anecdotes of al-Hariri of Basra*, London and Cambridge, 1859, p. 34.
2. O. Grabar, *The Illustrations of the Maqamat*, Chicago, 1984, p. 104.
3. Preston, *Makamat* . . ., p. 33.
4. Preston, *Makamat* . . .; T. Chenery, *The Assemblies of al-Hariri*, London, 1867; F.

Steingass, *The Assemblies of Ḥarīrī*, London, 1897 and 1989, Arabic and English text.

5. Preston, *Makamat . . .*, p. 9.

6. R. Ward, 'Evidence for a School of Painting at the Artuqid Court', *The Art of Syria and the Jazira*, 100–1250, (ed.) J. Raby, Oxford, 1985, p. 70.

7. Grabar, *Illustrations . . .*, p. 145.

Chapter 1

1. Steingass, *Assemblies . . .*, Arabic text, pp. 54–5.

2. M. M. Ahsan, *Social Life Under the 'Abbāsids, 786–902 AD*, London, 1979, p. 32.

3. Ahsan, *Social Life . . .*, p. 278; A. Mez, *Renaissance of Islam*, London, 1937, p. 427.

4. Al-Ṭabarī, iii, 1012 ff., cited R. Levy, 'Notes on Costume in Arabic Sources', JRAS, 1935, p. 325, note 10; Ibn al-Athīr, viii, pp. 101, 150, cited Levy, 'Notes . . .', p. 337, note 3; Ibn Iyās, V, iv, p. 143, lines 5ff., cited Levy, 'Notes . . .', p. 333, note 4; Ibn Jubayr, *Travels . . .*, cited Levy, 'Notes . . .', p. 333, note 6.

5. Al-Ṣābī, *The Rules and Regulations of the 'Abbasid Court*, Beirut, 1977, p. 111, note 1.

6. T. J. al-Janābī, *Studies in Mediaeval Iraqi Architecture*, Baghdad, 1982, p. 192.

7. E. Whelan, 'The Origin of the *miḥrāb mujawwaf*', IJMES, Vol. 18, 1986, p. 222, note 73.

8. Al-Janābī, *Studies . . .*, Plate 194; pp. 194–5.

9. Whelan, 'Origin . . .', pp. 206, 209, 211, 215.

10. Ettinghausen, 'The Beveled Style in the Post-Samarra Period', *Archaeologica Orientala in Memoriam Ernst Herzfeld*, (ed.) G. Miles, New York, 1952, Plate XIII.

11. Al-Janābī, *Studies . . .*, p. 243; p. 37, Fig. 7; p. 47, note 57.

12. D. Brandenburg, *Islamische Baukunst in Agypten*, Berlin, 1966, Figs. 2, 4, Miḥrāb, al-Azhar, Fig. 1 Mausoleum of Qalāwūn; F. Sarre and E. Herzfeld, *Archäologische Reise im Euphrat und Tigris Gebiet*, Berlin, 1911–1920, III, Table Va.

13. Al-Janābī, *Studies . . .*, Fig. 43; Plates 160A, B; Plate 16.

14. Preston, *Makamat . . .*, p. 239.

15. G. von Grunebaum, *Muhammadan Festivals*, London, 1981, pp. 63, 56, 58.

16. Grabar, *Illustrations . . .*, p. 64; J. Dickie (Ya'qūb Zakī), 'Allah and Eternity: Mosques, Madrasas and Tombs', *Architecture of the Islamic World* (ed.) G. Michell, London, 1978, p. 35; J. Lassner, T*he Topography of Baghdad in the Early Middle Ages: Texts and Studies*, Detroit, 1970, p. 194, Appendix C, al-Tanūkhī recounted that his father told him how he was 'sitting in the presence of 'Aḍūd al-Dawla'. He continued, 'We were encamped close to the *muṣallā* of the Festivals on the east side of Madīnat al-salām (Baghdad)'; p. 114.

17. E. W. Lane, *Arabic-English Lexicon*, Reprint, London, 1984, Vol. 1, p. 872, s.v. *dari'a*; Ahsan, *Social Life . . .*, p. 36; L. A. Mayer, *Mamluk Costume: a Survey*, Geneva, 1952, p. 288.

18. Al-Mas'ūdī, *Murūj al-dhahab wa ma'ādin al-jawhar*, vii, p. 402, cited Ahsan, *Social Life . . .*, p. 36; *al-Rāghib*, cited Levy, 'Notes . . .', p. 327.

19. R. Ettinghausen and O. Grabar, *The Art and Architecture of Islam*, 650–1250, London, 1987, p. 334; al-Ṣābī, *Rules and Regulations . . .*, p. 78.

20. R. B. Serjeant, 'Material for a History of Islamic Textiles up to the Mongol Conquest', AI, IX-XVI, Reprint, Beirut, 1972, p. 78; al-Tha'ālibī, *The Book of Curious and Entertaining Information*, Edinburgh, 1968, p. 129; E. Ashtor, *Histoire des prix et des salaires dans l'orient médiéval*, Paris, 1969, p. 150.

21. E. Kuhnel and L. Bellinger, *Catalogue of Dated* Ṭirāz *Fabrics in the Textile Museum*, Washington, 1952, p. 102.

22. von Grunebaum, *Festivals . . .*, p. 63.

23. S. Wiklund and C. J. Lamm, 'Some Woollen Girths from Egypt', AI 6, 1939, pp. 149, 143, 150.
24. J. Jenkins and P. R. Olsen, *Music and Musical Instruments in the World of Islam*, London, 1976, p. 84.
25. Ward, 'Evidence . . .', Fig. 8; Jenkins and Olsen, *Music* . . ., p. 55.
26. P. Kahle, 'Schattenspielfiguren', *Der Islam* 1, 1910, Figs. 58, 59.
27. R. Ettinghausen, *Arab Painting*, New York, 1977, p. 97; D. Talbot Rice, *Islamic Art*, London, 1984, Fig. 66, Victoria and Albert Museum, Brangwyn Collection.
28. M. Rosen-Ayalon, 'The Problem of the "Baghdad" School of Miniatures and its connection with Persia', *Israel Oriental Studies* 3, 1973, Plate 6.
29. Preston, *Makamat* . . ., p. 419.
30. Al-Tha'ālibī, *Curious and Entertaining* . . ., p. 142.
31. E. W. Lane, *Manners and Customs of the Modern Egyptians*, p. 475.
32. Al-Ṣābī, *Rules and Regulations* . . ., pp. 76–7; R. Ettinghausen, *Turkish Miniatures from the 13th to the 18th century*, London, 1965, Plates 1, 2.
33. London, BL or. 1200, ff. 85v, 86r, red and blue; and Abu Zayd sometimes wears a blue turban, as in f.100r, or a red one on f.110r; London BL or. 9718, f.72r; P. K. Hitti, *History of the Arabs*, London, 1982, p. 353; Mez, *Renaissance* . . ., p. 58, note 1.
34. R. P. A. Dozy, *Dictionnaire détaillé des noms des vêtements chez les Arabes*, Amsterdam, 1845, cited Ahsan, *Social Life* . . ., p. 50, note 19.
35. *Tārīkh al-rusul wa al-mulūk*, iii, 1368, cited Ahsan, *Social Life* . . ., p. 52.
36. R. Ettinghausen, *Arab Painting*, New York, 1977, p. 91, Vienna, Natbibliothek A.F.10.
37. Ettinghausen, *Arab Painting*, p. 117; D. S. Rice, 'The Oldest Dated "Mosul" Candlestick', *The Burlington Magazine* 91, 1949, Fig. F.II, V, X; Rosen-Ayalon, 'The problem . . .', Plate 2, *mīnā'ī* plate, private collection; Plate 8, Beaker, Freer Gallery of Art, Washington, No. 28.2; Plate 6, Kāshān polychrome glazed tile, Museum of Fine Arts, Boston, No. 31.495.
38. N. Nassar, 'Saljuq or Byzantine: Two related styles of Jaziran Miniature Painting', *The Art of Syria and the Jazira*, 1100-1250, (ed.) J. Raby, Oxford, 1985, pp. 92–3.
39. S. B. Ṣamadī, 'Some Aspects of the Arab-Iranian Culture from the Earliest Times up to the Fall of Baghdad', IC, 26 Oct. 1952, p. 39; D. Haldane, *Mamlūk Painting*, Warminster, 1978, p. 3.
40. *Encyclopaedia of Islam* 1, Leiden, 1960, pp. 443–4 , s.v. *amīr al-ḥajj* (J. Jomier); Ṣamadī, 'Some Aspects . . .', p. 39; von Grunebaum, *Festivals* . . ., p. 37; *Tārīkh*, iii, 1383–4, cited Ahsan, *Social Life* . . ., p. 280.
41. Ibn Baṭṭūṭa, *Travels in Asia and Africa*, 1325–54, London, 1929, p. 101.
42. Hitti, *History* . . ., p. 136, note 1; R. Ettinghausen, 'Notes on the Lustreware of Spain: to Ernest Kuhnel on the occasion of his seventieth birthday', AO I, 1954, p. 136, note 9; Hitti, *History* . . ., pp. 656–7, 676.
43. Abū al-Fidā', *The Memoirs of a Syrian Prince*, Wiesbaden, 1983, p. 77.
44. von Grunebaum, *Festivals* . . ., p. 38.
45. Ibn Jubayr, *The Travels of Ibn Jubayr*, London, 1952, p. 65.
46. R. Ettinghausen, 'Painting in the Fatimid Period: A Reconstruction', AI, IX, 1942, Fig. 12.
47. Ibn Baṭṭūṭa, *Travels* . . ., p. 73, note 63.
48. Preston, *Makamat* . . ., pp. 419–20.
49. Ahsan, *Social Life* . . ., p. 29, note 3; *Tāj* 154, attributed to al-Jāḥiẓ, cited p. 34; von Grunebaum, *Festivals* . . ., p. 26.
50. Ibn Khallikān, *Biographical Dictionary*, Karachi, 1961, p. 125.

51. E. Schroeder, 'Aḥmad Mūsa and Shams al-Dīn: a Review of Fourteenth-century Painting', AI VI, 1939, Figs. e, h, j, o, jj.

52. Ettinghausen, *Arab Painting*, p. 91; Arts Council of Great Britain, *The Arts of Islam*, Hayward Gallery Catalogue, London, 1976, p. 179, Fig. 196, Ewer, beaten brass, inlaid with copper and silver, Mesopotamia, 1232, British Museum, 66 12–69 61; Ettinghausen, 'Lustreware . . .', Plate 1, Fig. 2, Ivory, Cairo, Musee Arabe; A. U. Pope and P. Ackerman, *A Survey of Persian Art from Prehistoric Times to the Present*, London and New York, 1938-9, Vol. X, Fig. 647a, lustreware figure of camel.

53. Ibn Baṭṭūṭa, *Travels* . . ., p. 104.

54. Ibn Jubayr, *Travels* . . ., pp. 127–8.

55. Ibid., p. 65.

56. Lane, *Manners* . . ., p. 441.

Chapter 2

1. Al-Ghazālī, *Counsel for Kings*, London, 1964, p. 95; Niẓām al-Mulk, *The Book of Government or Rules for Kings*, London 1978, p. 31; S. Lane-Poole, *The Art of the Saracens in Egypt*, London, 1886, p. 23.

2. Mez, *Renaissance* . . ., p. 147.

3. Al-Sābī, *Rules and Regulations* . . ., p. 75.

4. G. Makdisī, 'An Eleventh-century Historian of Baghdad', *Bulletin of the School of Oriental and African Studies*, XIX, 1956, p. 19; XX, 1957, p. 29; al-Dhahabī, *The Dynasties of Islam*, Damascus, 1979, pp. 2–3.

5. J. Lassner, *Topography* . . ., pp. 91, 88.

6. Ettinghausen and Grabar, *Art and Architecture* . . ., Plate 388; Brandenburg, *Islamische* . . ., Figs. 1, 2; Ettinghausen, *Arab Painting*, pp. 98–9, 101; A. al-R. M. al-Gailānī, 'The Origins of Islamic Art and the Role of China', PhD thesis, University of Edinburgh, 1974, Figs. 169A, B, C; Ettinghausen, 'Beveled . . .', p. 75.

7. Al-Tanūkhī, *The Table Talk of a Mesopotamian Judge*, London, 1922, pp. 133–4, 29.

8. Hitti, *History* . . ., 327 note 6; Lane, *Lexicon* . . ., ii, 2768, s.v. *najada*.

9. Niẓām al-Mulk, *Book of Government* . . ., pp. 240–1.

10. Al-Gailānī, 'Origins . . .', Figs. 82B, C; T. Arnold and A. Grohmann, *The Islamic Book*, London, 1929, Fig. 10.

11. Levy, 'Notes . . .', p. 334.

12. D. S. Margoliouth, 'Meetings and Salons under the Caliphate', IC 3, Jan. 1929, p. 7.

13. Al-Tanūkhī, *Table Talk* . . ., p. 25.

14. Ibid., pp. 266–7.

15. Lane-Poole, *Saracens* . . ., p. 23; *Dīwān lughat al-turk*, cited B. Lewis, *Islam from the Prophet Muḥammad to the Capture of Constantinople*, Vol. II, *Religion and Society*, London, 1979, p. 215.

16. E. Esin, 'The Hierarchy of Sedent Postures in Turkish Iconography', *Kunst des Orients* 7, 1970–71, pp. 1, 23.

17. *Rasā'il ikhwān al-ṣafā*, cited Lewis, *Islam* . . ., p. 215.

18. Ettinghausen, *Arab Painting*, p. 85; Arnold and Grohmann, *The Islamic Book*, Fig. 32; Rosen-Ayalon, 'The Problem . . .', Figs. 4, 8.

19. W. H. Worrell, 'On Certain Arabic Terms for Rug', AI I, 1934, pp. 221–2.

20. Al-Ghazālī, *Counsel for Kings*, p. 86.

21. Al-Ghazālī, 'They Lived Once Thus in Baghdad', *Mediaeval and Middle Eastern Studies in Honor of Aziz Suryal Atiya*, (ed.) S. A. Hanna, Leiden, 1972, p. 42.

22. G. Marcais, *La grande mosquée de Kairouan*, Paris, 1934, Fig. 64.

23. Ibn Jubayr, *Travels* . . ., p. 237; Paris BN 6094, f.31r, *Maqāma* 10; London BL 22.114, f.66r, *Maqāma* 23; Ettinghausen, *Arab Painting*, pp. 65, 91, Istanbul, F. E. 1566, *Kitāb al-aghānī*, c. 1218–19, Vienna, A. F. 10, *Book of Antidotes*, mid-13th century, respectively; D. S. Rice, 'The Aghānī Miniatures and Religious Painting in Islām' B M 95, 1953, Fig. C; Nassar, 'Saljūq or Byzantine . . .', Figs. 2 c, d, 'Blacas ewer', British Museum, No. 66.12–69.61, Fig. 2e, Ewer, Walters Art Gallery, Baltimore, No. 54–456, Fig. 2f, 'Cup', Istanbul, Turk ve Islam Eserlei Muzesi, No. 102.

24. A. S. Melikian-Chirvani, 'Le Roman de Varque et Golshāh', *Arts Asiatiques* xxii, 1970, Istanbul, Hazine 841, Figs. 40, 6, 29, 64.

25. Hitti, *History* . . ., p. 326; Mez, *Renaissance* . . ., p. 141.

26. Al-Rāwandī, p. 18, cited Lewis, *Islam* . . ., p. 208.

27. Ibn Baṭṭūṭa, *Travels* . . ., p. 158; al-Ṣābī, *Rules and Regulations* . . ., p. 74; Niẓām al-Mulk, *Book of Government* . . ., pp. 103–4.

28. F. Rosenthal, *Four Essays on Art and Literature in Islam*, Leiden, 1971, pp. 66, 67, 75, 77; Rice, 'Aghānī'. . ., p. 130.

29. E. Whelan, 'Representations of the Khāṣṣakīya and the Origins of Mamlūk Emblems', *Content and Context of Visual Arts in the Islamic World*, (ed.) P. P. Soucek, Pennsylvania State University and London, 1988, pp. 219–20; Ettinghausen, *Arab Painting*, p. 91, *Kitāb al-tiryāq* of Pseudo-Galen, Vienna, Nationalbibliothek, A. F. 10, f.1r; Ettinghausen, *Arab Painting*, p. 148, *Maqāmāt*, probably Egypt, 1334, Vienna, Nationalbibliothek A. F. 9, f.1r; E. Atil, *Renaissance of Islam: Art of the Mamlūks*, Washington D. C., 1981, Fig. 20, Brass bowl, inlaid with silver and gold, c.1290–1310, Paris, Musée du Louvre, MAO 331, Bequest of Marquet de Vasselot, 1956; P. Kahle, 'The Arabic Shadow Play in Mediaeval Egypt', *Journal of the Pakistan Historical Society*, 1954, p. 97, shadow play figure of a merchant vessel with a Mamlūk blazon, denoting the *fūta* (napkin) of the office of jandar, (jamdar?) c.1290–1370; Whelan, 'Representations . . .', Fig. 2, p. 222, note 25, carved stone niche from the Gu' Kummet in Sinjār showing eight youths in military dress carrying appropriate items of rank, now in Iraq Museum, Baghdad, Fig. 9, p. 222, note 31, Artūqid 6th/12th-century stone bridge built by Qara Arslān at Ḥiṣn Kayfa with figures in Turkish military dress.

30. Al-Ghazālī, 'They Lived . . .' , pp. 42–3.

31. Al-Muqaddasī, cited Mez, *Renaissance* . . ., pp. 317–18.

32. H. Buchtal, '"Hellenistic" Miniatures in Early Islamic Manuscripts', AI 7, 1940, Fig. 30. Al-Idrīsī, cited Lewis, *Islam* . . ., pp. 113, 154. Lassner, *Topography* . . ., p. 91.

33. Buchtal, '"Hellenistic" . . .', Fig. 23, Paris, BN 3465.

34. Al-Ṣābī, *Rules and Regulations* . . ., pp. 75, 152–3.

35. Al-Jāḥiẓ, *The Epistle of Singing-Girls* of Jāḥiẓ, Warminster, 1980, pp. (20), 20, V (25), 22.

36. Al-Ṣābī, *Rules and Regulations* . . ., p. 73.

37. Al-Tha'ālibī, *Curious and Entertaining* . . ., p. 142.

38. Hitti, *History* . . ., p. 334; Niẓām al-Mulk, *Book of Government* . . ., p. 219.

39. Levy, 'Notes . . .', pp. 333, 334, 335.

40. *Kitāb al-aghānī*, v, 60, 109, cited Levy, 'Notes . . .', p. 335.

41. Ashtor, *Histoire* . . ., p. 172; Serjeant, 'Material . . .', p. 99.

42. Ahsan, *Social Life* . . ., p. 30; al-Jāḥiẓ, *Bayān*, iii, 100, cited Ahsan, *Social Life* . . ., p. 32.

43. Niẓām al-Mulk, *Counsel for Kings*, London, 1964, p. 83.

44. Levy, 'Notes . . .', p. 333; Quatremere, I, i, p. 133 ff. cited Levy, 'Notes . . .', p. 334.

45. Al-Tanūkhī, *Table Talk* . . ., I, p. 125, cited Ashtor, *Histoire* . . ., p. 54.

46. Al-Tanūkhī, *Table Talk* . . ., pp. 125–6.

47. Yāqūt, *Irshād*, i, p. 254, cited Levy, 'Notes . . .', p. 326; al-Ṭabarī, iii, p. 627, cited Levy, 'Notes . . .', p. 326; al-Maqrīzī, *Khiṭaṭ*, i, p. 390, ll. 6ff., cited Levy, 'Notes . . .', p. 326.

48. Al-Māwardī, cited Mez, *Renaissance* . . ., pp. 233, 234; R. Levy, *The Social Structure of Islam*, Cambridge, 1957, pp. 343 ff.

49. Mez, *Renaissance* . . ., p. 234; al-Tanūkhī, *Table Talk* . . ., p. 179.

50. Mez, *Renaissance* . . ., p. 224; Levy, *Social Structure* . . ., p. 346.

51. K. D. al-Dūrī, 'Society and Economy of Iraq under the Seljuqs (1055–1160 AD) with Special Reference to Baghdad', PhD thesis, University of Pennsylvania, 1970, p. 145; al-Samarqandī cited Mez, *Renaissance* . . ., p. 218.

52. D. S. Margoliouth, 'The Table Talk of a Mesopotamian Judge', Part II, *Islamic Culture*, 5, July 1931, p. 187.

53. *Sefer-Nāme*, p. 161, cited Ashtor, *Histoire* . . ., p. 228.

54. Al-Tanūkhī, *Table Talk* . . ., p. 125.

55. Al-Tha'ālibī, *Curious and Entertaining* . . ., p. 51; Ibn al-Jawzī, p. 193a, cited Mez, *Renaissance* . . ., p. 136.

56. Al-Ghazālī, *Counsel for Kings*, pp. 114–16.

57. *Al-Ṣiḥāḥ*, cited Lane, *Lexicon* . . ., Vol. i, p. 500; Hayward Gallery Catalogue, Plate 183, David Collection, no. 32/1970; Esin, 'Hierarchy . . .', Fig. 10; Mez, *Renaissance* . . ., p. 225.

58. Mez, *Renaissance* . . ., p. 230; al-Kindī, cited Mez, *Renaissance* . . ., p. 227.

59. Makdisī, 'Eleventh-Century Historian . . .', BSOAS, XIX, 3, p. 436.

60. H. Buchtal, 'The Painting of the Syrian Jacobites in its Relation to Byzantine and Islamic Art', *Syria* 20, 1939, Plate XXIII, Figs. 1 and 2, BM Add. 7170, f.145, Christ before Caiaphas; BN 5847, f.107r, *Maqāma* 34; Buchtal, '"Hellenistic" . . .', Figs. 27–8, Paris BN 3465, ff.55r, 69v.

61. Al-Ṭabarī, cited Ahsan, *Social Life* . . ., p. 183, Ibn al-Nadīm cited p. 181; al-Tha'ālibī, *Curious and Entertaining* . . ., cited pp. 48, 128.

62.Al-Muqaddasī, cited Mez, *Renaissance* . . ., pp. 335, 336.

63. Al-Sharīshī, ii, 318, cited Ahsan, *Social Life* . . ., p. 181; Rosen-Ayalon, 'The Problem . . .', Plate 4, polychrome plate.

64. Al-Ghazālī, *Counsel for Kings*, pp. 69, 58.

Chapter 3

1. Ibn Munqidh, *An Arabian-Syrian Gentleman and Warrior in the Period of the Crusades: Memoirs of Usāma ibn Munqidh*, London, 1987, p. 38.

2. Buchtal, '"Hellenistic" . . .', Fig. 35; T. Arnold, *Painting in Islam*, New York, 1968, Plate XIX a.

3. Ettinghausen, 'Lustreware . . .', p. 135, note 6; Plate 1, Fig. 2; Plate 1, Fig. 3, Fatimid wood carving; Plate 1, Fig. 4, Inlaid brass platter.

4. Ibn Khallikān, *Biographical* . . ., p. 318.

5. St Petersburg S.23, p. 288, *Maqāma* 43; BN 3929, f.173r, *Maqāma* 21; Istanbul EE 2916, f.77r, *Maqāma* 23; BL 1200, f.120v, *Maqāma* 37, and BN 5847, f.156r, *Maqāma* 47; E. Baer, *Metalwork in Mediaeval Islamic Art*, New York, 1983, Fig. 2, *De Materia Medica*, Freer Gallery of Art, 32.20, 1224, and *Na'at al-Ḥayawān* of Ibn Bakhtīshū', BL or. 2784, Fig. 3; Ettinghausen and Grabar, *Art and Architecture* . . ., Plate 374.

6. Ibn Jubayr, *Travels* . . ., p. 18.

7. Ibn Taghrībirdī, *Egypt and Syria under the Circassian Sultans, 1382–1468 AD*, Berkeley and Los Angeles, 1930–42, p. 27; P. A. Andrews, 'The Felt Tent in Middle Asia: the Nomadic Tradition with Princely Tentage', PhD thesis, SOAS, University of London, 1980, p. 997.

8. BN 5847, f.77r, *Maqāma* 26; St. Petersburg, S.23, p. 166, *Maqāma* 26; BN 6094, f.84r, *Maqāma* 26; Andrews, 'Felt Tent . . .', Plate 95; D. Talbot Rice, The Illustrations of the 'World History' of Rashīd al-Dīn, (ed.) B. Gray, Edinburgh, 1976, Edinburgh University, Arab ms. 20; al-Bīrūnī, *al-Athār al-bāqiya 'an al-qurūn al-khāliya* [*Chronology of Ancient Peoples*] Edinburgh University, Arab ms. 161; Andrews, 'Felt Tent', Plates 91, 92; C. Welch, Royal Persian Manuscripts, London, 1978, Plate 45, Haft Awrang of Jāmī', 1556–65 AD; Plate 28, *Khamsa* of Niẓāmī, 1539–43 AD; Rosen-Ayalon, 'The Problem . . .', Plate 8.

9. Ibn Khallikān, *Biographical Dictionary*, p. 73; D. S. Margoliouth, 'The Renaissance of Islam: Trade', IC 7, 1933, p. 321; *Book of Songs*, verse 119, cited Margoliouth, 'Renaissance . . .', p. 321, note 9.

10. Miskawayh, *The Experiences of the Nations*, London, 1921, p. 249; Al-Dhahabī, *Dynasties* . . ., p. 15; Margoliouth, 'Trade . . .', p. 315.

11. S. B. Ṣamadī, 'Social and Economic Aspects of Life under the 'Abbasid Hegemony at Baghdad', IC 29, 1955, p. 242; Ibn Taghrībirdī, *Egypt and Syria* . . ., p. 27; *Qābūs-nāma*, 162, cited al-Dūrī, 'Society and Economy . . .', p. 319.

12. Niẓām al-Mulk, *Book of Government* . . ., p. 67.

13. F. Klein-Franke, *Iatromathematics in Islam*, Hildesheim, 1984, p. 18.

14. C. E. Bosworth, *Mediaeval Arabic Culture and Administration*, London, 1982, VI, 10.

15. C. E. Bosworth, *The Mediaeval Islamic Underworld: the Banū Sāsān in Arabic Society and Literature*, Part 1, Leiden, 1976, pp. 83, 115.

16. B. Farès, 'Un herbier arabe', *Archaeologica Orientala in Memoriam Ernst Herzfeld*, New York, 1952, (ed.) G. Miles, p. 87, Fig. a; Lane, *Lexicon* . . ., i, 259, s.v. *banj*; Bosworth, *Underworld* . . ., pp. 126, 145, 145, note 40; P. E. Kahle, 'Shadow Play . . .', p. 93.

17. Lewis, *Islam* . . ., p. 161.

18. Al-Dhahabī, *Dynasties* . . ., p. 231.

19. Ḥamd Allāh Mustawfī al-Qazwīnī, *The Recreation of Hearts*, p. 75.

20. S. D. Goitein, 'Urban Housing in Fatimid times as illustrated by the Cairo Geniza Documents, *Studia Islamica* 47, 1978, p. 9.

21. Al-Dūrī, 'Society and Economy . . .', p. 222.

22. E. Herzfeld, 'Damascus: Studies in Architecture' II, AI 10, 1943, p. 24; E. Herzfeld, 'Damascus . . .' I, AI 9, 1942, p. 48.

23. Al-Janābī, *Studies* . . ., pp. 255, 256; Mez, *Renaissance* . . ., p. 122; S. D. Goitein, 'The Rise of the Near-Eastern Bourgeoisie in Early Islamic Times', *Journal of World History* 3, 1957, p. 596.

24. Mez, *Renaissance* . . ., p. 117; Ibn Jubayr, *Travels* . . ., pp. 317, 318; I. Fatḥī, *The Architectural Heritage of Baghdad*, London, 1979, p. 23; V. Strika and J. Khalīl, 'The Islamic Architecture of Baghdad; the Results of a Joint Italian-Iraqi Survey', *Istituto Universitario Orientale, Supplemento* No. 52 annali, Vol. 47, 1987, fasc. 3, p. 77.

25. Lewis, *Islam* . . ., p. 127.

26. Al-Tanūkhī, *Table Talk* . . ., pp. 109–10.

27. Mez, *Renaissance* . . ., p. 481.

28. D. S. Margoliouth, 'Wit and Humour in Arabic Authors', IC 1, 1927, p. 528; al-Janābī, *Studies* . . ., Plate 195b, p. 255; p. 255, note 425.

29. Ibn Taghrībirdī, *Egypt and Syria* . . ., p. 29; Ibn Jubayr, *Travels* . . ., pp. 380, 262.

30. Ibn Khallikān, *Biographical Dictionary*, p. 83; Miskawayh, *Experiences* . . ., London, 1921, pp. 405–6.

31. Lewis, *Islam* . . ., p. 127; Mez, *Renaissance* . . ., pp. 16–1; Ṣamadī, 'Some Aspects . . .', p. 46; al-Tha'ālibī, *Curious and Entertaining* . . ., pp. 140–1.

32. Al-Dūrī, 'Society and Economy . . .', p. 309; Hitti, *History* . . ., p. 386; al-Dūrī, Society and Economy . . .', p. 308.

33. G. Le Strange, *Baghdad during the 'Abbasid Caliphate*, Oxford, 1924, p. 68; Lewis, *Islam* . . ., pp. 236–7.

34. Lewis, *Islam* . . ., p. 239.

35. Niẓām al-Mulk, *Book of Government* . . ., p. 117.

36. Mez, *Renaissance* . . ., pp. 160, 161.

37. S.16:73; S.12:31; Yūsuf; Ahsan, *Social Life* . . ., p. 31; Mez, *Renaissance* . . ., p. 169; *Encyclopaedia of Islam*, II, 1965, p. 26, s.v. *'abd* (R. Brunschvig).

38. Ashtor, *Histoire* . . ., p. 111; Goitein, 'Near-Eastern Bourgeoisie . . .', p. 590.

39. Lane-Poole, *Saracens* . . ., p. 27.

40. S. H. Nasr, *Islamic Science: an Illustrated Study*, London, 1976, p. 143, Figs. 67a, b, 68, 69; Miskawayh, *Experiences* . . ., pp. 202, 203.

41. B. Farès, *Le livre de la Thériaque: manuscrit arabe à peintures de la fin du XIIIe siècle*, Cairo, 1953, Plate XI; J. Allan, *Islamic Metalwork: the Nuhad Es-Said Collection*, London, 1982, p. 51, Ewer from Herat, late 12th or early 13th centuries.

42. Al-Ghazālī, 'They Lived . . .', p. 45.

43. *Jāmi' al-tawārīkh* [*Universal History*], iii, pp. 239–41, cited Lewis, *Islam* . . ., pp. 171, 172.

44. D. P. Little, 'The Ḥarām Documents as Sources for the Arts and Architecture of the Mamlūk Period', *Muqarnas: An Annual on Islamic Art and Architecture*, Vol. 2, 1984, Plate 4.

45. Mez, *Renaissance* . . ., p. 161; Le Strange, *Baghdad* . . ., pp. 68, 123; Lassner, *Topography* . . ., pp. 72–3, 99; G. Makdisī, 'The Topography of Eleventh-century Baghdad: Materials and Notes (1)', *Arabica* 6, 1959, pp. 191–2.

Chapter 4

1. Margoliouth, 'Trade . . .', p. 309.

2. Al-Tanūkhī, *Table Talk* . . ., pp. 101–2.

3. A. Mazaheri, *La vie quotidienne des Musulmans au Moyen-Age*, Paris, 1951, p. 195.

4. Ibn Riḍwān, *Mediaeval Islamic Medicine: Ibn Riḍwān's Treatise 'On the Prevention of Bodily Ills in Egypt'*, Berkeley and Los Angeles, 1984, p. 66.

5. H. Kamal, *Encyclopaedia of Islamic Medicine*, Cairo, 1975, pp. 204, 205.

6. M. Ullman, *Islamic Medicine*, Edinburgh, 1978, p. 73.

7. Bosworth, *Underworld* . . ., Part 1, p. 127.

8. E. G. Browne, *Arabian Medicine*, Cambridge, 1962, p. 12.

9. Nasr, *Islamic Science* . . . , p. 174.

10. Nasr, *Islamic Science* . . ., p. 176; Browne, *Arabian Medicine*, p. 42, Part VII concerning general and special pathology, including phlebotomy, p. 43, concerning Discourse 12 (20 Chapters), including baths, and the indications afforded by the pulse and urine.

11. Ullmann, *Islamic Medicine*, p. 45.

12. Goitein, *A Mediterranean Society* . . ., Vol. 1, 91.

13. Ahsan, *Social Life* . . ., p. 294, note 132.

14. Ullmann, *Islamic Medicine*, p. 112.

15. J. M. Rogers, *The Topkapi Saray Museum: the Albums and Illustrated Manuscripts*, London, 1976, Plate 11, Ahmet III, 3472, dated 1206; Z. M. Ḥasan, *Madrasa Baghdad fī al-taswīr al-Islāmī*, Sumer, 2, 1955, Fig. 13 (d).

16. Goitein, 'Near Eastern Bourgeoisie . . .', p. 589, note 12.

17. Ibn Munqidh, *Memoirs . . .*, p. 175.

18. Ettinghausen, *Arab Painting*, p. 159, Istanbul, Suleymaniye Mosque Kala Ismail 565 manuscript.

19. Ibn Jubayr, *Travels . . .*, p. 262.

20. Buchtal, '"Hellenistic" . . .', Fig. 35; Melikian-Chirvani, 'Varqué et Golshāh . . .', Fig. 1.; Ahsan, *Social Life . . .*, p. 150, notes 665–8.

21. Makdisī, 'Topography . . .', pp. 182, 195.

22. Arnold and Grohmann, *The Islamic Book*, Fig. 32; Fares, *Thériaque . . .*, Figs. VII-VIII; Ettinghausen, *Arab Painting*, p. 87.

23. Ettinghausen, *Arab Painting*, pp. 98–9; M. S. Simpson, 'The Role of Baghdad in the Formation of Persian Painting', *Art et Société dans le Monde Iranien*, (ed.) C. Adle, Paris, 1982, Fig. 50; p. 94.

24. BN 5847, f.122v, *Maqāma* 39; Rosen-Ayalon, 'The Problem . . .', Plate 4; Melikian-Chirvani, 'Varque et Golshāh', Fig. 1; D. S. Rice, 'Inlaid Brasses in the workshop of Aḥmad al-Dhakī al-Mawṣilī, AO II, 1957', Figs. 23–4.

25. J. Pedersen, *The Islamic Book*, Princeton, 1984, pp. 116, 129; Nasr, *Islamic Science . . .*, Plate 65, Istanbul F.1404.

26. Ibn Abī Uṣaybi'a, *'Uyūn*, cited Pedersen, *The Islamic Book*, p. 125.

27. Mez, *Renaissance . . .*, p. 173.

28. Al-Janābī, *Studies . . .*, Plate 187, Mosul, al-Mujāhidī Mosque, stucco ornamented *mihrāb*, and Fig. 6, terracotta decoration on exterior of mausoleum of Sitt Zubayda.

29. M. Kabīr, 'Libraries and Academies during the Buwayhid Period, 946 AD to 1055 AD', IC 33, 1959, pp. 31, 32.

30. Makdisī, 'Topography . . .', pp. 195–6.

31. Ibn Khallikān, *Biographical Dictionary*, p. 139.

32. Pedersen, *The Islamic Book*, p. 128; Mez, *Renaissance . . .*, p. 172.

33. M. E. Pauty 'L'architecture dans les miniatures islamiques', *Bulletin de l'Institut d'Egypte* XVII, 1935, p. 28.

34. Le Strange, *Baghdad . . .*, p. 92; Ibn Khallikān, *Biographical Dictionary*, p. 271.

35. Al-Dūrī, 'Society and Economy . . .', p. 263.

36. Ullman, *Islamic Medicine*, p. 73; Ibn Ṭiqṭāqa, *On the Systems of Government and the Muslim Dynasties*, London, 1947, p. 2.

37. Al-Tanūkhī, *Table Talk . . .*, p. 289.

38. Steingass, *Assemblies . . .*, Arabic text, p. 378, lines 9–12.

39. J. Sadan, 'Kings and Craftsmen: a Pattern of Contrasts on the History of a Mediaeval Arabic Humoristic Form', Part 2, *Studia Islamica* LVI, 1982, p. 120: Ahsan, *Social Life . . .*, p. 21, note 72; S.2:282.

40. Al-Tha'ālibī, *Curious and Entertaining . . .*, p. 13; Bosworth, *Underworld . . .*, Part One, p. 65.

41. Hitti, *History . . .*, p. 409, note 5.

42. Al-Tanūkhī, *Table Talk . . .*, pp. 260–1.

43. F. Rosenthal, *Four Essays . . .*, Leiden, 1971, pp. 90 ff; Ḥasan, 'Madrasa Baghdad . . .', Fig. 5, al-Jazarī's automata manuscript dated 1304 AD, Minassian Collection; G. M. Meredith-Owens, *Persian Illustrated Manuscripts*, London, 1973, pp. 20–1, and Plate XIII.

44. E. Herzfeld, 'Die Tabula Ansata in der Islamischen Epigraphik und Ornamentik', *Der Islam*, VI, 1916, Figs. 4–13; 11th-century alabaster headstone from Yazd, B.M. Collection A. Upham-Pope, Brooke Sewell Fund, 1982 6-23 1; Herzfeld, 'Damascus . . ., III, AI 11–12, 1946, p. 57; A. J. Spencer, *Death in Ancient Egypt*, London, 1984, Fig. 44. This was a small wooden label, some 12 cm. by 5 cm. in size which was attached to an individual mummy as a new means of identification before it was released for interment. A short text in Greek or demotic script gave the name and age of the deceased, and sometimes the names of the parents. This was the only means of identifying bodies in a communal tomb when mummification became widely available.

45. Baer, *Metalwork* . . ., p. 240, note 300; Baer, *Metalwork* . . ., 240-1; Hayward Gallery Catalogue, London, 1976, Fig. 344, lustreware plate; R. Hillenbrand, *Imperial Images in Persian Painting, Scottish Arts Council Catalogue*, Edinburgh, 1977, p. 14, Victoria and Albert Museum, ms. 359-1885, Layla and Majnūn, copied by Mulla Mīr Bakharzī.

46. Niẓām al-Mulk, *Book of Government* . . ., p. 154; Ibn Jubayr, *Travels* . . ., p. 283.

47. G. Awad, 'The Mustanṣiriya College, Baghdad', *Sumer* I, 1945, p. 18, viz. the teacher would have received seven *arṭāl* of bread, two dishes of rice a day, and three *dīnārs* per month; the reciter four *arṭāl* of bread, one dish of rice and one *dīnār* twenty *qīrāṭs* per month, and the boys three *arṭāl* of bread, one dish of rice a day and thirteen *qīrāṭ* per month; p. 15.

48. Al-Ghazālī, 'They Lived . . .', p. 44.

49. Ettinghausen, *Arab Painting*, p. 71, Topkapi Saray Museum, Istanbul, manuscript Ahmet III, 2127.

50. Hayward Gallery Catalogue, Fig. 344.

51. *New Grove Dictionary of Music and Musicians*, London, 1980, pp. 306, 307.

52. *New Grove Dictionary of Musical Instruments*, Vol. 2, London, 1984, p. 554.

53. NGDMI, p. 515.

54. Al-Fārūqī, 'The Golden Age of Arab Music', *The Genius of Arab Civilization*, (ed.) J. R. Hayes, 2nd edition, Henley on Thames, 1983, p. 142.

55. Al-Kumayt, *Ḥalbat*, Ch. xiv, cited E. W. Lane, *Arabian Society in the Middle Ages: Studies from the Thousand and One Nights*, (ed.) S. Lane-Poole, New edition, London, 1971, p. 168.

56. NGDMI, p. 552.

57. 'Blacas ewer', B.M. no. 66.12-69-61; F. Sarre, *Der Kiosk von Konya*, Berlin, 1936, Plate 7a, star tile with lutanist; A. J. Racy, 'Music', *The Genius of Arab Civilization*, (ed.) Hayes, p. 135.

58. Al-Tanūkhī, *Table Talk* . . ., p. 46.

59. Margoliouth, 'Wit and Humour . . .', p. 525.

60. Al-Jāḥiẓ, *Epistle* . . ., p. 23.

61. NGDMI, p. 552.

62. Ibid., p. 516.

63. Al-Jāḥiẓ, *Epistle* . . ., pp. 31–2.

64. S. Cary Welch, *Royal Persian Manuscripts*, London, 1978, Plate 10.

65. Grabar, *Illustrations* . . ., p. 48.

66. Ibn Ṭiqṭāqā, *On the Systems* . . ., p. 116.

67. Al-Jāḥiẓ, *Epistle* . . ., p. 26.

68. Jenkins and Olsen, *Music* . . ., p. 56, BL or. add. 22.114, f.26r, *Maqāma* 12; A. J. Racy, 'Music', *The Genius of Arab Civilization* (ed.) Hayes, p. 125; Racy, 'Music', p. 133, V and A Inv no 10 1866; Baer, *Metalwork* . . ., f.188, Louvre 3681.

69. A. Schimmel, *As Through a Veil: Mystical Poetry in Islam*, New York, 1982, p. 77.

70. Lane, *Manners* . . ., 374 - He mentions boatmen accompanying their earthenware drums

with a 'double reed pipe' (*zummāra*); this is related to the root of *mizmār*.

71. E. J. Grube, *Islamic Pottery, of the Eighth to the Fifteenth Century in the Keir Collection*, London, 1976, Fig. 213.

72. NGDMI, p. 511.

73. Ibn Khallikān, *Biographical Dictionary*, p. 282.

74. Rice, 'Inlaid Brasses . . .', p. 200, Fig. 25b; Grube, *Islamic Pottery* . . ., Figs. 211–4; Ettinghausen, 'The Mesopotamian Style in Luster Painting', *Islamic Art and Archaeology, Collected Papers*, (ed.) M. Rosen-Ayalon, Berlin, 1984, Fig. 5, Capella Palatina, Palermo, lutanist; Welch, *Royal Persian Manuscripts*, Plates 18, 27.

75. D. S. Rice, 'The Oldest Illustrated Arabic Manuscript', BSOAS 22, 1959, pp. 214–15; D. James, 'Space Forms in the Work of the Baghdad *Maqāmāt* Illustrators, 1225–58', BSOAS 37, 1974, pp. 314–17.

76. S. Masliyah, 'Mourning Customs and Laments among the Muslims of Baghdad', IC 54, Jan. 1980, p. 20; Ashtor, *Histoire* . . ., p. 222.

77. Masliyah, 'Mourning Customs', p. 21.

78. Al-Bukhārī, lxviii, pp. 46–7, cited Y. Stillman, *Encyclopaedia of Islam* V, Leiden, 1986, p. 735, s.v. *libās*.

79. Stillman, EI V, p. 735.

80. Al-Dhahabī, *Dynasties* . . ., pp. 99–100.

81. M. Jastrow, 'Dust, Earth and Ashes as Symbols of Mourning among the Ancient Hebrews', *Journal of the American Oriental Society*, 1899, p. 142.

82. O. Grabar, 'Notes on the Iconography of the Demotte *Shāh-nāma*', *Paintings from Arab Lands*, (ed.) R. Pinder-Wilson, Oxford, 1969, p. 39. The *Shāh-nāma* tells how when Farīdūn went out to greet his favourite son, Irāj, 'the troops all rent their clothes', and Farīdūn noticed 'their banners rent, their kettledrums reversed'; Grabar, 'Demotte', Fig. 13—The mourners at Isfandiyār's funeral wore purple/blue dresses. V. V. Bartol'd, *O Pogrebenii Timura*, Iran, 1974—following the untimely death of Muḥammad Sulṭān, the governor of north-western Persia, in 1403, Tīmūr and his army wore garments of 'black or dark blue'.

Chapter 5

1. Chenery, *Assemblies* . . ., pp. 246–7.

2. BN 3929, f. 34v, *Maqāma* 12; D. S. Rice, 'The Oldest Dated Mosul Candlestick, AD 1225', BM XCI, 1949, Figs. C (IV), (VII) and (IX); Ettinghausen, *Arab Painting*, p. 129, Biblioteca Apostolica, Vatican ar. 368, *Ḥadīth Bayāḍ ū Riyāḍ*, Spain or Morocco, 13th century, f.10r. The musical aspect is dealt with further elaborated upon in the analysis of al-Wāsiṭī's tavern scene in *Maqāma* 12, at the section on 'Drinking' in Chapter 7.

3. Ibn Taghrībirdī, *Chronicles* . . ., p. 27.

4. Schimmel, *Mystical Poetry* . . ., pp. 143, 144.

5. Rice, 'Aghānī . . .', p. 129; M. Bahrami, *Gurgan Faiences*, Cairo, 1949, Plate 51.

6. Makdisī , 'Topography . . .', pp. 189–90.

7. Ettinghausen, *Arab Painting*, p. 91.

8. Al-Dūrī, 'Society and Economy . . .', pp. 186, 187.

9. Ettinghausen, *Arab Painting*, p. 97.

10. Al-Janābī, *Studies* . . ., p. 203; Ya'qūbī, *Buldān* . . ., p. 238, cited Ahsan, *Social Life* . . ., p. 178; Ettinghausen, *Arab Painting*, p. 108.

11. Ettinghausen, *Arab Painting*, pp. 85, 93; Oxford, Bodleian, Marsh 458, f.29v, *Maqāma* 13; Istanbul, EE 2916, f.211v, *Maqāma* 50.

12. Al-Janābī, *Studies* . . ., pp. 257–8; Plates 161, 163.

13. Ibid., pp. 201, 202, 207–8; Plate 161; P. Waley and N. M. Titley, 'An Illustrated

Persian Text of *Kalīla wa Dimna* Dated 707H/1307-8', *British Library Journal* 1, 1975, Figs. 4, 10–13 and 18–20; Istanbul EE 2916, f.211v, *Maqāma* 50.

14. Al-Janābī, *Studies* . . ., p. 208, Fig. 11; Plates 15, 17, 21, 24.

15. Ibid., Plates 36, 45, 97.

16. Yāqūt, *Mu'jam al-buldān*, Vol. I, pp. 395, 461; Vol. II, pp. 23, 116–17, 546, cited al-Dūrī, 'Society and Economy . . .', p. 186.

17. Ibn al-Athīr, cited Preston, *Makamat* . . ., p. 267.

18. Steingass, *Assemblies* . . ., p. 39.

19. Dozy, *Dictionnaire* . . ., p. 200.

20. Abū Tammām, *Ash'ār al-Ḥamāsa*, p. 171, cited Hitti, *History* . . ., p. 25.

21. R. Wellsted, *Travels to the City of the Caliph*, cited al-Dūrī, 'Society and Economy . . .', p. 305.

22. Yāqūt, *Mu'jam al-buldān*, cited M. Rosen-Ayalon, 'The Problem . . .', p. 162.

23. Al-Dūrī, 'Society and Economy . . .', p. 194.

24. Preston, *Makamat* . . ., p. 268.

Chapter 6

1. Preston, *Makamat* . . ., pp. 218, 219.

2. Al-Muqaddasī, *Ahsan al-taqāsim*, pp. 128—9, cited Ahsan, *Social Life* . . ., p.195; Ahsan, *Social Life* . . ., p. 192, note 201.

3.Al-Janābī, *Studies* . . ., p. 239, note 232; J. Warren, 'Syria, Jordan, Israel, Lebanon', *Architecture* . . ., (ed.) Michell, pp. 232, 233; H. Philon, 'Iraq' in *Architecture* . . ., (ed.) Michell, pp. 247, 249.

4. James, *Arab Painting* . . ., Plate 6.

5. Goitein, 'Urban Housing . . .', p. 14, note 1.

6. Lane, *Arabian Society* . . ., pp. 238, 239; D. Talbot Rice, 'Two Islamic Manuscripts in the Library of Edinburgh University', *Scottish Arts Review* VII/I, 1959, Fig. 1; D. Talbot Rice, *The Art of Byzantium*, London, 1959, Plate 5, Roman silk textile, c. 800 A.D. in Museo Sacro, Vaticano, Rome; B.W. Robinson, *Persian Drawings from the Fourteenth through the Nineteenth Century*, New York, 1965, reprint, Plate 20, Herat painting of Jamshīd teaching the crafts, dated 1469. The spinning woman wears a shoulder length headdress of the *khimār* type, which is commented upon in *Maqāma* 40 in BN 3929, f.134r.

7. Ettinghausen, *Arab Painting*, pp. 107, 138, 99, 98.

8. Ullmann, *Islamic Medicine*, p. 108; J. C. Sournia, *Médecins Arabes Anciens Xe et XIe Siècles*, Paris, 1986, p. 101.

9. L. H. Gray, 'Iranian Miscellanies', *Journal of the American Oriental Society* 33, 1913, p. 291; Meredith-Owens, *Persian Illustrated Manuscripts*, Plate XIII (c), BL or. 3299, f.119a, probably 16th century, Timūrid.

10. EI I (1960), p. 722, s.v. *asṭurlab*; the linear type was known as the 'staff of Tūsī' after its inventor, Muẓaffar Sharaf al-Dīn al-Tūsī, and there was also a spherical form of instrument; Nasr, *Islamic Science* . . ., Plates 73, 74, 75, 77.

11. Klein-Franke, *Iatromathematics* . . ., p. 19.

12. Buchtal, '"Hellenistic" . . .', Fig. 36, BN 3465, f.78; Farès, *Thériaque* . . ., Plates VII, VIII, XI.

13.Shaykh Uways, *History*, The Hague, 1954, p. 45; F. Keshavarz, 'The Horoscope of Iskandar Sultan', *JRAS*, 1984, p. 201.

14. Sournia, *Médecins* . . ., p. 97; M. Z. Siddiqi, *Studies in Arabic and Persian Medical Literature*, Calcutta, 1959, p. 123.

15. Al-Tha'ālibī, *Curious and Entertaining* . . ., p. 126.

16. Sournia, *Médecins . . .*, pp. 97, 105.
17. Sournia, *Médecins . . .*, p. 95.
18. Klein-Franke, *Iatromathematics*, p. 72; D. Pingree, 'Astronomy and Astrology in India and Iran', *Isis* 54, 1963, p. 229.
19. Talbot Rice, *Islamic Art*, Fig. 6, Edinburgh University Universal History, Fig. 121, Paris, BN suppl. pers. 332; Robinson, *Persian Drawings . . .*, Plate 78, Timurid provincial style, c. 1450.
20. Ullmann, *Islamic Medicine*, p. 109; Nasr, *Islamic Science . . .*, Fig. 84, Plates 103, 105, 106, 107.
21. F. R. Martin, *The Miniature Painting and Painters of Persia, India and Turkey from the 8th to the 18th Century*, London, 1912, Plate 6a.
22. Esin, 'Hierarchy . . .', Plate 11, Figs. 4, 5, 7, 9.
23. Esin, 'Hierarchy . . .', Figs. 4, 5; Baer, 'A Brass Vessel from the Tomb of Sayyid Baṭṭal Ghāzī', *Artibus Asiae* 39, 1977, Fig. 5.
24. Ceramics: Ettinghausen, 'Early Shadow figures . . .', Fig. 2, Bowl, end of 12th century, Persia; Talbot Rice, *Islamic Painting*, Fig. 132, 13th-century bowl from Fusṭāṭ, Egypt, a version of a type which was also manufactured in Syria. Glass: Hayward Gallery Catalogue, Fig. 136, Pilgrim flask, c.1250–60, Syria (possibly Aleppo), in London, British Museum, No. 691-203; Kuhnel, *The Minor Arts of Islam*, Fig. 179, Glass beaker, 'The Luck of Edenhall', 13th century, Aleppo, Syria, in British Museum. Ivory: Grube, *World of Islam*, Fig. 29, Casket, 12th century, Egypt, in Berlin, Staatliche Museen. Metalwork: Rice, 'Inlaid Brasses . . .', Figs. 23, 24; Rice, 'Oldest . . .', Figs. 5, 6. Textiles: Ettinghausen, *Arab Painting*, 84; Ḥasan, *Madrasa Baghdad . . .*, Fig. 12; Talbot Rice, *Islamic Painting*, Plates 105, 106; Buchtal, '"Hellenistic" . . .', Fig. 36; Waley and Titley, 'Illustrated Persian Text . . .', Figs. 7, 10. Woodcarving: Kuhnel, *Minor Arts . . .*, Figs. 201, 202; Simpson, 'The Role of Baghdad . . .', Fig. 50; similar vegetal motifs were also noted on spandrels in the *Marzubān nāma* dated 1299, f.5r.
25. Asad, *The Message of the Qur'ān*, Gibraltar, 1980, p. 52, note 224.
26. Ashtor, *Histoire . . .*, pp.153, 165.
27. M. Raḥmatallāh, *The Women of Baghdad in the 9th and 10th Centuries as Revealed in the History of Baghdad of al-Khaṭīb*, MA thesis, University of Pennsylvania, published by Baghdad University, 1952, p. 49.
28. Ibn Munqidh, *Memoirs . . .*, p. 8.
29. Miskawayh, *Experiences . . .*, pp. 77, 79; Meredith-Owens, *Persian Illustrated Manuscripts*, Plate 1, BL Add. 18113, *Rauzat ul-anvar*, f.85b, Plate 13.
30. Al-Ghazālī, 'They Lived . . .', p. 45.
31. Martin, *Miniature Painting . . .*, Plate 6A, lower figure; BN 5847, f.107r, *Maqāma* 34; Buchtal, 'Syrian Jacobites . . .', p. 148; Simpson, 'The Role of Baghdad . . .', Fig. 50.
32. Baer, *Metalwork . . .*, pp. 145, 294; Rice, 'Aghānī . . .', p. 134.
33. Ibn Ṭiqṭāqa, *On the Systems . . .*, p. 198 cited Goitein, 'Near-Eastern Bourgeoisie . . .', p. 599, note 71; al-Tanūkhī, *Table Talk . . .*, p. 52.
34. Al-Tanūkhī, *Table Talk . . .*, p. 271; Miskawayh, *Experiences . . .*, pp. 63, 45; Ṣamadī, 'Some Aspects . . .', 43, note 67; Shaykh Uways, *History*, p. 81; Abū al-Fidā', *Memoirs . . .*, p. 78; D. G. Hogarth, *Arabia* (Oxford, 1922), p. 63, cited S. B. Ṣamadī, 'Social and Economic . . .', IC 26, 1955, p. 33, note 5.
35. Ahsan, *Social Life . . .*, p. 72; Lane, *Manners . . .*, p. 45; Ashtor, *Histoire . . .*, pp. 54, 71; Ahsan, *Social Life . . .*, p. 71.
36. Buchtal, '"Hellenistic" . . .', Fig. 38; Haldane, *Mamluk Painting*, Fig. 6; D. Goldstein, *Hebrew Manuscript Painting*, London, 1985, Plate 33.

37. L. Mayer, '*Mamlūk Costumes . . .*', p. 330; Melikian-Chirvani, 'Varqe et Golshāh . . .', Plate 41; Ettinghausen, *Arab Painting*, pp. 116, 117.

38. Grabar, *Illustrations . . .*, p. 142; Talbot Rice, *Islamic Art*, Fig. 69; Rosen-Ayalon, 'The Problem . . .', Plates 2, 8.

39. Preston, *Makamat . . .*, 135, note 1, S.2:96, a reference to the witchcraft of Babylon, explained by Steingass, *Assemblies . . .*, Arabic text, p. 135, note 40.

40. Mayer, '*Mamlūk Costumes . . .*', p. 298; Baer, *Metalwork . . .*, p. 243, Fig. 198; Ettinghausen, *Arab Painting*, pp. 99, 101, *Epistles of the Sincere Brethren*; Rosenthal, *Four Essays . . .*, p. 88: bread wrapped in a *mandīl* might be carried in the sleeve (*kumm*) of official civilian dress.

41. Al-Dhahabī, *Dynasties . . .*, p. 146; Lane, *Lexicon . . .*, ii, p. 2359, s.v. *faraja*; Al-Ṭabarī, III, 968; *Kitāb al-aghānī*, 239–40, cited Ahsan, *Social Life . . .*, p. 40; Y. K. Stillman, 'Female Attire of Mediaeval Egypt according to the Trousseau lists and Cognate Material from the Cairo Geniza', PhD thesis, University of Pennsylvania, 1972, p. 78.

42. E. Kuhnel, 'Abbasid Silks of the 9th Century', AO II, 1957, pp. 367–71, Fig. 6; Serjeant, 'Material . . .', AI IX, p. 84 and AI XV–XVI, p. 67.

43. Al-Jāḥiẓ, p. 154, cited Ahsan, *Social Life . . .*, p. 34, note 43; Dozy, *Dictionnaire . . .*, cited Ahsan, *Social Life . . .*, p. 68, note 334.

44. Ashtor, *Histoire . . .*, p. 235; Preston, *Makamat . . .*, p. 402. Ṣamadī, 'Some Aspects . . .', p. 26.

45. Oxford, Bodleian 2806, cited Ashtor, *Histoire . . .*, p. 145.

46. Lane, *Lexicon . . .*, ii, p. 3026, s.v. *mala*; Serjeant, 'Material . . .', AI XV–XVI, p. 67; Hitti, *History . . .*, p. 334; Guest and Ettinghausen, 'Kashān Lustre Plate . . .', p. 632.

47. Serjeant, 'Material . . .', *AI* XV-XVI, p. 67.

48. N. Titley, *Plants and Gardens in Persian, Mughal and Turkish Art*, London, 1979, p. 5.

49. Al-Tanūkhī, *Table Talk . . .*, pp. 286–7; S.80:31; Ṣamadī, 'Some Aspects . . .', p. 43.

50. Lane, *Manners . . .*, p. 55.

51. J. W, Allan, *Nīshāpūr: Metalwork of the Early Islamic Period*, New York, 1982, Figs. 83, 84, 85.

52. British Museum, 1958 10–13 2, Persian, 12th-13th centuries, pair of cast gold bracelets with bands of dedicatory inscriptions and niello work, unhinged and open ended; British Museum, 19 6-21 4, Egyptian, 14th-century silver bracelet, dragon head finials, geometric design and inscription. Chinese influence.

53. Ashtor, *Histoire . . .*, pp. 220, 222.

54. Lane, *Lexicon . . .*, i, p. 779, s.v. *khalla*; Isaiah 3:16.

55. Ashtor, *Histoire . . .*, p. 220; Lane, *Lexicon . . .*, p. 323, s.v. *ṭūma*; Cambridge University Taylor-Schechter, 10, J.21, 4a, cited Ashtor, *Histoire . . .*, p. 220.

56. Pope and Ackerman, *Survey* XII, Plate 1300, A, B; Hayward Gallery Catalogue, p. 179, Fig.184.

57. Pope and Ackerman, *Survey*, XIII, p. 1302, Figs. A, B, D, H; London BL 1200, f.89r, 5 'kings' looking down from niches representing the upper storey of the Wāsiṭ *khān*; Ashtor, *Histoire . . .*, p. 222.

58. Pope and Ackerman, Survey XIII, p. 1310, f.47v; B. Gray, *A World History of Rashīd al-Dīn*, Edinburgh, 1976, Plate 29, p. 36.

59. *Nihāyāt al-'Arab fī funūn al-adab*, cited Hitti, *History . . .*, p. 334, note 7.

60. Ibn Khallikān, *Biographical Dictionary*, p. 224.

61. Al-Bukhārī, x, 155, cited R. Levy, *Sociology of Islam*, Vol. I, London, 1957, p. 186; Ṣamadī, 'Some Aspects . . .', p. 42.

62. Ibn Jubayr, *Travels . . .*, cited Levy, *Sociology . . .*, Vol. I, p. 186; S. D. Goitein,

'Urban Housing . . .', SIsl 47, 1978, p. 18.

63. Serjeant, 'Material . . .', *AI* XV/XVI , p. 79,

64. Stillman, 'Female Attire . . .', p. 142; Mayer, '*Mamlūk Costumes* . . .', p. 302.

65. M. Bahrami, *Gurgan Faiences*, Cairo, 1949, Plate 5(a); Waley and Titley, 'Illustrated Persian Text . . .', p. 49, Fig. 6, 12th-century bowl, B. M. 1914 3-18 1; Talbot Rice, *Islamic Art*, Fig. 69. *mīnā'ī* bowl, 12th-13th centuries; Allan, *Nīshāpūr*, p. 47, Herati ewer, late 12th or early 13th centuries; Ettinghausen, *Arab Painting*, p. 174, Qur'ān of Arghūn Shāh, Egypt, c.1368–1388, Cairo, National Library, ms. no. 54. 1388.

66. Serjeant, 'Material . . .', AI IX, p. 84; Ṣamadī, 'Some Aspects . . .', pp. 42–3.

Chapter 7

1. D. S. Rice, 'Deacon or Drink: Some Paintings of Sāmarra Re-examined', *Arabica* V, 1958, p. 33.

2. Rosenthal, *Four Essays* . . ., p. 76; Ettinghausen, p. 146, BL or. add. 22114, f.94r, *Maqāma* 28—worshipper in the Samarqand jāmi' overcome by Abu Zayd's sermon; D. R. Hill, 'Mechanical Technology', The Genius of Arab Civilization . . ., (ed.) Hayes, p. 148, Al-Jazarī's automatata manuscript, Istanbul, Topkapi Palace Museum,A. 3472, dated 1206, Iraq, f.98r - mechanical boat with drinking men and musicians.

3. Rosenthal, *Four Essays* . . ., p. 93; Baer, *Metalwork* . . ., p. 214; Ward, 'Evidence . . .', Fig. 4; Rosenthal, *Four Essays* . . ., p. 82.

4. Kahle, 'Shadow Play . . .', p. 97; Lane, *Lexicon* . . ., i, p. 389, s.v. *jadara*.

5. M. Rosen-Ayalon, 'Themes of Sasanian Origin in Islamic Art', *Jerusalem Studies in Arabic and Islam* 4, 1984, Plate 9, Ivory casket, Victoria and Albert Museum, London, 10-1986, dated 969-70; Ivory casket, Louvre, Paris, dated 969; Ettinghausen, *Arab Painting*, p. 45, Ceiling panel, Cappella Palatina, Palermo, 12th century; Baer, *Metalwork* . . ., Fig. 143, Candlestick, 13th century, possibly Mesopotamian, Cairo Museum of Islamic Art, 15.121, where there appears to be a drinking figure with glass and flower; BL or. add 22114, f.26r, *Maqāma* 12.

6. Ibn Khallikān, *Biographical Dictionary*, p. 282, note 2; Steingass, *Assemblies* . . ., Arabic text, p. 92, line 2; Lane, *Arabian Society* . . ., p. 161; Schimmel, *Mystical Poetry* . . ., p. 77.

7. Talbot Rice, *Islamic Art*, Fig. 83; Rice, 'Oldest . . .', p. 337, Figs. C (I), (IV); Rosen-Ayalon, 'Themes . . .', Plate 2; K. Weitzmann, 'Islamic Scientific Illustrations', *Archaeologica Orientala* . . ., (ed.) Miles, Fig. 4, al-Jazarī manuscript in Boston, dated 1354.

8. O. Grabar, 'The Illustrated *Maqāmāt* of the thirteenth century: the Bourgeoisie and the Arts', *The Islamic City*, (eds.) A.H. Hourani and S. M. Stern, Oxford, 1970, p. 219, note 20.

9. Al-'Umarī, *Masālik al-abṣār*, pp. 321 ff, cited D. S. Rice, 'Deacon or Drink . . .', p. 29, note 3.

10. Ibn Munqidh, *Memoirs* . . ., pp. 164, 165.

11. EI IV (1978), p. 995, s.v. *khamr*, (A. J. Wensinck); Rice, 'Deacon or Drink . . .', pp. 32, 28, note 1; Schimmel, *Mystical Poetry* . . ., p. 78; Lane, *Arabian Society* . . ., p. 38.

12. *Kitāb al-aghānī*, X, p. 135, cited Rice, 'Deacon or Drink . . .', p. 23; Abū Nuwās, *Dīwān*, p. 214, cited Rice, 'Deacon or Drink . . .', p. 26, note 6; Ibn al-Fāriḍ, *The Wine Song of Shaykh 'Umar ibn al-Fāriḍ (572–632 AH)*, BSOAS 2, 1934, pp. 235 ff; Al-Firūzābādī, *Kitāb al-jālis fī taḥrīm al-handāris*, B.M. Or. 9200, cited Rice, 'Deacon or Drink . . .', p. 32, note 1.

13. Lane, *Arabian Society* . . ., pp. 148, 149.

14. Preston, *Makamat* . . ., p. 189, note 9.

15. S.16:67, S.16:69, S.2:216, S.4:46, S.5:92.

16. Rice, 'Deacon or Drink . . .', p. 28; H. G. Farmer, 'The Origin of the Arabian Lute and Rebec', *Sumer*, 1930, p. 773.

17. Al-Tanūkhī, *Table Talk* . . ., p. 107.

18. Farmer, 'Origin . . .', pp. 773, 774, 768; Ettinghausen, *Arab Painting*, p. 91.

19. BN 5847, f.3v, *Maqāma* 1; Rice, 'Deacon or Drink . . .', pp. 17, 23.

20. Rice, 'Deacon or Drink . . .', p. 24; Sadan, 'Kings and Craftsmen . . .', Part II, p. 116.

21. Rice, 'Deacon or Drink . . .', p. 27.

22. EI IV (1978), p. 997, s.v. khamr, (J. Sadan); Rice, 'Deacon or Drink . . .', p. 26.

23. Lane, *Arabian Society* . . ., 157, note 2.

24. O. Grabar, *The Formation of Islamic Art*, New Haven, 1973, Plate 98; M. S. Dimand, 'Dated Specimens of Mohammedan Art in the Metropolitan Museum of Art, Part II: Manuscripts and Miniature Painting', *Metropolitan Museum Studies*, Vol. I, part 2, 1928-29, Acc. no. 13.152.6; Baer, Metalwork . . ., p. 229, Fig. 189, Istanbul, Tv.IEM, T.I.109.

25. E. Atil, *Renaissance of Islam Art of the Mamlūks*, Washington, D.C. 1981, p. 76, brass bowl inlaid with gold and silver, c.1290–1310, made by Ibn al-Zayn, Louvre, MAO, 331, bequest of Marquet de Vasselot, 1956; Allan, *Islamic Metalwork* . . ., p. 101, wine pourer, Egypt or Syria, 1347–61; Hayward Gallery Catalogue, Fig. 199, metal wallet, mid-13th century, North Mesopotamia; Baer, *Metalwork* . . ., p. 325, note 279; N. M. Titley, *Sports and Pastimes: Scenes from Turkish, Persian and Mughal Paintings*, London, 1979, Plate 10A, BL or. 4125, *Dīvān* of Neva'ī, f.109a.

26. Rice, 'Deacon or Drink . . .', p. 27.

27. Nassar, 'Saljūq or Byzantine . . .', Fig. 3a, candlestick, private collection, UK; Kashān lustreware flagon, V and A Museum, Ades Bequest, c.165–1977.

28. J. R. Hayes (ed.), 'The Genius of Arab Civilization: Source of Renaissance', p. 133; Hayward Gallery Catalogue, Fig. 135.

29. Kahle, 'Schattenspielfiguren', Figs. 52, 53.

30. Lane, *Arabian Society* . . ., p. 157.

31. Ibn al-Fāriḍ, *Wine Song* . . , p. 246.

32. Ettinghausen, *Arab Painting*, p. 87; Rice, 'Deacon or Drink . . .', p. 16.

33. Martin, *Miniature Painting* . . ., Plate 7b.

34. Kahle, 'Schattenspielfiguren', Fig. 51; Kahle, 'Shadow Play . . .' , p. 97.

35. Al-Ghazālī, 'They Lived . . .', p. 38.

36. *Maqāmāt* 1, 2, 5, 7, 14, 18, 30, 44.

37. Al-Tanūkhī, *Table Talk* . . ., p. 282.

38. *Arabic Proverbs*, I, 134, cited, Chenery, *Assemblies* . . ., p. 517.

39. D. Waines, *In a Caliph's Kitchen*, London, 1989, p. 11, Oxford, Bodleian, Hunt, ms. No. 187, late 9th-10th centuries; al-Warrāq, *al-Ṭabīkh wa Islām al-aghdhiya wa al-ma'kūlāt*; Nasr, *Islamic Science* . . ., p. 166.

40. Al-Mas'ūdī, *Meadows of Gold and Mines of Gems*, London, 1841, vii. pp. 170–1; *Qutūb al-surūr*, pp. 290–1, cited Ahsan, *Social Life* . . ., p. 112, note 324.

41. Al-Jāḥiẓ, *Epistle* . . ., p. 22.

42. Al-Isfahānī, *Conquête de la Syrie et de la Palestine par Saladin*, Paris, 1972, p. 117.

43. Abū al-Fidā', *Memoirs* . . ., p. 28.

44. Ibn Khallikān, *Biographical Dictionary*, p. 293.

45. Lane, *Manners* . . ., p. 109.

46. Al-Ghazālī, *Counsel for Kings*, p. 58.

47. Lane, *Manners* . . ., p. 109.

48. Steingass, *Assemblies . . .*, Arabic text, p. 10, note 22, *Maqāma* 1, and p. 223, note 10, *Maqāma* 29.; Chenery, *Assemblies . . .*, p. 516; Preston, *Makamat . . .*, p. 42.

49. Al-Mas'ūdī, *Meadows . . .*, p. 54; Ibn Qutayba, *'Uyūn al-akhbār*, iii, pp. 265–9 and others, cited Ahsan, *Social Life . . .*, p. 120, note 392; al-Baghdādī and others, cited Ahsan, *Social Life . . .*, p. 120, note 393; Le Strange, *Lands of the Eastern Caliphate*, pp. 429; 471, cited Ahsan, *Social Life . . .*, p. 121, note 408; al-Isfahānī, *Conquest . . .*, p. 300.

50. Margoliouth, 'Wit and Humour . . .', p. 526.

51. Gray, *World History . . .*, Fig. 36; B. Gray, 'An unknown fragment of the *Jāmi' al-tawārīkh* in the Asiatic Society of Bengal', *AO* I, 1954, Fig. 17; Welch, *Royal Persian Manuscripts*, Plate 28, B.M. or. 2265, *Khamsa* of Niẓāmī, 1539-43, f.157v, Layla and Majnūn; R. Ettinghausen, *Turkish Miniatures from the Thirteenth to the Eighteenth Century*, London, 1965, Plate 3, Istanbul, Top. Sar. 2153, Album of the Conqueror, 2nd half 15th century. The lid and the high metal trivet are incongruous and too sophisticated in a scene with sinuous, half-clad people; the simpler utensils noted elsewhere are more in keeping with a genre setting.

52. Steingass, *Assemblies . . .*, Arabic text, p. 315, line 7, *Maqāma* 37; al-Baghdādī, *al-Ṭabīkh* (BL or. 5079), cited Ahsan, *Social Life . . .*, p. 119, note 379; Steingass, *Assemblies . . .*, Arabic text, p. 315, note 80.

53. Ashtor, *Histoire . . .*, p. 255; p. 113, he also received 12 *dīnārs* per month, 600 *arṭāl* of bread and 150 *arṭāl* of meat and vegetables.

54. Ṣamadī, 'Some Aspects . . .', p. 43.

55. A. Papadopolou, *Islam and Muslim Art*, London, 1980, p. 99, Fig. 581.

56. Miskawayh, *Experiences . . .*, p. 314.

57. Ibn Khallikān, *Biographical Dictionary*, p. 170.

Select Bibliography

Abū al-Fidā', *The Memoirs of a Syrian Prince* [*al-Mukhtaṣar fī akhbār al-bashar*] (transl. P. M. Holt), Wiesbaden, 1983
M. M. Ahsan, *Social Life under the 'Abbāsids, 786–902 AD*, London, 1979
J. W. Allan, *Islamic Metalwork: The Nuhad Es-Sa'īd Collection*, London, 1982
——*Nīshāpūr; Metalwork of the Early Islamic Period*, New York, 1982
T. Arnold and A. Grohmann, *The Islamic Book*, London, 1929
E. Ashtor, *Histoire des prix et des salaires dans l'Orient médiéval*, Paris, 1969
E. Atil, *Renaissance of Islam: Art of the Mamluks*, Washington, DC, 1981
E. Baer, *Metalwork in Mediaeval Islamic Art*, Albany, NY, 1983
E. Blochet, *Les peintures des manuscrits orientaux de la Bibliothèque Nationale*, Paris, 1914–20
——*Les enluminures des manuscrits orientaux—Turcs, Arabes, Persans—de la Bibliothèque Nationale*, Paris, 1926
C. E. Bosworth, *The Mediaeval Islamic Underworld: The Banu Sasan in Arabic Society and Literature*, Part 1, Leiden, 1976
——*Mediaeval Arabic Culture and Administration* (reprint), London, 1982
E. G. Browne, *Arabian Medicine*, Cambridge, UK, 1962
P. J. Chelkowski (ed.), *Studies in the Art and Literature of the Near East in Honor of Richard Ettinghausen*, New York, 1974
T. Chenery, *The Assemblies of al-Hariri* (transl. from the Arabic), London, 1867
K. A. C. Creswell, *Early Muslim Architecture*, Vols 1 & 2, New York, 1979
al-Dhahabi, *Les dynasties de l'Islam: traduction annotée des années 447/1055–6 à 656/1258* [*Kitāb duwal al-Islām*] (transl. A. Nègre), Damascus, 1979
R. Ettinghausen, *Arab Painting*, New York, 1977
H. G. Farmer, *The Sources of Arabian Music: An Annotated Bibliography of Arabic Manuscripts which Deal with the Theory, Practice and History of Arabian Music*, Cairo, 1932
I. Fathi, *The Architectural Heritage of Baghdad*, London, 1979
G. Fehervari, *Islamic Metalwork of the 8th–15th Centuries in the Keir Collection*, London, 1976
M. Gaudefroy-Demombynes, *La Syrie à l'époque des Mamloukes*, Paris, 1923
al-Ghazāli, 'They Lived Once Thus in Baghdad' [*Al-adab fī al-dīn*] (transl. J. Badeau) in S. A. Hanna (ed.), *Mediaeval and Middle Eastern Studies in Honor of Aziz Suryal Atiya*, pp. 38-49

H. A. R. Gibb, *Studies in Arabic Literature*, London, 1962
S. D. Goitein, *Mediaeval Arabic Culture and Administration*, London, 1982
O. Grabar, *The Illustrations of the Maqamat*, Chicago, Ill./London, 1984
E. J. Grube, *Miniature Islamische*, Padua, 1975
—*Islamic Pottery of the Eighth to the Fifteenth Century in the Keir Collection*, London, 1976
G. E. von Grunebaum, *The Spirit of Islam as Shown in its Literature, Essays in the Nature and Growth of a Cultural Tradition*, 2nd edn, London, 1961
—*Muhammadan Festivals*, London, 1981
—*Themes in Mediaeval Islamic Literature* (reprint), London, 1981
G. E. von Grunebaum (ed.), *Unity and Variety in Muslim Civilization*, Chicago, Ill., 1955
S. Guthrie, 'Everyday Life in the Near East: The Evidence of the 7th/13th-century Illustrations of al-Ḥarīrī's Maqāmāt', PhD thesis, University of Edinburgh, 1991
D. Haldane, *Mamluk Painting*, Warminster, 1978
J. R. Hayes (ed.), *The Genius of Arab Civilization: Source of Renaissance*, 2nd edn, London, 1983
R. Hillenbrand, *Imperial Images in Persian Painting* (Scottish Arts Council Catalogue), Edinburgh, 1977
P. K. Hitti, *History of the Arabs*, London, 1982
R. L. Hobson, *A Guide to the Islamic Pottery of the Near East*, London, 1932
A. Hourani and S. M. Stern (eds), *The Islamic City*, Oxford, 1970
Ibn Baṭṭūṭa, *Travels in Asia and Africa, 1325-1354* [*Kitāb riḥlat ibn Baṭṭūṭa al-musamma tuḥfat al-nuẓẓar fī gharā'ib al-amṣār wa 'ajā'ib al-asfār*] (transl. H. A. R. Gibb), London, 1929
Ibn Jubayr, *The Travels of Ibn Jubayr* [*Al-riḥla*] (transl. R. J. C. Broadhurst), London, 1952
Ibn Khallikān, *Biographical Dictionary* [*Wafayāt al-a'yan wa anbā' abnā' al-zamān*] (transl. M. de Slane; ed. S. Moinul Haq), Karachi, 1961
Ibn Taghrībirdī, *Egypt and Syria under the Circassian Sultans, 1382–1468 AD* [*Ḥawādith al-duhūr fī mada al-ayyām wa al-shuhūr*] (transl. W. Popper), Berkeley/Los Angeles, Calif., 1930–42
Ibn Ṭiqṭāqa, *On the Systems of Government and the Muslim Dynasties* [*Al-fakhrī fī ādāb al-sulṭāniyya*] (transl. C. E. J. Whitting), London, 1947
R. Irwin, *The Middle East in the Middle Ages: The Early Mamluk Sultanate, 1250-1382*, Carbondale and Edwardsville, 1986
al-Isfahānī, Conquête de la Syrie et de la Palestine par Saladin [*al-Fatḥ al-qussī fī al-fatḥ al-qudsī*] (transl. H. Masse), Paris, 1972
al-Jāḥiz, *The Epistle of Singing-Girls of Jāḥiẓ* [*Risalat al-qiyān*] (transl. A. F. L. Beeston), Warminster, 1980
D. James, *Arab Painting*, Bombay, 1977
T. J. al-Janābī, *Studies in Mediaeval Iraqi Architecture*, Baghdad, 1982
J. Jenkins and P. R. Olsen, *Music and Musical Instruments in the World of Islam*, London, 1976
A. Lane, *Early Islamic Pottery; Mesopotamia, Egypt and Persia*, London, 1947

——*Later Islamic Pottery; Persia, Syria, Egypt, Turkey*, London, 1957
E. W. Lane, *Manners and Customs of the Modern Egyptians*, Paisley/London, 1895
——*Arabian Society in the Middle Ages: Studies from The Thousand and One Nights*, new edn (ed. S. Lane-Poole), London, 1971
S. Lane-Poole, *The Art of the Saracens in Egypt*, London, 1886
I. M. Lapidus (ed.), *Middle Eastern Cities: Symposium on Ancient, Islamic and Contemporary Middle Eastern Urbanism*, Berkeley, Calif., 1969
J. Lassner, *The Topography of Baghdad in the Early Middle Ages: Texts and Studies*, Detroit, Mich., 1970
R. Levy, *A Baghdad Chronicle*, Cambridge, UK, 1929
——*The Social Structure of Islam*, Cambridge, UK, 1957
——*The Sociology of Islam*, 2 vols, London, 1957
B. Lewis, *Islam from the Prophet Muhammad to the Capture of Constantinople*, Vol. 2: *Religion and Society*, London, 1979
F. R. Martin, *The Miniature Painting and Painters of Persia, India and Turkey from the 8th to the 18th Century*, 2 vols, London, 1912
H. Mason, *Two Statesmen of Baghdad*, The Hague, 1972
al-Mas'ūdī, *Meadows of Gold and Mines of Gems* [*Murūj al-dhahab wa ma'ādin al-jawhar*] (transl. A. Sprenger), London, 1841
L. A. Mayer, *Mamluk Costume: A Survey*, Geneva, 1952
A. S. Melikian-Chirvani, *Islamic Metalwork from the Iranian World, 8th-18th Centuries*, London, 1982
A. Mez, *Renaissance of Islam*, London, 1937
G. Michell (ed.), *Architecture of the Islamic World*, London, 1978
G. C. Miles (ed.), *Archaeologica Orientala in Memoriam Ernst Herzfeld*, New York, 1952
Miskawayh, *The Experiences of the Nations* [*Tajārīb al-Umām*] (transl. D. S. Margoliouth), London, 1921
W. Montgomery Watt, *The Majesty that was Islam: The Islamic World 661–1100*, London, 1974
Niẓām al-Mulk, *Counsel for Kings* [*Naṣihāt al-mulūk*] (transl. F. R. L. Bagley), London, 1964
——*The Book of Government or Rules for Kings* [*Siyar al-mulūk* or *Siyāsat al-mulk*] (transl. H. Darke), 2nd edn, London, 1978
Ibn Munqidh [Usāma ibn Murshid] [Mu'ayid al-Dawla called Ibn Munqidh], *An Arab-Syrian Gentleman and Warrior in the Period of the Crusades: Memoirs of Usamā ibn Munqidh* [*Kitāb al-I'tibār*] (transl. P. K. Hitti), London, 1987
S. H. Nasr, *Islamic Science: An Illustrated Study*, London, 1976
A. Papadopoulo, *Islam and Muslim Art* (transl. R. E. Wolf), London, 1980
J. Pedersen, *The Islamic Book*, Princeton, NJ, 1984
A. U. Pope and P. Ackerman, *A Survey of Persian Art from Prehistoric Times to the Present*, London/New York, 1938-9
T. Preston, *Makamat or Rhetorical Anecdotes of al-Hariri of Basra* (transl. from the Arabic), London, 1850
Ḥamd Allāh Mustawfī al-Qazwīnī, *The Recreation of Hearts* [*Nuzhat al-Qulūb*]

(transl. G. Le Strange), Cambridge, UK, 1905

J. Raby (ed.), *The Art of Syria and the Jazira, 1100–1250*, Oxford, 1985

B. W. Robinson, *Islamic Painting and the Arts of the Book*, London, 1976

M. Rosen-Ayalon (ed.), *Islamic Art & Archaeology: Collected Papers*, Berlin, 1984

F. Rosenthal, *Four Essays on Art and Literature in Islam*, Leiden, 1971

—*The Classical Heritage in Islam*, London, 1975

Hilāl al-Ṣābī', *The Rules and Regulations of the 'Abbasid Court* [*Rusūm dār al-khilafā'*] (transl. E. A. Salem), Beirut, 1977

D. Sourdel, *Mediaeval Islam* (transl. J. Montgomery Watt), London, 1983

F. Steingass (ed.), *The Assemblies of Ḥarīrī* (Arabic text), London, 1897; *The Assemblies of Ḥarīrī* [*Maqāmāt al-Ḥarīrī*] (English transl.), London, 1898.

G. le Strange, *Baghdad during the Abbasid Caliphate*, Oxford, 1924

D. Talbot Rice, *Islamic Art*, London, 1984

al-Tanukhī, *The Table Talk of a Mesopotamian Judge* [*Nishwār al-muḥaḍara wa akhbār al-mudhakira*] (fragmented manuscripts, transl. D. S. Margoliouth), London, 1922

al-Tha'ālibī, *The Book of Curious and Entertaining Information* [*al-Laṭā'if wa al-ma'ārif*] (transl. C. E. Bosworth), Edinburgh, 1968

al-'Umarī, *L'Afrique, moins l'Égypte* [*Masālik al-abṣar fī mamālik al-amṣar*] (transl. M. Gaudefroy Demombynes), Vol. 1, Paris, 1927

Index

Sources of Illustrations

Bibliotheque Nationale, Paris
BN *arabe* 5847, Cover

BN *arabe* 5847, Plates 1,2,5,6,10,11,12,16,19,20
Illustrations 1,2,4,8,9,11,12,13,15,16,17,18

BN *arabe* 3929, Plates 14,17,18
Illustrations 3,5,6,14

BN *arabe* 6094, Plates 7,13

British Library, London
BL or. 1200, Plate 15
Illustrations 7,10

Academy of Science, St. Petersburg
S.23, Plates 3,8

Suleymaniye Mosque, Istanbul
Esad Efendi 2916, Plates 4,9